DISASTER AND THE MILLENNIUM

DISASTER
AND THE
MILLENNIUM

Michael Barkun

New Haven and London, Yale University Press, 1974

Published with assistance from the foundation established in memory of Henry Weldon Barnes of the Class of 1882, Yale College.

Library of Congress catalog card number: 73-86884
International standard book number: 0-300-01725-1

Designed by Sally Sullivan and set in Times Roman type.
Printed in the United States of America by The Colonial Press Inc., Clinton, Mass.

Published in Great Britain, Europe, and Africa by Yale University Press, Ltd., London.
Distributed in Latin America by Kaiman & Polon, Inc., New York City; in Australasia and Southeast Asia by John Wiley & Sons Australasia Pty. Ltd., Sydney; in India by UBS Publishers' Distributors Pvt., Ltd., Delhi; in Japan by John Weatherhill, Inc., Tokyo.

FOR JANET

Contents

Acknowledgments

My interest in millenarian movements was piqued a decade ago by a chance encounter with Norman Cohn's seminal work, *The Pursuit of the Millennium*. My response—shared, I suspect, by many others—was to partake in Cohn's own excitement with a dramatic but neglected subject. As I grew more conversant with the diffuse body of millenarian scholarship, spread over several disciplines, I was also drawn to the pioneering and imaginative theoretical work of Anthony F. C. Wallace. While succeeding pages note many points on which I dissent from both Cohn and Wallace, this should not obscure my debt to them; a systematic understanding of the subject is scarcely possible without the most serious consideration of their work.

Research began in earnest in 1970–71, when a Ford Foundation Faculty Fellowship in Political Science provided the time for uninterrupted work. Completion of the manuscript itself was greatly expedited by a timely grant from the Appleby-Mosher Fund of the Maxwell School, Syracuse University. During both the research and writing, my demands for ever more esoteric materials from the staff of the Ernest Stevenson Bird Library at Syracuse were met with unfailing kindness and cooperation.

Several of the principal ideas developed here received preliminary expression in a paper, "Millenarian Movements and Political Order," presented at the 1971 Annual Meeting of the American Sociological Association. I am most appreciative of Elise Boulding for providing me with this forum. I have since modified many of the concepts presented in that paper, in large measure because of the helpful and often vigorous comments of many who took the trouble to respond to it; particularly, Edwin Bock, Adda Bozeman, Norman Cohn, David Greenstone, Robert McClure, and Richard Wilsnack.

As my commitment to the subject grew, I soon found that, obscure as the subject seemed to some, its fascination was shared by many others of whom I had not initially been aware. The existence of a kind of "millenarian underground" among colleagues in several disciplines at Syracuse led to the formation of a discussion group which was the source of invaluable stimulation. I am most appreciative of the efforts of Ephraim Mizruchi and D. Glynn Cochrane in organizing these sessions.

I am grateful to two individuals for generously permitting me to see unpublished materials: Ann S. Kliman of The Center for Preventive Psychiatry, who made available preliminary reports of her work with disaster victims in Corning, New York; and David Bennett, who gave me access to his work in progress on the history of American nativism.

Several individuals read the entire manuscript, and its readability and freedom from the most glaring errors are due in no small measure to their diligence. Margaret Mead and Glynn Cochrane, besides reading the entire manuscript, were especially helpful in suggesting improved ways of treating the material on Melanesia. Jeffrey B. Russell brought to the manuscript the historian's traditional concern for stylistic clarity. Where I went astray despite these individual and collective urgings, I am wholly responsible. Marian Neal Ash of the Yale University Press has been a constant and valued source of assistance and encouragement.

But of the many who have helped shape this book, there is one whose contributions I most prize, with whom I discussed and tested ideas in their earliest, most tentative formulations, and who with marvelous acuteness and unending patience read and commented upon successive drafts: my wife, Janet, to whom I dedicate this book.

Introduction

This study explores the relationships between two concepts: disaster and the millennium. At first sight, one could hardly imagine two more dissimilar ideas. The first suggests death and desolation, the second, salvation and fulfillment. Yet the two intertwine again and again. Those who regard the millennium as imminent expect disasters to pave the way. The present order, evil and entrenched, can hardly be expected to give way of itself or dissolve overnight. From the perspective of the scholar who attempts to stand outside events, disaster has another significance: it is the very cause of the millenarian commitment itself. Men cleave to hopes of imminent worldly salvation only when the hammerblows of disaster destroy the world they have known and render them susceptible to ideas which they would earlier have cast aside. The pages that follow explore both these levels.

Disaster and millennium, upheaval and promise—between these polarities we find a kind of group life that has fascinated historians, sociologists, and anthropologists. It is the world of millenarian movements, those collective endeavors to anticipate, produce, or enter a realm of human perfection. Its hallmarks are nervous anticipation, withdrawal from normal social commitments, and bitter renunciation of the established order. Led by all manner of prophets and messiahs, these movements flicker briefly in the wake of disaster. Although they rarely appear to make an enduring mark, we shall see that the brevity of their active lives is deceptive. Their true consequences are often far greater than their conventionally minded adversaries are willing to admit.

The kinship between disaster and millenarian movements also extends to the manner in which they have been studied. Until recently, neither received much systematic scholarly attention. The neglect of both resulted from the fact that they are, beyond anything else, atypical kinds of events. A disaster

1

is by its very definition a break in the accustomed patterns of human life. Disasters "are so rare in comparison with the events that make up the generality of human experience that their existence as a class is less evident than their abnormality with respect to other classes." [1] In the same way, intense longing for the consummation of human history runs at odds with the workaday routines of life. To be sure, all existence is punctuated with microdisasters, the tragedies and pitfalls of individual existence: death, illness, economic insecurity. But insofar as our concern here is with the great stresses that distort entire communities, disaster both is and is expected to be uncommon. Diffuse hopes and desires counterbalance the ills of life. Insofar as we place any faith in "progress," we subscribe to a greatly diluted millenarianism. But here, too, precisely in proportion to its diluted character, vague longings for improvement are very different from true millenarianism: those instances in which human beings band together and actually act upon a belief in imminent and total transformation.

Scholarship, particularly in the social sciences, dwells upon pattern and regularity; and properly so, for only by an understanding of the commonplace can we achieve any systematic explanations of social life. Every strategy of inquiry, however, exacts its price. The price of a detailed understanding of the routine is relative ignorance of the exceptional. And so these two great pattern breakers, disaster and millenarianism, have had to wait while the bulk of resources were expended on "the generality of human experience." It need only be added that the generality of human experience is both shaped by and understood through its exceptions. The characteristics of behavior in disaster and its millenarian by-products illuminate the wellsprings of human activity in more tranquil times.

Systematic disaster research, minus a few early exceptions, began in the early 1950s. Significantly, the stimulus was World War II, a protracted period in which that contradiction in terms, "normal disaster," entered the lives of millions of people.[2] By 1961 the Disaster Research Group was able to inventory systematic studies of 103 disasters, described through 21,600 interviews.[3] The systematic study of millenarian movements, too, had its early, isolated figures: Ralph Linton and Bernard Barber come most quickly to mind. But the feeling that this was a separate phenomenon worthy of large-scale study began with the publication in 1957 of Norman Cohn's *The Pursuit of the Millennium*. Where disaster research grew out of the bombardment of civilian centers in World War II, Cohn's book owed its inspiration to the related historical puzzle posed by the rise of totalitarianism. At the same time that Cohn was at work, anthropologists increasingly noted the presence of millenarian themes among non-Western peoples. Some sense of a potential synthesis of materials from different areas and disciplines appeared in 1960 in a conference sponsored by the journal *Comparative Studies in Society and History*.[4] By the early 1970s a large and complex literature was already in existence.[5]

The complexity of the work on millenarian movements is not the result of impenetrability of its vocabulary or methods. Rather, it simply results from the fact that the movements have been understood through the constructs of the people who have studied them: as predominantly Western by the European historian, as a reaction to culture-shock by the anthropologist, as instances of mental stress by the psychiatrist, as sects by the sociologist of religion, as revolutionary movements by the political scientist. Each has seen in the movements that which he has been trained to recognize. It is equally clear that no one of these perspectives can justifiably claim full validity. To the extent that the following chapters betray such parochialisms, I expect no special charity from the reader. The need remains for ways of viewing these movements in a comprehensive fashion.

There are, however, a number of specific limitations to this work which do provide its emphasis. They also operate as criteria of exclusion, denying a fuller hearing to certain aspects of the subject. The principal concern of this book is, as stated at the beginning, the relationship between disaster and the millennium. That major thrust has necessitated cursory treatment for subjects that under other circumstances might have claimed a larger share of space. Second, the book is largely concerned with active as opposed to passive movements; that is, those that expect the millennium immi-

nently and take concrete actions on this basis. A consideration of passive movements consequently is less than complete.
I have alluded to them in chapter four but only in the context
of a larger discussion of the effects of prophetic disconfirmation.

My bias has similarly been in the direction of greater
concern for action than for ideology. My social science
training doubtless accounts for this. In any case, a full
treatment of millenarian ideas remains a pressing scholarly
need. Here I have only entered the realm of intellectual
history where it was essential for an understanding of social
conduct. By and large, this is limited to chapters one and six,
where I deal with millenarian movements in modern Western
society. The reader whose principal interest lies in the
intellectual or ideological realm will, therefore, be disap-
pointed. I share the regret that more could not have been
done with this dimension, but if nothing else perhaps the gap
will prove a spur to others.

I have tried to concentrate on those points at which
millenarian movements have impinged upon the stability of
the social and political order. In pursuing this aim, much
material from the sociology of religion, including anything
suggestive of the contemplative life, has had to be excluded.
The world of millenarianism contains themes of a less volatile
character than those which are considered here, but, again,
systematic and essential biases were operating.

The corpus of millenarian scholarship contains its share of
internecine warfare. Wherever possible I have tried to avoid
becoming embroiled. That has meant dealing in a cavalier
manner with problems that to some are pressing and significant. Thus I have not pursued the question whether these
movements are religious or political. It seems to me obvious
that they are both. Too often the "essence" of millenarianism
has turned out to be the essence of the discipline from which
the observer has come. We deal here not with movements
that must be categorized as political, social, economic, or
religious. Life does not come so neatly packaged. We deal
instead with aspects that, however accentuated, give partial
and simplified pictures of richly complex organizations.

Just as I have tried to steer clear of the religious-political dichotomy, I have tried to avoid problems of terminology. There has been no end of typologies and neologisms in this area,[6] most of them to little purpose. At one time or another these movements have been called: millenarian, chiliastic, millennial, nativist, transformative, messianic, revitalization, and crisis cults. I have chosen to avoid what for me are irrelevant distinctions, to principally rely upon the term *millenarian* and to use *messianic* and *chiliastic* as occasional synonyms. I recognize that these labels have had their own specific uses (thus, for some it is an important point that there have been millenarian movements without messiahs). However, I believe the argument will proceed in a more orderly fashion by minimizing verbal distinctions. The meaning I assign to *millenarian* will be made clear in chapter one. Finally, certain distinctions significant to historians of religion do not appear here. I do not distinguish, for example, between *premillennial* and *postmillennial* movements. These terms derive specifically from interpretations of Christian doctrine, and, since I look comparatively at both Western and non-Western movements, they seem antithetical to my purpose.

It is now time to sketch out the chapters and the broad lines of the argument. The first chapter attempts three functions: to present some representative examples of millenarianism in action, to clarify the usage of *millenarian* adopted throughout the remaining chapters, and to indicate some larger implications. The subject, despite recent interest in it, remains fairly exotic and unfamiliar. I have therefore chosen four movements to describe, less for the answers this might provide than as a way of giving added concreteness to the later chapters: the so-called Vailala Madness in Melanesia; the Taiping Rebellion in China; the Ghost Dance among the Sioux Indians; and the Taborites in late medieval Central Europe. The definitional section of the chapter disposes in what I hope is a satisfactory manner with those problems of special vocabulary not already dealt with here. The concluding section on larger contemporary implications will not be expanded upon until the final pages of the book, when I return to what must after all be a major concern.

Chapter two in many ways serves as the pivot upon which

the later argument turns. It begins with a review and critique of existing theories and tries to focus sharply upon the questions of explanation which millenarian movements pose; particularly, can they be caused by social change alone? I review in this context the available literature of social psychiatry, which deals with the psychological consequences of change. I conclude that on the basis of the available evidence social change qua social change is insufficiently disturbing a factor to engender millenarian movements, that it can do so only when the change involved radically destroys or reshapes an individual's most highly valued human and physical surroundings. This kind of change is, of course, a euphemism for disaster, and the chapter concludes with a discussion of the psychological and social consequences of catastrophic events. Disaster produces the questioning, the anxiety, and the suggestibility that are required; only in its wake are people moved to abandon the values of the past and place their faith in prophecies of imminent and total transformation.

But, obviously, disaster—as helpful a concept as it is—by itself gives us a necessary but hardly a sufficient condition. Chapter three attempts to delineate the additional factors required: there must be multiple rather than single disasters; a body of ideas or doctrines of a millenarian cast must be readily available; a charismatic figure must be present to shape those doctrines in response to disaster; and the disaster area itself must be relatively homogeneous and insulated. The combination of necessary and sufficient conditions suggests that millenarian movements are essentially rural-agrarian rather than urban-industrial. The city cannot provide the environment in which they can originate and take root. Only the disaster-prone, homogeneous countryside seems to call forth the pursuit of the millennium.

By way of summary, the fourth chapter begins with a sketch of the typical millenarian-prone area. This serves as an introduction to the balance of the chapter, which, accepting the environmental conditions as given, proceeds to an examination of psychological consequences. What impels individuals to jettison conventional values and modes of behavior? How and why do they remain affiliated with

chiliastic sects? This regress from the social to the psychological level is inescapable, given the pressures which disaster
exerts upon the human psyche. Chapter four focuses upon the
conversion process, the way from an old life to a new one.
Conversion is, of course, customarily thought to be an
exclusively religious act, yet the abrupt passage from one
value system to another can also be understood as conversion
in a broad, generic sense. That is the manner in which I have
chosen to see it, since it is the very commingling of religious,
political, and social categories which gives to millenarianism
its peculiar driving force. If conversion brings new members
in, socialization maintains them in their new existence.
Socialization proves a fitting point of entry to the question
whether these movements are in fact as swift and fleeting as
their chroniclers seem to believe. Are they indeed simply
transient spasms of discontent, or do they in fact lead longer,
more continuous, but perhaps less visible lives? The socialization process is seen as the link between psychological process
and the millenarian-prone environment. For multiple disasters are precisely the socializing agents which, over the years,
give to an area a special chiliastic tradition. Individual
movements may erupt into public view and die down, but
each springs from a common utopian propensity.

Of all the problems with which millenarian scholarship has
had to deal, surely the most vexing is the determination of
rationality. Are these movements instances of rational behavior or are they, as many observers seem to believe, instead
cases of mass psychopathology? Chapter five attempts to
grapple with the rationality problem through the three
perspectives most often utilized in support of judgments of
psychopathology: epidemic hysteria or behavioral contagion;
paranoia; and religious ecstasy. The ecstatic behavior of
millenarians is seen less as evidence of mental instability
than, first, as an energizing device which resocializes the
individual and, second, as a contrived means for recapturing
that curious phenomenon, the "disaster utopia." Disasters
paradoxically inflict deprivations but also confer benefits. In
the midst of disaster, its victims frequently experience moments of intense warmth, community, comradeship, and
fellow feeling absent from their workaday lives. How fre-

quently they say, "If only people could always be like this!"
Thus, curiously, the disaster itself appears to prefigure the
millennium, and the cultivation of ecstatic behavior becomes
a mechanism for reproducing the disaster utopia experience.

Chapter six returns to a point made much earlier: are
millenarian movements inherently the products of rural or
backward areas? A reexamination of the question is fundamental to an understanding of contemporary implications,
for if millenarianism is exclusively agrarian, its days are
numbered. In what I hope is not an excessively dialectical
manner, I attempt in this chapter to suggest ways in which the
agrarian-millenarian link has been broken in modern times.
In the first place, there are cases of millenarian movements in
apparently urban settings, and it is with these deviant cases
that the chapter begins: Münster under the Anabaptists;
Florence under Savonarola; London and the Fifth Monarchy
Men; and American black ghettoes in the twentieth century.
The burden of this discussion lies in the fact that all of these
cases occurred in settings which in significant ways are
unrepresentative of quintessentially urban life. The preindustrial city and the ghetto-as-urban-village leave the hypothesis
articulated in chapter three still intact.

Yet these cases do not dispose of the matter. Millenarian
ideas have become so widely diffused in modern times that
their compatibility with urban-industrial society must be
raised in a more serious way. Totalitarianism has become, as
Norman Cohn suggested, the key vehicle for the activation of
millenarian sentiments in modern times. Given the strictures
already made concerning urbanism, how can we account for
this turn of events? The remainder of chapter six deals with
the millenarian-totalitarian nexus in three cases: Russia at the
time of the Bolshevik Revolution; Germany during the rise of
nazism; and China at the advent of communism. All three
revolutionary upheavals were preceded by precisely the
lengthy disaster prologues we have been led to expect. All
three societies already possessed an ample store of millenarian motifs. And in all three a charismatic figure existed to
mold this doctrine. In all three, the movements originated
and spread from either small towns or rural areas or both. In
none were large cities early strongholds or enthusiastic

converts. Each occurred at a period when the technology of communication allowed for a breadth of distribution that had been denied to earlier movements.

Are these the only differentiating factors? Chapter seven takes up problems related to what one might call the modernization of millenarianism: Have patterns of disaster changed in modern times? Can individuals not directly affected by a disaster participate vicariously in it? Can disasters be induced, more or less at will, to serve conscious political or social purposes? The answer to the first, so far as it can be given with any certainty, is that indeed patterns of catastrophe have altered, such that they are characterized by increasing scale. They are more likely, too, to be the products of human actions, an artifact of growing human interdependence. The rural enclave vulnerable to natural disaster has given way to the world community prey to human frailties and malice. In addition, concentrating institutions, such as the ghetto, factory, and university, create enclaves of homogeneity that constitute anomalies in otherwise diverse urban societies. Media of communication, particularly television, offer the opportunity for vicarious participation unavailable in the past. Mass media make potential disaster victims, hence potential millenarian adherents, of even those remote from the nominal point of impact. Finally, the disaster environment that fostered millenarianism can itself be replicated almost at will through induced disasters, of which the Chinese Cultural Revolution is the most striking contemporary example. The use of terror by totalitarian movements constitutes an attempt, however futile in the long run, to maintain a dynamic of permanent revolution.

These conclusions are necessarily speculative. The recent events from which they are drawn lie too close to permit anything but provisional evaluation. Yet the burden of the final chapter is that qualitative characteristics of modern life, most of them linked to technological change, have abruptly transformed the prospects for millenarianism. Until the twentieth century all signs pointed to millenarian movements as essentially agrarian responses. Born of disaster, localized in origins, their salvationist yearnings seemed destined to pass away. National integration, industrialization, and the growth of urban centers appeared to have marked chiliasm as an early casualty. The twentieth century has shown the will to utopia to be a far more durable striving. Once the last recourse of the backward and downtrodden, it has apparently made the leap to establish itself in the modern world. Just as modern life has produced its own brand of disasters, so it too seems destined to reap a characteristically sinister type of collective consequence.

Chapter One

THE NATURE AND SCOPE OF MILLENARIAN MOVEMENTS

No matter how much men may desire to improve their present conditions, they rarely desire to see them totally changed. The known and familiar are comforting even when they are less than totally desirable. The idea that the entire social universe might be totally transformed overnight may be difficult to conceive, but it is not unknown. Indeed, at times it has exercised an obsessive fascination. Belief in the imminence of the millennium, while restricted in its occurrence, has a potency all its own. The messianic consummation can be awaited passively, but more often the expectation itself produces profound behavioral consequences, ranging from withdrawal from society to revolutionary violence. The bizarre behavior associated with both ecstatic religion and hysteria frequently appear along with it.

If chiliasm exerts a fascination for its adherents, it has proven hardly less intriguing to scholars. A vast descriptive and theoretical literature embraces political, social, religious, historical, economic, and psychological considerations. A rich descriptive literature has come from the pens of social scientists, missionaries, government officials, journalists, and travelers. Millenarian groups, once known only in their remote locales, have come within the view of outside observers. Groups already known in more conventional guise come to be recognized as millenarian with the addition of more sophisticated data. And as the total picture has grown richer and more complete, new efforts have been made to explain why the movements arise in the first place.

Millenarian movements are on the surface merely the curiosa and footnotes of world history, their origins obscure and their consequences uncertain. Since they so often lie outside what historians define as mainstreams of social and political activity, it is best to begin with a closer look at some

representative examples. We shall begin by examining four
that have the advantages of representativeness, geographical
dispersion, and relatively full descriptions: the Vailala Madness, an early example of the Cargo Cults of Melanesia; the
Taiping Rebellion, which shook the Manchu throne; the
Ghost Dance among the Sioux, the final convulsive Indian
resistance; and the Taborites of Central Europe. Let us look
now at the bare factual outlines and leave to a later point the
knotty problems of explanation which the facts pose.

The Vailala River is located in the Gulf Division of Papua
in New Guinea.[1] In this vicinity, in late 1919, the Australian
authorities came upon the movement which was to become
known as the Vailala Madness. The terms by which it was
known to the natives translate variously as "madness,"
"head-he-go-round," and "belly-don't-know"—the last stemming from the fact that the sensations experienced by
participants seemed to be felt in the belly and to occur
outside the control of the individual. In Pidgin English,
"head-he-go-round men" vividly described the combination
of excitement, ecstasy, and giddiness. However unusual the
natives' behavior appeared to themselves, it astounded Western onlookers. One such witness reported that

> these natives . . . were taking a few quick steps in front of
> them, and would then stand, jabber and gesticulate, at the
> same time swaying the head from side to side; also bending
> the body from side to side from the hips, the legs appearing
> to be held firm. Others would take the quick steps forward
> and stop, placing the hands on the hips, jabbering continu-
> ously, swaying the head from side to side, and moving the
> trunk of the body backwards and forwards, remaining in
> this position for approximately a minute . . .[2]

Whole villages would suddenly lapse into uncontrolled motor
activity, reeling about in a manner which suggests the
medieval European dancing manias.

The Vailala Madness proved to be neither transient nor
without content. The sect spread very rapidly and maintained
itself until about 1923, although evidences of it reemerged
from time to time up to 1931. It was, in any case, merely one
of a number of related movements which began in Melanesia

around the turn of the century and continue to crop up on Pacific Islands up to the present day. The Vailala movement occupies a singular place, however, since it introduced motifs which subsequently found their way into most of the successor groups. The prophets who led Vailala foretold that a ship would arrive bearing both the spirits of the dead ancestors and a "cargo" of European goods for the natives. The material wealth of the Europeans was believed to have been created in the spirit world, intended for the natives, and maliciously diverted by the whites for their own uses. The day would consequently come when the power of manufactured goods would find its way to its legitimate recipients.

In order to maintain contact with the spirits of the dead, large and frequent feasts were decreed; at the same time, the cult's members abandoned cultivation of their gardens, since the ancestors would provide food. The new ceremonials superseded traditional religious observance, and the paraphernalia associated with them, such as masks, were ostentatiously destroyed. The economic dislocation produced by new sources of consumption and reduced productivity was paralleled by social upheaval. Traditional conceptions of authority, work, and permissible behavior gave way. Cult prophets took up leadership roles. Economically productive labor was supplanted by ritualistic activity, such as military drills, which was carefully imitative of European behavior. The cults dispensed with traditional sexual taboos and at the same time introduced strict new norms concerning sexuality, theft, and personal adornment. The Vailala leaders purported to maintain contact with the ancestors through messages that fell from the sky or which were transmitted down flagpoles erected in the village for that purpose. In retrospect, it appears that the flagpoles were in fact inspired by radio antennas.

Finally, the message of the Vailala movement contained a barely suppressed motif of the elimination of European power and privilege. It is even now unclear whether there was at this time a firm belief that the arrival of the cargo would coincide with the disappearance of the Europeans, for it has not proved possible to disentangle what the natives believed from what panicky settlers thought they believed. But it does appear that some versions of the cargo were thought to include rifles and some versions of the ancestors' return made the ancestors white. In any case, the cargo ship—in later versions, cargo-bearing airplanes—would usher in an era of power, plenty, and autonomy. Those who had lived through the hectic years of the Vailala Madness maintained long afterward that the ground had shaken and that, while neither ancestors nor cargo had materialized, the phantom ship itself had been sighted near at hand.

The Taiping Rebellion, from 1851 to 1864, was the bloodiest civil war on record.[3] Hung Hsiu-ch'üan, the founder of the Taipings, in 1843 experienced conversion to a quite idiosyncratic form of Christianity. Six years previously, in 1837, he had undergone an acute mental disturbance, filled with complex and vivid visions, and he was regarded by those around him as mad. The 1843 transformation occurred when Hung connected the substance of his prior visions with the contents of a Christian missionary tract; each seemed to reinforce the other.

Notwithstanding his prior history, Hung made converts quickly, even from within his own family where his past behavior was well known. The rebellion against the Manchus broke out in 1852, at which time the rebels numbered 30,000. By the mid-1850s, they had reached 2 million. Since many of these had been members of bandit groups before, their new-found adherence to Taiping beliefs is questionable. However, Taiping society was a marked break with the traditional past—emphasizing common property, higher status for women, and sexual puritanism—and at least a sizable proportion regarded their new allegiance as total and regenerating. An elaborate conversion ceremony, modeled on the Christian baptism, provided a means of identifying the core of loyally committed adherents.

Hung's moments of mental instability appear to have persisted into the war years themselves. As his career drew to a close, his thinking became increasingly dominated by fixed ideas. However, he eventually appeared less a madman than a prophet to the alienated, resentful *lumpen* of South China. Entry into his "Heavenly Kingdom of great peace," with its promise of individual and communal renewal, took the follower from an old life of low status and impoverishment to assured position among the elect and, at least in promise, a life of plenty.

The rebels moved out of their rural center to eventually capture Nanking. Their defeat in Nanking came only after substantial military exertions by the Manchus. Especially in the early period of the movement, convulsive, ecstatic experiences were common. Although the Taiping movement arose among the ethnically separate and disadvantaged Hakka, it quickly spread to overwhelmingly Chinese areas. The promise was both of relief from Manchu oppression and of a coming era of social harmony.

The so-called Ghost Dance religion was very much a case of movements within movements.[4] In 1870, and then again in 1890, Paiute Indian prophets announced the message of the Ghost Dance: that performance of this new ritual must replace traditional observances; that if this were done, the spirits of the dead would return, the buffalo would once again be plentiful, and the earth would tremble. The prophet of the later Ghost Dance, Wovoka, in addition preached a doctrine of concord and harmony: the Indians were to avoid lies, love one another, and live in peace with the white man. This is at some variance with the sect's subsequent development, in which it was widely believed that the earthquake or related cataclysm that would usher in the ancestral spirits would also kill the whites.

The dance itself was performed in a white garment, the Ghost Shirt, and lasted several days. By the time of its completion most participants had collapsed from exhaustion and entered a trance state. From Wovoka's home in Nevada, the dance spread with extreme rapidity as far east as Kansas and Nebraska, north into Canada, and south into southern and Lower California and the Texas panhandle. Most Western tribes adopted the dance. Only the Pacific Northwest and areas of Arizona and New Mexico seemed immune. In particular, the relatively well off Navaho failed to participate.

Where the Ghost Dance did take hold, the result was a set of tribal variations upon Wovoka's message. Hence the movement took forms compatible with local usages and myths, filling in lacunae in the original doctrine. Of all the

tribes among whom the Ghost Dance religion was practiced,
the Sioux did so with the most devastating effect. The
medicine man Sitting Bull became the spokesman for Wovoka's message. He announced that the dance would preserve
Indians from white bullets and that a great landslide would
bury the whites. As the dancing continued, troops were
ordered in by frightened authorities. When the troops appeared, a large group of Sioux sought refuge by leaving the
Pine Ridge Reservation for the Dakota Badlands. Sitting Bull
himself did not join them; instead, he remained at his camp
on Grand River, where he was shot in a brief skirmish with
troops.

In the two weeks following Sitting Bull's death, the refugees
in the Badlands yielded to persuasion and coercion and
returned to the reservation. They camped, surrounded by
troops, at Wounded Knee. Attempts to disarm them were
only partially successful. The tragic conclusion is best con-
veyed by the government ethnologist, James Mooney, whose
investigation was made shortly after the event:

> While the soldiers had been looking for the guns Yellow
> Bird, a medicine-man, had been walking about among the
> warriors . . . urging them to resistance, telling them that
> the soldiers would become weak and powerless, and that
> the bullets would be unavailing against the sacred "ghost
> shirts." . . . It is said one of the searchers now attempted to
> raise the blanket of a warrior. Suddenly Yellow Bird
> stooped down and threw a handful of dust into the air,
> when, as if this were the signal, a young Indian . . . drew a
> rifle from under his blanket and fired at the soldiers, who
> instantly replied with a volley directly into the crowd of
> warriors.[5]

Two hundred men, women, and children were killed in the
Battle of Wounded Knee; it was the last major armed
confrontation between American Indians and the government during the period of Western settlement. Its power to
grip the imagination was made clear in the second confrontation at Wounded Knee, in 1973.

The Taborites of Bohemia present a yet more complex
picture, split as they were into a bewildering array of factions,

both joined to and distinct from the larger Hussite movement.[6] Unrest and dissension increased markedly in Bohemia
after the execution of Jan Hus in 1414. By 1419–20 an armed
clash between Hussite and Catholic forces was inevitable. A
radical Hussite group took shape at this time—the Taborites
—and for the next few years formed the millenarian wing of
the Hussite revolt.

The Taborite preacher, Martin Huska, gave to the revolt a
new, cosmic dimension by preaching the imminent destruction of a corrupt society. Only the Taborite towns were to be
spared when the apocalypse came, prophesied for between
February 10 and 14, 1420. The struggle at hand was to be the
final battle between good and evil, and the millennium to
follow victory would come not simply through a miracle but
through the active strivings of the militant faithful. The
Taborites, though they sought to establish five points of
refuge, in fact concentrated in two towns, Tabor and Pisek.
Curiously, their full development as millenarian communities
took place only after the predicted apocalypse had failed to
arrive.

The Taborite settlements emphasized a primitive communism in which private property and feudal obligations were
abolished. The sale of individual property served to fill the
communal coffers. Human authority was likewise dispensed
with. Simultaneously, the Taborites found themselves an
essential military element in the larger Czech uprising, under
the generalship of John Zizka. In time, a combination of
economic and military factors worked to subvert the Taborite
utopia. First, the resources gathered in the initial collectiviza-
tion of wealth were gradually expended, and the collection of
feudal rents became inevitable. Second, Zizka, who was
himself not a millenarian, organized the army on traditionally
authoritarian lines of command.

By 1421, as the ardor and ideological purity of the
Taborites began to wane, they found in their midst a yet more
militant faction, the Adamites. This group held themselves
destined for eternal life and free of the possibility of sin, their
mission to exterminate the impure. The Adamites' pursuit of
a sinless existence led them into the orgiastic sexual excesses
for which they are best known. In any case, they proved

extreme even by Taborite standards as they plundered and murdered in raids from their island haven. Zizka, though embroiled in the larger conflict with the Catholics, nonetheless felt compelled to deal with the Adamites and in a campaign from April to October, 1421, exterminated the cult's members.

What may we say of these and like movements? Superficially, they constitute peripheral episodes, emerging now and again, often in remote, faintly exotic locales, flaring briefly, only to be quickly and ruthlessly suppressed. They seem out of touch with the world's great, formative historical currents. There is also something almost touchingly naïve in the appearance they give, in their extravagant expectations and lack of awareness of the way the world "really works." Yet, as we shall soon see, millenarian movements, even when they are remote, still connect with larger, more consequential events. Even when they appear to have died out, they often live to fight another day. Even when they fail to achieve their ultimate goals, they set in motion effects felt long after they have disappeared.

Insofar as a capsule definition is possible, millenarian or chiliastic movements are social movements which expect immediate, collective, total, this-worldly salvation.[7] They anticipate the complete destruction of the existing social, political, and economic order, which is to be superseded by a new and perfect society. They frequently couple this anticipation with an active desire to speed the inevitable result, often through violent, revolutionary means. The old must be totally destroyed before a new and perfect society can be established in its place. This type of utopianism implies the potential for violent confrontation, with room for neither bargaining nor compromise.

The literature describing such movements is vast and spills over into political science, sociology, anthropology, religion, history, and psychiatry.[8] Even a cursory examination of that literature suggests that any millenarian movement might be characterized by most or all of the following: intense emotional expression; aims so sweepingly comprehensive that outsiders regard them as impossible to attain; claims to

esoteric knowledge and some measure of control of basic
social and historical processes; dependence upon charismatic
leadership; blanket condemnation of the existing social and
political order, coupled with a total renunciation of its claims
to legitimacy; association with periods of disaster, change,
and social upheaval; breach of accepted norms, laws, and
taboos; high risk-taking; and withdrawal from conventional
social, political, religious, and economic relationships. In
short, millenarian movements lay claim to a total, all-encompassing truth and make concomitantly broad demands upon
their members. Membership is neither nominal nor clearly
demarcated from other areas of life and thus differs from
traditional conceptions of, say, political party membership or
interest-group affiliation. The movement enfolds its members
in a belief system that provides meaning and explanation for
virtually all problems and in a round of activities that allays
feelings of personal insecurity and builds a new and strong
sense of identity.

Historical and ethnographic accounts make clear that
chiliasm has been very widely distributed over the globe.[9] In
addition to the four movements already sketched, we may
count among them the Ras Tafari in Jamaica, the so-called
separatist churches in sub-Saharan Africa, and the Andalusian anarchists. Millenarian movements need not be revolutionary. The passive ones leave the final battle between good
and evil entirely to supernatural forces or—the secular
equivalent—to inevitable historical tendencies. Either the
gods or progress will bring the transformation in their own
good time. Indeed, passivity is often a sign that a movement
has already had its moment of confrontation with existing
institutions and has been defeated; or passivity may mean
that predictions of anticipated changes have been seen to fail.
It is often difficult to distinguish between movements that are
trying to make things happen (to "force the end," in Martin
Buber's phrase) and those that are simply making what they
regard as prudent preparations. "Prudent preparations" may
themselves wreak social havoc. Millenarian movements often
so engage their followers' emotions that property is sold,
fields are left untilled, and productive economic activity
is abandoned.

Just as the passive-active distinction is sometimes difficult to make, so it is even harder to classify movements as "violent" or "nonviolent." The very judgments that millenarian movements make about the existing state of affairs and their predictions about the immediate future can lead unconsciously to violent clashes with the government.[10] Government officials, as might be imagined, take predictions of their imminent doom seriously, even when their annihilation is to be at the hands of vengeful ancestors. Then, too, people who view social institutions as irremediably evil have little disposition to comply with their demands, save as a tactical expedient.[11]

The most perplexing aspect of millenarian activity, one that has so often fascinated ethnographers and historians, has been their bizarre behavioral features. We come again and again upon references to what was once called "enthusiasm" [12] and is now more commonly referred to as ecstasy. Thus references abound to hallucinations; ecstatic dancing; trances; uncontrolled motor activity; feelings of persecution and conspiracy; extreme dependence on the leader; a sudden willingness to abandon the obligations and routines of everyday life; and feelings of rebirth and personality transformation.[13] Millenarians often behave unconventionally and may appear to present or mimic psychopathological symptoms. The Vailala Madness, already referred to, struck administrators and natives alike as unpredictable and strange.[14] Richard Hofstadter has popularized the notion of a "paranoid" political style, and while his usage of the term lies within a specifically American context, he makes plain his debt to studies of millenarian movements elsewhere.[15] We shall see that these surface phenomena have given rise to many rather facile attributions of madness and irrationality. Yet, however superficial these judgments may be, the prominence of unusual psychophysiological activity demands explanation.

What we have already seen of chiliasm serves only to reinforce the impression of its exoticism and remoteness from modern experience. How odd and alien these movements appear, hidden in the interstices of the modern world. Yet the

implications have a way of ramifying, drawing us progressively closer to mainstream social forces. The larger implications of millenarianism lie in four directions: in their bearing
on major revolutionary upheavals; in the continuing presence
of messianic themes even where movements are absent; in the
millenarian character of so many modern social movements;
and, finally, in its hypothesized influence on the rise of
modern totalitarianism.

We can best gain insight into the relationship between
millenarianism and revolution by examining revolution itself.
The term *revolution* is now used so freely that an approach to
the subject must necessarily begin with an examination of the
concept and of its cognate, *rebellion.* The term *revolution* has
had an unusual history. Until the seventeenth century, it was
used primarily by astronomers. By metaphorical extension, it
came to be associated with violent, abrupt political changes—
a coming around of the political system.[16] Once established as
part of the political vocabulary, it is again applied metaphori-
cally, this time to connote not simply sudden and violent
change in the form of government but any social change: thus
we find "revolutions of rising expectations," "Industrial
Revolution," "Cultural Revolution," and so on. In this welter
of diverse usages, revolution may best be understood in
counterpoint to rebellion. Rebellion, though it involves
collective violence, leaves the constitutional framework unaltered. New incumbents occupy old offices.[17] Indeed, the rebel
frequently sees himself as a defender of traditional values and
institutions against those who would betray them.

The interplay of rebellious violence and constitutional
acceptance is nowhere more evident than in so-called rituals
of rebellion, to which Max Gluckman has directed our
attention.[18] These rule-governed attacks upon the ruler in
certain African tribal societies are always hedged about with
mutually accepted limitations. They may occur at set times
and often serve to bind the society together by directing
separatist tendencies toward a common center. Rebellion
thus involves the paradox of violent change amid institutional
continuity, and this paradox ties together rituals of rebellion,
medieval peasant revolts, and military coups. The seizure of
power, unaccompanied by expectations of structural change,

necessarily leaves society pretty much as it was. Some rebellious or quasirebellious outbursts do not seem to be focused on the seizure of power at all. Rather, they serve to discharge hostility, express discontent, or seek the alleviation of very specific grievances: for example, slave revolts, seizures of open land, destruction of labor-saving machinery, commodity riots, and intercommunal brawling.[19]

The distinguishing characteristic of rebellion lies in its acceptance of the legitimacy of basic social and political arrangements. The quintessential rebellion *is* ritual, where adversaries fulfill structured roles and remain in agreement concerning basic values. But in point of fact rebellions only approximate this relatively benign picture. Most of the time, the elements of rebellion and revolution are intermixed. We must, consequently, conceive of a spectrum at one end of which lies the most ritualized, consensual rebellion; at the other lies millenarian revolution. Movement along this continuum, away from ritualized rebellion, takes us through an indefinite number of hybrids, each incorporating value disagreement and consensus in different proportions. As one moves in the direction of millenarian revolutions, the commitment to basic structural change increases, until at the farthest extreme, society is to be utterly and totally transformed.

Characteristics of millenarianism in fact show up even in the "classical" revolutions of France, Russia, America, England, and China.[20] The American Revolution, one of the least violent and disruptive, nonetheless generated a considerable literature concerning its own transcendent significance and outlining the role to be played by the new nation in the world's secular salvation. The margins of the English Civil War harbored many millenarian sects: Ranters, Diggers, Levellers, Fifth Monarchy Men. And, of course, the French, Russian, and Chinese revolutions took with utmost seriousness the possibility of individual and social perfectibility.

Why then do we draw a distinction between these revolutions on the one hand and, on the other, the millenarian movements discussed earlier? Here, as is so often the case, differences of degree have been converted into differences of kind. The distinction between *revolution* and *millenarianism* is thus largely artificial. Two circumstances appear primarily responsible. First, movements with an apparently religious character tend to be classified as millenarian, while those that are professedly secular are regarded as movements of political revolution. This is due in part to historical changes; most of the events we now regard as revolutions took place after Western society had become secularized, and as a result social discontent was expressed in secular terms. This secularization has not prevented the retention of essentially messianic themes, where "there are functional analogues of supernatural forces, like 'the force of history,' 'national destiny,' and so on." [21] Where a society does not clearly distinguish between secular and religious realms, millenarian movements quite naturally articulate political problems in what we would regard as religious terms.[22]

Second, the classification also comes to rest on the point a movement reaches in the revolutionary life cycle. Historians and ethnographers tend to describe movements as millenarian which were suppressed or went underground at a fairly early point.[23] The classical revolution, as Crane Brinton pointed out, runs through a cycle which leads from active opposition to the final "Thermidorean reaction," a period characterized by loosened revolutionary discipline, increased hedonism, and a renewed if partial acceptance of prerevolutionary norms and institutions.[24] Thermidor occurs only where a revolution has succeeded to governmental power; it is the price of success. Millenarian revolutions may in fact simply be those that have failed to attain power, through unrealizable goals, deficient resources, or poor leadership. In any event, they lacked the opportunity to pass into the relative normalcy of Thermidor, by which time their millenarian ardor would have cooled. Thus it is entirely possible that many successful revolutions were millenarian in their youth and that we call the Taborites, for example, "millenarians" largely because events cut short their full development.

The historiography of revolutions, because it concentrates so heavily upon successful assertions of opposition, tends to read back into the original revolutionary period the relative conventionality of the established revolutionary regime. Brinton has drawn our attention to the fact that after the fall of the old regime, the new regime becomes the arena of intense factional struggles. Revolutionary groups compete with each other with all of the earnestness they previously reserved for the old regime. The initial seizure of power is dominated by moderate men of secure position who seek fairly conventional institutional reforms.[25] There is consequently a gap between their attitudes and their flamboyant rhetoric. "The moderates . . . do not really believe in the big words they have to use. They do not really believe a heavenly perfection is suddenly coming to men on earth." [26] The administrative, social, and military problems which confront the new regime work against moderation and, in what amounts to a second revolution, the new regime comes to be dominated by the extremist faction.

The extremists now institute a period which in language, belief, and action is virtually indistinguishable from a millenarian movement. In this "Reign of Terror and Virtue," the ardent adherent receives satisfactions qualitatively different from those derived from normal political participation. He "finds in his devoted service . . . most of the psychological satisfactions commonly supplied by what we call religion." [27] The old evils must be extirpated and perfection instantly attained. All manner of surveillance, confession, ritual demonstrations, and punitive action are harnessed in the service of these twin aims. "What separates these revolutionaries from traditional Christianity is most obviously their insistence on having their heaven, here, now, on earth, their impatient intent to conquer evil once and for all. Christianity in its more traditional form has long since, not by any means given up the moral struggle, but given up its chiliastic hopes." [28]

Whatever the similarities between extremists within a larger revolution and millenarians on their own, we must face the question whether other differences exist. Granted the beliefs are very much the same, what of the men themselves? Michael Walzer argues that they are in fact different. The Puritan, whom he sees as the quintessential practitioner of radical politics, tended to have relatively high social status, as aristocrat, minister, gentleman, merchant, or lawyer—hardly the backward agrarians customarily identified with chiliastic movements. This recruitment pattern stems, he suggests, from the great personal exertions and self-discipline required in building the redeemed society, competences demanded not only of the Puritans but of such successor revolutionaries as the Jacobins and Bolsheviks.[29] Against such rigors, "laborers and peasants were more likely, if they were free at all from traditional ways, to adopt some more specific or chiliastic faith whose promise did not depend upon their own hard work, that is, upon the control of themselves and the cruel, unwearying repression of others." [30] These radical Puritan "saints" see their chosenness as a mandate for change. The destruction of evil and the perfection of society lie in their own hands. They must methodically and systematically transform the world and, however much their activities may conform to the requirements of a Divine Plan or the necessities of History, the actual constructive effort must be their own.

Walzer's model thus distinguishes between radical politics, which possesses a strong millenarian element but demands organizational skills, hard work, and enduring loyalties; and millenarian movements themselves, which subsist only so long as individual enthusiasms can be sustained and depend far more upon external agencies than upon human resources. The former presumably requires some prior habituation to hard work, a recognition of means-ends relationships, and a familiarity with instrumental social organizations—in short, the Puritan ethic. This distinction between the sophisticated revolutionary and the untutored millenarian begins to break down, however, when it is closely examined.

Where millenarians constitute a minority in the midst of a hostile culture, they have proven as adept as conventional revolutionaries at the art of concealment and survival. The history of heresy provides vivid examples of their ability to adapt to difficult circumstances. Like revolutionary cells, medieval heresy persisted, reappearing over and over again in the Low Countries, southern France, and northern Italy. The Cathars, whose growth gave them temporary hegemony over southern France, were crushed only by a genocidal crusade.[31]

The Islamic millenarians known to us as the Assassins fused revolutionary terrorism with preexisting forms of religious brotherhoods.[32]

This suggests that millenarians may have a wholly unappreciated ability to make significant innovations in social organization. Too often this has been missed by concentration upon a seemingly endless procession of military and political defeats. Traditional societies lack effective means for central decision making. Where their adversary is larger and better organized, segmented forms of social organization cannot cope. Millenarian movements attempt to solve this "problem of scale." [33] The prophet offers an alternative to traditional local leaders and preaches his message to new and ever-larger social groups. The prophet who responds to a societal crisis may provide the only means for organizational innovation. The conventional revolutionary generally emerges in less traditional societies where voluntary associations are already prevalent, and he has only to design another such organization, devoted to the forcible rearrangement of the political system. The traditional millenarian, for whom social forms are far less plastic, superimposes innovation on a normally static environment.

Thus far we have continued to employ *millenarian* and *revolutionary* as separate terms which refer to separate phenomena. This is, indeed, the conventional distinction, between the undisciplined chiliast who expects outside forces to provide the motive force and the calculating, energetic revolutionary who remakes the world by his own efforts. We have seen that the differing usages reflect the roots of the former in nonsecularized agrarian societies and the latter in more secularized modern settings. But neither modernization nor secularization proceeds in a wholly orderly way. And even if it did, old concepts have a way of reappearing in modern dress. The complexities of the millenarian idea emerge as we attempt to trace it through its various incarnations.

The original meaning of *millennium* refers, of course, to the passage in the Book of Revelation (20:4–6), which envisions a thousand-year messianic kingdom on earth to follow Christ's second coming. After his thousand-year reign, all earthly existence is to give way before the fury of the Last Judgment. The subsequent history of the millenarian idea in the West suggests something of its expanding influence. By the late Middle Ages, preoccupation with the theological millennium "joined forces with the active demands of the oppressed strata of society." [34] In the period which followed the Puritan Revolution, a procession of English theologians, scientists, and philosophers gradually transmuted religious concepts of judgment and salvation into the secular idea of progress. The significance of this transformation was twofold: First, it reversed a view widely held in the sixteenth century, that the earth was in the process of irreversible decay. This temporary emphasis on natural degeneration contrasts sharply both with the general teleological conception of Western history and with the millenarian philosophies then extant at the margins of "respectable" discourse.[35] The second and related consequence was that millenarianism was again made respectable. At least in England, the excesses of the Puritan sects had made religious enthusiasm a subject of disdain.[36] In addition, as we have seen, the natural world was viewed as inexorably "winding down." By the seventeenth century, "millennial thought has, so to speak, received the sanction of the Establishment, at least in England, and has again entered the main stream of Western religion and philosophy. This re-entry was necessary before a truly optimistic attitude towards the future could get established." [37] Progress, Ernest Tuveson argues, derives from the fusion of two intellectual streams: millenarian thought and Newtonian physics.

The long-term effect was both to dilute the strength of millenarian doctrine and at the same time to inject it wholesale into Western society. As the millennium came to be understood in terms of the gradual unfolding of scientific knowledge and human potential, it came to be regarded as less and less imminent. Progress might eventually function as a powerful stimulus to growth and achievement, but the distant, uncertain nature of the goal demanded a less emotional commitment. In short, by the eighteenth century what was at hand was not the Day of Judgment but the steady ascent of the human species. But despite the intellectual transformation, elements of the older salvationism survived. More importantly, they did so within the context of accepted intellectual discourse, not as part of the isolated lives of fringe sects. That millenarianism retained some of its original character is clear from the fact that elements of it were transmitted intact from Europe to America. The image of redeemed society, of America as the "New Jerusalem," bulks large in the colonial period.[38] Subsequently, an American messianism, a sense of corporate mission to the outside world, was to alternate with an isolationist withdrawal from the perceived evil outside.[39] A more direct exportation of millenarian ideas, however, lay in the emigration of European sectarians, a process vividly manifested in the establishment of American utopian communities.[40] "In America, and America alone, the religious socialism of the seventeenth century evolved without break into the secular socialism of the nineteenth. The communitarian sects were the links in this chain of continuity. The inspiration they drew from the Reformation and the Christian tradition in general, they passed on as a living force to the nineteenth century leaders of social reform in the United States." [41]

Meanwhile, in Western Europe itself the history of millenarian thought in the eighteenth and nineteenth centuries was dominated by France. Beginning shortly before the French Revolution, doctrines of inevitable progress and the total redemption of a corrupt society were being widely disseminated, most notably by Rousseau and Condorcet.[42] Although it is generally assumed that the outright millenarianism on the fringes of the Puritan Revolution was unknown in France before the nineteenth century,[43] it also seems that French thought was influenced by some of the same factors as English: the growth of empirical science and philosophical empiricism; a common, eschatologically oriented religious tradition; and the secularization of religious ideas. Thus whether French messianism derived from English influence, or whether similar forces produced similar developments that simply arrived later in France, is a moot point. In any event, J. L. Talmon argues that beginning in the late eighteenth century, Western European political discourse was dominated by two warring sets of ideas: one, a commitment to liberal democracy, incremental change, and a recognition of ineradicable human imperfections; the other, a utopianism which sought the final and ultimate attainment, by force if necessary, of totally harmonious human society. Over and over in these debates the same questions sound, of class privilege, property ownership, and the control of human passions. From Rousseau, Babeuf, and Saint-Simon the development of political millenarianism runs eventually to Fichte and, more particularly, to Marx.

The watershed of political messianism occurred in the mid-nineteenth century, when it ceased to take the form of a universal cure for universal human ills and began to be reshaped as an instrument of national aspirations. "The real victor of Political Messianism was neither the conservative Right nor liberalism, neither capitalism nor democracy, but nationalism, which in the early days of a common struggle against the same enemy, dynastic absolutism, appeared as an integral part of Political Messianism." [44] To a certain extent, the concept of messianic nationalism has proved to be exportable to the non-Western world. It is a commonplace of millenarian scholarship to fasten on the Christian missions as the principal means by which chiliastic ideas were introduced into traditional societies. In fact, the picture is much more complex, for messianic ideas came from three sources: indigenous myths, Christian doctrine brought by the missionaries, and—most germane to the present discussion—Western ideas concerning the secular, politicized millennium. Elie Kedourie argues that medieval millenarianism, intellectually sanitized as the idea of progress, has made its mark even on the non-Western world. He, alongside J. L. Talmon, regards the French Revolution as the great entering wedge by which millenarian ideas came finally and irreversibly to enter Western, and world, politics. "What we may call *sans-culott-isme* has become a striking element in the European political tradition." [45] From there, the tradition of revolutionary messianism has moved outward to become "the mainspring of nationalism in Asia and Africa." [46] We shall have occasion later to critically examine this assertion, for it contradicts much current thinking about the political significance of chiliasm. The traditional line of argument has it that millenarianism precedes, follows, or stands apart from political activity;[47] and that it commonly serves as a stepping-stone to nonmillenarian nationalist movements.[48] If Kedourie is correct, one millenarianism is merely exchanged for another.

Millenarian themes have thus come to permeate Western and non-Western societies alike—albeit in the highly attenuated form of belief in inevitable progress or national mission. Yet even the most cursory examination of the scholarly literature bears out the observation that twentieth-century movements have flourished most in colonial or newly independent areas. This clustering has led to all manner of postulated agents of change, on the assumption that only the introduction of Western ideas could produce chiliasm.[49] While this is a welcome if indirect proof of the importance such ideas have had in the West, it implies that the West alone is the fountainhead of messianic ideas. A few writers, like Kedourie, look to the Western themes of progress and national independence; even more identify the rise of non-Western millenarianism with the introduction of Christianity by missionaries.[50] "Messiah," "Second Coming," and "millennium" itself flow freely and naturally out of Christian eschatology.

We cannot, however, yield too readily to a belief in Western "contagion." The historical problem is acute, for reliable knowledge about non-Western societies itself is a product of Western penetration. Certainly so far as nonliterate peoples are concerned, we know little enough about their history before contact with the West. What if, in fact, they possessed rich indigenous millenarian traditions of their own? Orally transmitted traditions picked up by early Portuguese explorers suggest the existence of millenarian movements in Indian Brazil,[51] and few societies can be found which lack belief in the eventual return of a culture hero.[52] It has been easy to postulate Western influences, for those are the influences about which we know the most. Native traditions, even when at first glance they appear inhospitable to messianic ideas, often turn out to harbor heresies, variations, or subordinate doctrines which in willing hands may be turned to the purpose. "Even in situations where Christian influences have been clearly established . . . it seems probable that the absence of reliable or readily available data in relation to the more traditional ideologies has resulted in an over-emphasis of the Christian influences." [53] Even Buddhism, so contemplative and changeless in its dominant aspect, provided the ideological support for millenarianism in Ceylon.[54]

Consequently, millenarian ideas flow from many sources; the choice can never be clearly between diffusion and independent invention. Marginally different ideas have cropped up too often in too many places for us to attribute them all to a single source. They spread, fission, and combine in a host of syncretic variations. If the emphasis here has been on intellectual life in the West, it is only because it is here that the history of ideas has so far made its deepest probes.

Given the spread of messianic themes, it is difficult to find any period of time wholly without expression of them. The twentieth century has proven particularly fertile. We have only to glance at the array of diverse social movements active in the United States alone: the Townsendites, the Jehovah's Witnesses, the Weathermen, the Black Muslims. Despite the enormous differences among them, each has held to a vision of an old society destroyed, a new one created, and mankind's ills finally cured. The United States does not constitute a unique case. The Cultural Revolution in China, the German youth movements between the wars, Sokka Gakai in Japan, the Social Credit movement in Canada, the Kimbangu movement in the Congo, and the Melanesian Cargo Cults which proliferate to the present day—all have organized men around concepts of ultimate good and evil, in an attempt to exchange the one for the other. Hardly a region has proven immune. The more historians burrow, the more movements come to light—in Latin America, the Caribbean, the South Pacific, the United States, South Asia, sub-Saharan Africa, the Middle East, Central Asia, Europe.

The most audacious attempt to trace millenarianism into modern times, however, remains the hypothesis advanced by Norman Cohn.[55] Cohn's position, most simply put, is that nazism and communism are the direct descendants of late medieval and Reformation chiliasm. The ramifications of this position are sufficiently extensive so that detailed discussion of them will be held for a later chapter. However, it might be

well at this point to sketch in Cohn's view. His own account
of European messianism concludes with the destruction of
the Anabaptists' "New Jerusalem" at Münster in 1535, the
unsuccessful attempt by Jan Willemsen to reestablish it in
1567, and Willemsen's execution in 1580. Yet, Cohn asserts,
the story did not end there:

> That peculiar faith which is of the very essence not indeed
> of chiliasm as such but of militant, revolutionary chiliasm
> —the tense expectation of a final, decisive struggle in which
> a world tyranny will be overthrown by a "chosen people"
> and through which the world will be renewed and history
> brought to its consummation—this did not disappear with
> the fall of the New Jerusalem at Münster. It continued a
> dim, subterranean existence down the centuries, flaring up
> briefly in the margins of the English Civil War and the
> French Revolution, until in the course of the nineteenth
> century it began to take on a new, explosive vigour, now in
> France, now in Germany, now in Russia.[56]

We have already had occasion to discuss the concept of a
millenarian tradition; we shall return to it in chapter four.

For Cohn, its reappearance in secularized form has been its
most sinister incarnation, for it carries into modern times the
same ideological content that, on a smaller scale, imparted
such destructive intensity to the late medieval sects: The
world stands on the verge of destruction, brought there by the
machinations of the powerful, the Jews, and the clergy.
Should this conspiracy be thwarted, the new emergent society
will offer "a state of total community, a society wholly
unanimous in its beliefs and wholly free from inner conflicts." [57] Finally, in the hands of Hitler and Rosenberg on the
one hand and Marx and Lenin on the other, the old themes
take on a form palatable to a nonreligious age.

Here is the final transmutation of millenarian scholarship:
from exotic sects on the margins of society (in that pregnant
phrase, "the lunatic fringe") to forces at the very center of
great events. A full assessment of the social and political
significance of millenarianism depends upon knowing, first,
the circumstances that stimulate its occurrence; second, the

means by which millenarian movements grow and survive; and, third, the relationship between the movements and canons of rationality. Consequently, the following chapters address themselves primarily to these three questions.

Chapter Two

THE DISASTER ORIGINS OF MILLENARIAN MOVEMENTS

Most attempts to explain millenarian movements may be assimilated to a single idea: that the movements result from the clash of dissimilar cultures. For want of a better term, I call this the *colonial hypothesis*. It asserts that contact between technologically unequal cultures produces social changes, and that these changes in turn give rise to millenarian movements. This very general relationship embraces a number of more specific explanations. Two have been particularly widely noted and will be discussed in detail. The first, *relative deprivation theory*, is both more widely held and more flawed; while the second, Anthony Wallace's *revitalization theory*, suffers principally from incompleteness. The discussion which follows a critical analysis of these two approaches goes on to seek some confirmation for the colonial hypothesis. Is acculturation disruptive? What kind of disruption occurs? I have chosen to seek evidence on these points from the realm of social psychiatry, both because the evidence is available and because it relates so closely to the problem of millenarian ecstatic behavior.

Why have millenarian movements occurred where and when they have? The standard explanation for them, as for revolution in general, has been relative deprivation. Relative deprivation provides a simple and logical answer to the origin of many forms of individual and social discontent, and it is small wonder that an idea at once so broad and so flexible should eventually have been applied to millenarianism. As the gap widens between what an individual perceives to be his legitimate expectations on the one hand and the means for satisfying them on the other, he becomes progressively more discontented. The continuation of this discontent, where it simultaneously affects many individuals, produces collective social and political violence. The gap between expectations

34

and capabilities exists and rankles only if we accept the validity of three assumptions: First, we must assume that human wants are in principle limitless; there is no natural ceiling to human desires, even where our biological equipment places limits on the realization of desires. Second, legitimate expectations are also not a fact of nature; they are the product of social and cultural definitions. One learns which expectations are considered reasonable and right and which are accounted irrational, unjustifiable, and, as it were, "unnatural." Finally, social and cultural change can disrupt definitions of legitimate expectations. Just as these expectations emerge from society and culture, so changes in society and culture may alter the expectations.[1]

Relative deprivation requires that the individual utilize some reference point to gauge his own position. That benchmark, filtered through his own perceptions and desires, bears no necessary relationship to the "objective" yardstick with which an outside observer might measure conditions in a society. Knowing per capita income statistics does not tell you how a particular individual judges his own life condition. Relative deprivation involves an essentially subjective individual judgment, and only where many individual judgments of life conditions coincide is it possible to anticipate social action.

Relative deprivation takes many forms, limited only by the variations in curves of expectations and capabilities. Millenarian movements seem to result most often from situations of *decremental deprivation.*[2] Decremental deprivation occurs when the expectations of a group concerning its overall well-being remain basically unchanged, but its perceived capabilities for realizing these expectations decline. As in other cases of relative deprivation, it is not particularly important that the participants' views of the matter be validated by the outside observer's. Indeed, it is perfectly possible to imagine a situation in which an outside observer notes a rise in capabilities, while the social actors themselves see the capabilities declining. Nathan Glazer has demonstrated that the statistical evidence on the condition of American blacks shows steady, sometimes dramatic, upward movement; but the statistical picture seems quite at variance with how many blacks themselves see their situation.[3] The participants do not, of course, reach their conclusions in a vacuum. Their own analysis grows out of perceived events around them, to which they attach a sinister significance. The decrementally deprived person feels that his progress is blocked; he feels he deserves something and suddenly finds that he will not get it.[4]

Decremental deprivation often occurs in situations such as industrialization and colonization, where a new distribution of values consigns some groups to economic, social, or political marginality. The small businessman, the family farmer, and the elite landowner in a developing country have all found themselves in this predicament.[5] Extremist movements have been prominently associated with a fall into marginal statuses. Decremental deprivation constitutes a particularly strong theme in accounts of millenarian movements. In the non-Western world, millenarian activity clusters in areas of intense colonial pressure: sub-Saharan Africa, the South Pacific, South China. It is only fair to observe that the tie may be coincidental, since few non-Western areas have been free of colonialism. It is also true that frequently colonial expansion confronted relatively stable, static societies with unimaginable military and economic power and an abrupt loss of autonomy. The millenarian reservoir in Western societies themselves has been made up of precisely those groups whose expectations have frequently been frustrated: religious, racial, and ethnic minorities; the lower middle class; artisans and shopkeepers; lower-echelon clergy; and the peasantry. At various times and in varying degrees, each of these groups has found its opportunities thwarted and its legitimate expectations juxtaposed with decreasing resources for their fulfillment.

Yet relative deprivation, decremental or otherwise, fails to provide a full explanation of millenarianism. As David Aberle notes, "It would seem . . . that a knowledge of the severity and type of deprivation, and of the date and place of its occurrence would make it possible to predict when, where, and with what ideology a social movement would arise. Such a claim cannot be sustained." [6] Why do some depressed conditions produce volatile political activity, while other circumstances, at least as bleak, yield only political apathy? Why do millenarian movements occur at some times of relative deprivation and not at others? What triggers them, and why does their content depart so significantly from conventional forms of political action? Finally, what explains the bizarre features so often remarked upon in descriptions of millenarian discontent? Descriptions of millenarian movements are replete with references to ecstatic activities.[7] These phenomena suggest some kind of breakpoint, a qualitative difference, between millenarianism and other forms of social and political dissidence. Yet nothing in relative deprivation theory prepares us for such a quantum leap, only for the comparatively graceful rise and descent of curves of expectations and capabilities.

Relative deprivation theory arms us with a necessary but not a sufficient condition, for severe relative deprivation may come and go without producing any significant social movement. The general passivity of American slaves and, more recently, of concentration camp inmates are cases in point. The dominant tendency among students of millenarian movements has been to point to culture contact as the great generator of relative deprivation in modern times, and no doubt in some highly general sense that is true. Having said that, however, we still have relatively little explanation for the peculiar form millenarianism takes. Relative deprivation, after all, is a well-nigh universal phenomenon, built into the human animal and his relationship to the environment. Millenarian movements, while widespread, are by no means universal, and it remains to separate those relative deprivations that induce millenarianism from those that engender apathy, reform, or unfocused rioting.

In an effort to connect deprivation as a cause to millenarianism as an effect of it, Anthony F. C. Wallace has chosen to introduce an additional variable, *stress*. The introduction of stress has enabled him to construct a rich if incomplete theory for the rise of certain kinds of social movements. He defines stress "as a condition in which some part, or the whole, of the social organism is threatened with more or less serious damage."[8] The only problem with this concept of stress is its ambiguity. For Wallace, to be sure, it is something that individuals and societies try to avoid, a source of deprivation, pain, and distortion. We can see in his usage a biologically derived concept of system maintenance: stress is a threat to the integrity of the organism, and the organism must adapt to it or die. However, it is just as true that organisms seek stress under certain conditions. The annals of exploration, sport, and military history are filled with instances of human beings deliberately seeking contact with conditions to which adaptation may not be possible. Nonetheless they seek stress "to increase the intensity of emotion or level of activations of the organism." [9] In an effort to evade this ambiguity, Wallace moves finally to a physiological definition of stress, operationalized in medical terms. He finds in Hans Selye's general adaptation syndrome the physiological evidences of stress, set forward in a way that purports to free them from the tension between stress-as-threat and stress-as-stimulation.[10] We must look, he tells us, at what happens to the body under stress, not at what led to the contact with stressful conditions in the first place.

On this basis, Wallace argues that many social movements, particularly those of a millenarian cast, partake of a single social process, which he terms *revitalization*. The essence of revitalization lies in the need of a society under excessive stress to either reinforce itself or die. The key to an understanding of the individual's predicament in such a society lies in Wallace's concept of the *mazeway*. The mazeway is simply "nature, society, culture, personality, and body image as seen by one person." [11] It is a shorthand term for the way perceptions are ordered. A society may be conceived as a group of individuals whose mazeways largely coincide, for these cognitive maps must possess high levels of internal communication, internal consistency, and correspondence with reality. "The higher the degree of order in the mazeway system . . . the lower the level of chronic stress, because the rate of experience of uncertainty, conflict, or error . . . will be correspondingly lower." [12]

But the mazeway is not beyond challenge. Events outside the control of either individual or society can confront persons with circumstances in which uncertainty, conflict, and error multiply. When mazeways can no longer reduce stress or produce pleasure for large numbers of people, we have entered a situation in which a revitalization movement may arise. Wallace postulates a process of consecutive though occasionally overlapping stages in which a society moves from homeostasis to crisis to revitalization and back to a "steady state." In between the two points of relative stability, mounting stress and the inability of existing cultural mechanisms to relieve it produce a radical resynthesis of existing beliefs and values, in essence the abrupt creation of a new culture. When a society can no longer effectively shield its members from the consequences of political subordination, acculturation, economic dislocation, or similar stresses, it faces either "societal death" or the need to restructure itself through the revitalization process.

The revitalization movement's first task is the reformulation of the mazeway, to explain the previously inexplicable changes and to restore individual senses of meaning. This task falls to a prophet-figure. The content of his vision provides the raw material for a new model of the world. Converts repeat the prophet's own personal transformation in countless individual conversions. A feeling of rebirth takes them from past stresses into a new relationship with "reality," built around innovative doctrines and charismatic leadership. If the movement proves effective in reducing feelings of malaise, what was once a fringe group becomes progressively more routinized and culturally dominant.

Notwithstanding its richness and subtlety, Wallace's model leaves open its own category of significant questions. We wonder but are not told precisely what kind of stress must be involved, over how long a period of time, involving what proportion of a population. At some points Wallace relies heavily on physiological data: heartbeat, adrenal secretions, and so on. At others, he accepts forms of social pathology as evidence of stress: crime, drunkenness, declining productivity.

Both relative deprivation and revitalization have been utilized as variants of the colonial hypothesis, although neither is inherently limited to culture-contact situations. The application of these approaches to the collision of cultures rests on a strong initial plausibility. The line of reasoning goes roughly as follows: In the last two hundred years, Western industrial society has progressively impinged upon more and more of the world beyond Europe. In so doing, it has confronted and overwhelmed many different societies, all less technologically sophisticated. Defeated, impoverished, and oppressed, they have suffered precisely the decrements that relative deprivation theory predicts and the stresses that revitalization theory assumes. The confrontation has proved traumatic for the sense of meaning and self-regard of many members of non-Western societies, and, as traditional modes of action and belief have been discredited, these individuals have sought cultural alternatives. Millenarian movements, with their dual emphasis on the destruction of Western power and the elevation of indigenous peoples to high status in a redeemed world, have proven popular solutions to these feelings of powerlessness and anxiety.

What questions remain? Regarding relative deprivation theory, the major question is always, How much is enough? How much relative deprivation is required to produce a particular effect? And why does millenarianism crop up only in certain times and places? Decremental deprivation can be blamed for everything from the Cargo Cults to the Daughters of the American Revolution. Surely, we must be able to discriminate between them. Decremental deprivation provides a beginning, a necessary condition, a general population of social circumstances. The focus must be narrowed and if only some situations are ripe, then which ones? Revitalization theory, by being much more specific about the initial conditions and about the dynamics of millenarian activity, begins to accomplish this task. But we still do not learn as much as we would like to know about the relationship between high levels of stress and millenarian activity. Wallace tells us that some individuals possess a heightened capacity for effecting creative resyntheses of old ideas under the pressure of stressful circumstances.[13] These persons then emerge as the prophet-figures who bring salvationist doctrines to a weary, confused populace. We would like to know more about their followers. Do they recapitulate the leader's personality transformation? Does stress simply erode their ability to cope, or do they too make a kind of quantum leap to a new definition of the situation?

These and other questions will occupy us in the pages to follow. But before we begin to fill in the interstices left by existing explanations, some cautionary notes are in order. The field of millenarian activity has proven unusually resistant to the efforts of social scientists. More than in most areas of human behavior, we seem always to be at the periphery, while the core remains stubbornly elusive. Methodological barriers stand between the observer and his subject, and at least part of the task of breaking through those barriers involves an understanding of what created them in the first place.

There is, to begin with, the very general problem of comparing cultures and historical epochs. Is there really enough that is shared by twentieth-century Melanesian Cargo Cults and fourteenth-century European chiliastic sects? As soon as the question has been posed, however, it collapses of its own weight: How can any two Cargo Cults be compared, or two medieval movements, or two of anything else? We can, if we choose to do so, always find something that makes a person, group, or act unique. We can also, if we will it, as easily find something that apparently disparate things have in common. Someone once said that the world of scholarship can be divided into the takers-apart and the putters-together. It is very much a matter of how we draw the boundaries of our categories. This question of like and unlike is much more a matter of how we choose to see and group things than of their inherent characteristics.

If we are willing to grant the possibility that comparison across time and space is possible, then we enter a realm of special difficulties encountered in the investigation of chiliasm. In the first place, social science has tended to be preoccupied with the nature and maintenance of social order. That is a laudable research question, to be sure, but since millenarian movements produce disorder and indeed arise under conditions of social change, they have proven difficult for contemporary social science to handle.[14] Since they

constitute breaks in the pattern, they can only be regarded as
nuisances for those whose principal interest lies in the pattern
itself.

In the interests of parsimony, it has also been common to
attribute the rise of millenarian movements throughout the
world to some single historical process. Our task would be
easier if we knew that all of these activities resulted from a
single source. It is the old battle between diffusion and
independent invention, refought. The culture-contact perspective reflects the appeal of diffusionism, for if the Europeans had not come, bringing their power and culture with
them, millenarianism would never have run rampant through
parts of Asia, Africa, and Oceania. In one of its less
sophisticated forms, the appeal to parsimony has ended up by
making millenarianism simply an unintended by-product of
Christianity. The missionaries, unknowingly, brought millenarian doctrines from the West to people who had no
salvationist beliefs of their own.[15] The Bible becomes a
subversive document, without which the natives would have
remained subdued and passive. This poses a difficult historical problem. How is it possible to secure reliable knowledge
of millenarian movements that might have arisen in nonliterate societies before the arrival of Westerners? What might
have happened in these societies had the Westerners never
come? We simply do not, and in the latter case cannot, know.
The Ghost Dance may in fact have arisen initially out of
purely native concerns; data that might finally decide the
question is not available.[16]

The larger question is one of the adequacy and reliability of
information. In any attempt to write the natural histories of
millenarian movements, the record is often so spotty that it is
impossible to reconstruct a sequence of events. These movements, so often made up of the ignorant and inarticulate,
rarely leave a satisfactory written record behind.[17] What we
know of specific movements frequently comes from outsiders.
European movements often involved people no more able or
disposed to produce a written record than their Asian and
African counterparts. What does survive frequently comes
from the hands of their adversaries,[18] clerics and government

officials who come to know the movements only when they constitute perceived threats to their own positions. The occasional traveler or journalist who happens upon a movement in some remote area is another source of partial and only intermittently reliable information.[19] Ethnographic studies (e.g. of the Cargo Cults) constitute an apparent exception to this haphazard picture, but even here the quality of data is subject to wide fluctuations.

Millenarian movements hence enter the historical record only at those points where outsiders stumble upon them or where they reach a level of high public visibility. Occasionally social scientists move in quickly to examine an otherwise obscure cult, as Festinger, Riecken, and Schachter and Lofland and Stark did in the cases of two American end-of-the-world movements.[20] But these are exceptional cases, which do not add up to the representative picture that is required. As a result, millenarian movements live an underground existence most of the time. They may be of central significance in the lives of their members, but this centrality often coexists with public obscurity.

Even where more or less adequate data becomes available, the interpretation of it is peculiarly vulnerable to bias. What is one to do with a movement's ecstatic manifestations? The initial tendency is usually to apply some concept of "normality," and what does not seem normal is readily categorized as the result of "neurosis," "psychosis," "hysteria," "fanaticism," or the like. Notwithstanding the generally rationalist emphasis of contemporary social science, millenarian movements have lent themselves to facile and usually unflattering politicopsychiatric labels.[21] These attributions imply a concept of "abnormality, . . . on the one hand . . . a judgment of value, of goodness or badness; on the other, there is reference to the statistical average . . . It is desirable, therefore, when we say that a man is abnormal to specify firstly, how he departs from the average; and secondly, how he falls short of the ideal, then we are immediately faced with the problem, what average? and whose ideal?" [22] Behavior which in the West is evaluated negatively, such as hallucinations, might possess quite positive connotations elsewhere.[23]

The individual who in one society is sufficiently deviant to require hospitalization might in another setting find a socially acceptable niche as a prophet or shaman.[24]

As far as most outside observers are concerned, the movements are "only" religious, "only" social, or "only" political. If the debate has had any dominant polarity, it has been between those who view millenarian movements as preeminently religious phenomena and those who see in them as both religious and secular strivings. Many movements do in fact express themselves in nominally religious terms, and the very language they employ gets them classified at the outset. The political scientist happily exiles them to the domain of the student of religion, in the interests of an intellectual division of labor. The student of religion concentrates upon the aspects that interest him and ignores the others. But of course there are many societies which do not make our conventional distinction between "secular" and "religious" realms, and for them "politics" or "social protest" does not have a separate existence. Where these distinctions are not made, millenarian movements quite naturally articulate political and social problems in what we would regard as religious terms.[25] Where a society has become secularized, it may retain essentially messianic themes but associate them with an allegedly natural but irresistible force, such as "History" or "National Mission." [26]

The religiosity of a movement is no guarantee the movement will avoid political issues. Quite the contrary, its religiosity may impel it toward an even greater insistence that its social goals be attained. The religious idiom of the Taiping Rebellion amplified rather than muted its political intensity. Taking the problem from the other direction, when we wish to emphasize the intensity with which a political movement pursues its goals, we frequently do so by referring to it in religiously derived terms: *fanaticism, apocalypse, messianic, charismatic, fervent,* and so on. David Apter uses the phrase "political religions" to refer to regimes which, while outwardly secular, attach transcendent significance to their acts.[27] We might just as easily speak of "religious politics." The point is that millenarian movements inhabit that border area where the religious and political fuse and interpenetrate, such that it no longer serves a useful analytic purpose to hold them separate. To exclude the one or the other only diminishes the phenomena.

Let us attempt to take these problems into account as we explore apparent uniformities in the emergence of millenarian movements. When we examine descriptions of them, we quickly come upon a stubborn likeness which they bear to one another: Millenarian movements almost always occur in times of upheaval, in the wake of culture contact, economic dislocation, revolution, war, and natural catastrophe.[28] Depredations such as the Black Death, as well as the man-made disaster of colonization, appear to have spawned volatile chiliastic cults. Millenarian movements do not flourish during periods that are otherwise stable; a catalyst is required. "Ordinary life" produces ordinary politics, while millenarian politics seem confined to "abnormal" situations. There are, to be sure, occasional exceptions. Upstate New York was relatively tranquil during the period 1825–60, yet was so often swept by millenarian fervor that it came to be known as the "Burned-Over District." [29] We shall deal with these exceptions in the next chapter. For the vast majority of cases, however, some instability in the environment seems to call the movement into existence.

The first question raised by this observation concerns the consequences of social change: Can social change, in and of itself, produce millenarian movements? That question cannot very well be answered without specifying, first, what we mean by social change and, second, what impact social change has upon those individuals touched by it. *Social change* is sometimes understood to mean the planned alteration of society and in this sense connotes forward movement. As it is applied to millenarianism, developing societies, and related topics, its meaning is a good deal broader, referring to any "broad and basic changes in the nature of society" which alter fundamental institutions and organizations.[30] The prevalent view states that social change induces personal disorganization. The colonial hypothesis, in effect, holds that there is a causal sequence at work: culture contact–social change–mental disturbance–millenarian movements. If this chain of inference is correct, it is reasonable to expect that we should be able to detect some evidence of the traumata of acculturation or modernization. Wallace anticipates that a society under stress eventually enters a period of "cultural distortion" as it attempts unsuccessfully to deal with its problems. Time-honored modes of doing and seeing, piecemeal innovation, and massive social change together produce a host of pathological forms of behavior. Among these effects, he points to alcoholism, passivity, indolence, dependency relationships, intragroup violence, violation of mores, irresponsibility in public officials, neurotic and psychosomatic disorders, and feelings of guilt and depression.[31]

Can social change produce these effects? The last two—neurotic and psychosomatic disorders, and feelings of guilt and depression—offer a particularly useful starting point. They easily relate to the ecstatic behavior and attributions of group hysteria so often found in descriptions of millenarianism. There is, in addition, a very extensive body of research directed to the hypothesized relationship between social change and psychic functioning. However, this literature itself makes abundantly clear that cross-cultural psychiatric research faces a forbidding set of methodological hurdles. There is, to begin with, the problem of the normal-abnormal dichotomy, to which reference has already been made. In addition, the most readily obtainable data—hospital admissions—are likely to be the least useful. In non-Western societies, and to a lesser extent in the West itself, different segments of the population possess differential access to Western-style medical treatment. Even where hospital data are available, they may be of poor quality. However, recent studies increasingly utilize specially constructed diagnostic tests and survey data to supplement or supplant admissions figures. One overriding difficulty transcends even questions of data quality, the very validity of modern psychiatric categories in cross-cultural research. The dominant tendency is to regard standard types of mental disorder as "ubiquitous." [32] Nonetheless even those who take this position concede the existence of certain culture-specific syndromes, which appear with regularity in one area but nowhere else, for example, *latah* and *amok* in Southeast Asia and the Windigo psychosis among Northeastern Algonkian hunters.[33]

With these caveats in mind, let us examine the conclusions of existing research. There is a widely diffused common understanding on the matter of the relationship between social change and psychological disorder. Most people are prepared to grant as self-evident the proposition that social change unhinges mental life. The research findings, however, produce almost the opposite conclusion, to the one which intuition and methodological shortcomings would suggest. The findings do not follow the biases, suggesting that however unfortunate the data and design faults might be, they do not in the end mold the findings to their own shape.

Acculturation shows a complex relationship: Mental hospitalization rates rise, as we should expect, as contact with Western culture increases. However, the most Westernized members of a non-Western society still show *less* mental pathology than members of Western societies themselves. This suggests that the original increase may not be due to social change per se; rather, it may be due to the fact that as non-Westerners become Westernized, they take on the illnesses of their role models.[34] This implies that the occurrence of "mental illness" in Westernizing societies may not be attributable to social change at all—at least not in a direct sense. Individuals do not necessarily lose their ability to cope because they are under novel stress, but rather an inability to cope which was once expressed in indigenous forms now appears in a manner more congenial to Western diagnostic categories. In short, "being sick is a cultural phenomenon in itself." [35] As one society absorbs a culturally different one, the latter's conception of being sick changes, too, whether or not the fusion of cultures has produced unusual stress. The commonsense attribution of mental illness to acculturation and attendant social change very likely confounds the variables, mistaking changing conceptions of the form of illness for acute culture-shock.

Migration, too, seems to have no clear-cut psychic impact. Neither refugees nor urbanites of rural origin show a disproportionate rate of psychological disorders.[36] Alex Inkeles and David Smith studied the frequency of psychosomatic symptoms in six modernizing societies: Argentina, Chile, India, Israel, Nigeria, and Pakistan. Their findings, which are not dependent upon hospitalization statistics, indicate that "of the modernizing experiences frequently indicated as likely to induce individual disorganization through disruption of personality, creation of strain, introduction of disturbing stimuli and the like, none consistently and significantly brings about increased maladjustment as measured by the Psychosomatic Symptoms Test."[37] Neither education, factory employment, city residence, exposure to mass media, nor migration itself was associated with a high rate of psychosomatic disorders (insomnia, trembling limbs, body pains, etc.).[38] There is even some reason to believe, on the basis of this research, that in the societies studied city living may be *more* conducive to individual harmony than traditional rural life.

Early research on migration and mental hospitalization seemed to demonstrate that migrants were far more likely than natives to require medical attention for psychological disturbances. More extensive study has rendered this early conclusion untenable. Migrants must be viewed from a number of perspectives: their own characteristics, the characteristics of the society from which they have come, and the characteristics of the society which receives them. When all the data have been examined, the net result can only be a sense of bewilderment and complexity. Whatever influence migration has upon behavior, the influence is subject to so many qualifications that no single generalization is possible.[39] Migration does not, in simple linear fashion, produce mental illness. Those instances in which migrants appear more prone to illness are frequently attributable to the nonrepresentative character of the immigrant population or the stressful character of their reception in a new environment.

There seems to be mounting evidence attesting to the notion that the development of mental illness in migrant groups is not so much due to qualities inherent in the migrants, but rather to the interaction between migrants and the societies that receive them. Stress seems to be most intense for those migrants whose original culture differs radically from the new, where there are no available familiar groups to join . . . and where the receiving society most actively emphasizes rapid assimilation.[40]

Even this analysis must be regarded as far more a hypothesis than a well-tested explanation.

Finally, certain social-change situations even appear to be associated with remission of previous psychological disorders, a point that can be inferred from the Inkeles and Smith study. In the many psychological studies of concentration camp inmates, a frequently noted paradoxical finding is that previous neuroses and physical illnesses of psychological origin disappeared after imprisonment.[41]

In the light of this evidence, it is no longer possible to say simply that social change produces mental disorder; if there is any relationship, it is far more complex. Acculturation, migration, and industrialization all seem to leave the individual in a far healthier condition than is customarily realized. If the relationship does not hold in the way once thought, it is equally impossible to state in the facile manner so long employed that changing societies produce individual stress, and individual stress produces social and political disruption. "There seems no way of clearly and inevitably differentiating between situations that promote 'normal' stress and those that develop 'disorganizing' stress." [42]

Presumably, however, people might show no observable mental disorders and yet flock to bizarre and violent social movements. Indeed, such a view is buttressed by extensive writing on the psychotherapeutic functions of group membership. Honigmann suggests that both the Cargo Cults and the Ghost Dance were the functional equivalents of group therapy, permitting "disturbed individuals to repair morale through an intense group experience." [43] Perhaps social movements in general are so effective in the performance of their therapeutic functions that they soak up, as it were, the individual discontents of their societies. And yet it is unlikely in the extreme that social movements, even at the peak of their success, can succeed in blocking the emergence of all of the singular and individual forms of psychological disorientation. It is far more likely that if social change produced mental disorder through increased stress, the evidence of disorder would survive even the simultaneous growth of social movements. It thus becomes more and more difficult to accept the common belief that social change per se produces collective behavior.

If social change in general does not produce detectable consequences for mental health, does any particular kind of social change? The data we have already examined would seem to rule this out. Imprisonment, acculturation, migration, industrialization—none seems a more likely candidate than another. This particular classification is not, however, the only one possible. While we can differentiate social change in terms of its various causes, we can also differentiate it in terms of varying intensity. Surely neither all wars nor all migrations produce social change of the same intensity. Perhaps millenarian movements are the result neither of social change caused in a particular manner nor of social change in general but of social change at a particular level of intensity. This approach is implied by H. B. M. Murphy when he speculates that the only time social change can possibly create mental disorder is when that change occurs within and severely threatens what Murphy calls an individual's "true society." "To a baby, the 'true' society . . . may consist only of the mother and itself; to a child it may consist only of the family; to an adult it may consist of face-to-face contacts only, or his whole nation, or may even be largely imaginary. Which is the perceived 'true' society will depend partly on the personality, partly on what society teaches." [44] It is worth noting, however, that people do not simply divide the perceived world dichotomously, into a true society which must be preserved and the balance which is psychologically expendable. Rather, the sense of personal identification moves outward from the individual in concentric circles of increasing radius and decreasing strength. The strength of identification does not diminish simply as a function of physical distance. It is likely to undergo sharp drops across kinship lines, at national boundaries, and from one religious community to another.

It should be clear at once that Murphy's "true society" and

Wallace's "mazeway" are much alike. Both are internalized pictures of the perceived primary environment, that combination of people and things that an individual regards as inseparably linked to his own sense of meaning and well-being. However, there are differences of emphasis. The mazeway provides explanation for and presumably takes in aspects of existence that are negatively valued; it is as much a world view as it is a statement of value. The true society is that aspect of the perceived world that the individual feels he must preserve. The collapse and destruction of the true society closely resembles the cultural crisis that Wallace refers to as "mazeway failure." More accurately, the destruction of the true society of many individuals at once is likely to bring about mazeway failure through the inability of existing cultural categories to explain the destruction.

Social change likely to destroy the true society must be highly focused and intense. Waves of social change sweep large areas of the world without, except in isolated cases, having these effects. In fact, when we talk about social change that destroys the true society, we are talking about events that are quite literally disasters for those who undergo them. A disaster is perhaps easier to recognize than it is to define. For purposes of analysis, we shall take a disaster to be "a severe, relatively sudden, and frequently unexpected disruption of normal structural arrangements within a social system, or subsystem, resulting from a force, 'natural' or 'social,' 'internal' to a system or 'external' to it, over which the system has no firm 'control.' [45] It is a particularly intense form of collective stress situation.[46] Most empirical disaster studies deal with natural or accidental catastrophes, such as hurricanes, tornadoes, and explosions. However, these well-studied disasters represent only a small and partially representative segment of the definable disaster universe.[47] By and large these have been community studies, based on events that are sharply limited in the time and space of their effects. The impact of a tornado on a small town can be more easily examined than the consequences of war, famine, or industrialization on an entire society. Where the scope is thus broadened, there is no reason to believe that a disaster's social and psychological effects will be diminished and (as

will be seen) some a priori reason to believe they will be
considerably greater.[48]

Thus natural catastrophes, demographic shifts, the rise and
fall of cities, alterations in the status system, economic
depression, industrialization—all might constitute disaster. It
is equally clear that disasters can constitute a potent if
unexpected form of social change. Specifically, they can
produce precisely the intense form of social change most
likely to produce major psychological consequences, in short,
that form of social change most likely to destroy an individual's true society. To anticipate the argument a bit, millenarian movements emerge as the artifacts of disaster situations,
and to the extent that we can identify the consequences of
disaster, to that extent we can identify many of the circumstances that cause millenarian movements to emerge.

What are the effects of disaster? When circumstances inflict
deprivations on a single individual, through loss of his
livelihood, social position, or loved ones, the event is likely to
be of limited political effect. His stresses are customarily
shifted to his family, friends, work group, or community
welfare institutions.[49] When disaster strikes an entire community, the consequences differ, for institutions to which stresses
might be shifted may themselves be unable to function.
Aggregated individual cases of deprivation are now on the
way toward becoming a social phenomenon, particularly as
individuals grasp the fact that many others are in identical
positions. As we examine the consequences, we must bear in
mind, too, that the findings grow primarily out of community
studies, where the outside environment has been quickly
mobilized to repair the damage.

Close observers of disaster have repeatedly noted the
presence of a characteristic cluster of psychological reactions
in a significant number of survivors. This complex has been
labeled the *disaster syndrome*.[50] While it is to be expected that
disaster leaves many persons momentarily dazed, large numbers continue to manifest a stunned condition. They are
relatively passive, withdrawn, and suggestible. They operate
with diminished mental efficiency and can no longer "perceive reality correctly." [51] Panic is rare; rather, individuals
attempt to interpret the unfamiliar in terms of the familiar

and, when that fails, lapse into behavior patterns that are nonrational and reflexive. While severe emotional disturbances are rare, psychosomatic aftereffects "are almost universal." [52] Small numbers show anxiety, fatigue, psychotic episodes, recurrent catastrophic dreaming and depression; while the disaster syndrome itself may include as many as one-third of the impact population. [53]

Psychological observations most frequently come from studies of small-scale disaster in which a well-defined population has been involved. The period of impact is brief and the rehabilitation swift. Societal disasters—colonization, industrialization, or plague, for example—have been far less studied. Their impact period is often reckoned in months or even years and may transcend available resources for rehabilitation. The disaster syndrome as observed in community studies lasts from a few hours to a few weeks. Recovery from it depends upon the rapidity with which the environment is reestablished. A town hit by a tornado suffers greatly, but the most conspicuous damage is usually quickly repaired and normal routines reestablished. Disasters of greater scope cannot hope to lead to rapidly renewed normalcy. Total disaster that destroys the physical environment and ruptures the fabric of interpersonal relationships might be expected to produce at least the functional equivalent of mental illness, simply as a consequence of isolation and sensory deprivation. [54]

On the basis of these considerations, we can see why the literature on the psychological consequences of social change has bypassed disaster phenomena. In the first place, the clinical signs are often so short-lived that the individual never seeks professional help. He is rarely hospitalized and hence does not become an analyzable statistic. To the extent that many others around him behave similarly, he may not be regarded as "abnormal" or "sick." His reactions are assumed to be normal, given the situation. Only community mental health programs or the chance presence of social scientists are likely to bring these transient phenomena to a level of visibility. Where the disaster is very intense and widespread, diagnostic and treatment facilities suffer along with the rest. Medical resources are quickly overloaded, so that large numbers of people may receive little or no treatment at all. Records may be destroyed. Time pressure prevents adequate diagnoses. All other things being equal, the more unstable and disrupted the situation, the less likely that social scientists will be tempted or able to enter it for the purpose of systematic research. The surveys that so often provide an invaluable supplement to hospital admissions data cannot very well be conducted in the midst of war or plague. Where a disaster covers an entire society, its medical establishment —whether folk or Western—may be as much at a loss to deal with the problems as anyone else. Finally, the disaster syndrome, although recognizable to those looking for it, does not constitute a disabling mental illness. It is almost always short-lived and permits those suffering from it to retain some minimal capacity to cope. As a relatively minor, short-lived nervous disorder, occurring in a person who may be cut off from sources of treatment, the disaster syndrome is thus unlikely to be noted as a consequence of a particular kind of social change. It is not a mental illness traceable to unresolved conflicts early in life but rather its temporary equivalent induced by extraordinary environmental stresses. Consequently, it is quite possible to accept in a literal sense the conclusion that social change does not directly cause mental illness and still recognize the existence of the disaster syndrome in certain social-change situations.[55]

Why does disaster have these effects? We normally harbor assumptions concerning the general stability of the true society and the rate at which it can be expected to change. Cultures differ on the matter of the size and frequency of incremental change but agree that there is for each some level of acceptable change. When changes occur within culturally defined limits, explanations for them come readily to hand. It is a major function of the mazeway to provide these explanations, and the internalized conception of the true society is predicated upon the continued existence of limits on change. The disaster syndrome occurs precisely because these limits have been abruptly violated, and it recedes to the extent that familiar surroundings return and the limits are restored. When the individual's reference points in life are lost, feelings of suggestibility, anxiety, and depression follow.[56]

The circumstances of a disaster are particularly likely to induce suggestibility. This is so because a disaster combines two factors, each of which separately is known to produce suggestibility, sensory deprivation, and sensory overstimulation. While they appear to be polar opposites, both occur in a disaster setting and both prepare the individual for the reception of strong new beliefs. The period of the immediate disaster impact is a time of involuntary sensory overstimulation. "The organism has been flooded with stimuli." [57] He is suddenly confronted by a large number of powerful, unanticipated pieces of sense data. When the impact period has passed, and the individual becomes aware of the extent of the desolation, he moves abruptly to a condition of relative sensory deprivation. William Sargant notes that insofar as the acquisition of new belief systems is concerned, the process seems equally well facilitated by either overstimulation or deprivation. The literature on religious and political conversion makes clear that both extremes induce a condition of greatly enhanced suggestibility.[58] The presence of both in disasters suggests that these situations offer unusual natural circumstances for the sudden adoption of new beliefs.

We can see in disaster a potent form of social change. While it seems to provide some with circumstances of optimal stress, a larger number emerge in a state of less than optimal intellectual functioning. A disaster population suffers a temporary sense of incapacity, vulnerability, and confusion. The collapsed social structure renders traditional authority relationships less effective and traditional statuses less meaningful. Under these conditions, millenarian movements appear.

Millenarian movements constitute, as it were, the artifacts of disaster. They thus cannot be seen simply as the product of stress or deprivation. The stress must involve a radical change in what we have called the true society, that portion of the environment most significant to an individual. Only that kind of upheaval produces the psychological correlates of disaster. Anxiety and meaninglessness create the need for millenarian movements, while the dissolution of traditional groups and a state of enhanced suggestibility make membership easy. Relative deprivation is tolerated by all of us in some form or another; only that deprivation which deprives us of the most valued environment produces millenarian activity. The disaster victim, for whom the ordinary cues and landmarks of living have been removed, is left passive, receptive to suggestion, and in need of a substitute environment. He requires a new configuration of social relationships and values to explain his new predicament.

He first seeks to understand his problems by assimilating them to the ideas he already possesses. If the problems bear some resemblance to those with which he or others around him are used to dealing, they can be dealt with in conventional ways. The modes of explanation already possessed will suffice. But if the problems are genuinely beyond common experience, they are much less easy to understand and manage. "In the absence of reliable guides from past experience for perceiving or acting, suggestibility is heightened." [59]

Millenarian beliefs are a form of explanation: they tell us why we are in the dreadful circumstances of the present. They also respond to the failure of a disintegrating society: they tell us that problems that appeared insoluble will be dealt with totally, favorably, and summarily, "in the twinkling of an eye." These ideas, diverging so radically from those to which people are accustomed, no doubt appear particularly suited to the circumstances. But, more importantly, they fall on the ears of a peculiarly susceptible audience, that of disaster victims. Disaster has both caused their problems and made of them potential converts. They have, as it were, been brainwashed by circumstances. That critical ability which, Hadley Cantril tells us, differentiates the suggestible from the skeptical no longer functions at its previous level.[60] Disaster, by removing the familiar environment, removes precisely those frames of reference by which we normally evaluate statements, ideas, and beliefs. Belief systems which under nondisaster conditions might be dismissed, now receive sympathetic consideration. The disaster victim is not "mentally ill," and millenarianism is not a form of collective psychopathology. Rather, disaster victims constitute a population among whom many show the functional analogues of mental illness,

transient conditions induced by sudden environmental instability. It is small wonder that among persons so situated
doctrines of imminent salvation should find such ready
acceptance.

In attempting to assess the role disaster plays, we must gain
some clearer idea of what a disaster is and how it comes
about. One aspect of this—multiple versus single disasters—is
the principal focus of the next chapter. Before reaching that
question, however, there are more fundamental and difficult
problems: Can disasters be anticipated? If so, do the anticipations constitute self-fulfilling prophecies? What kinds of
deprivations need an event inflict upon individuals in order to
induce the disaster syndrome?

On the most general level, an anticipated disaster is a
contradiction in terms. Without the element of surprise,
defenses, both material and psychological, may be erected.
Much of the force of a disaster comes from the sudden
manner in which it assaults unprepared societies, institutions,
and psyches. The more one prepares for future contingencies,
the less likely that these contingencies will inflict disorganizing damage. Even where uncontrollable forces of nature are
concerned, the mere existence of forewarning constitutes a
defense. The prospective hurricane victim may be able to
partially secure his possessions, reach high ground, and have
some time to adjust to the prospect of material loss. The
desire to minimize damage has led all manner of public
agencies, both civil and military, to attempt various kinds of
preventive measures: warning systems, first-aid training, civil
defense organizations, indoctrination programs, and so forth.
What is accomplished by preparing populations for disaster?
The manifest function, and the one to which we have so far
given the most attention, is that of taking actions which
neutralize the effects of stress: moving people out of harm's
way, tending the injured, preserving civil order, transmitting
and receiving messages. Without in any way minimizing the
importance of these activities, it is important to recognize the
existence of a latent function as well: preserving elements of
structure in a destabilized environment.[61] We have seen that
the psychological consequences of disaster result from the
destruction of the valued environment. The purpose of much

disaster preparation, however unrecognized, is to maintain elements of familiarity and structure to neutralize the effects of sudden, novel stress.

> Any stability in the present environment and one's place in it, whether it be narrow to include only a limited area of activity, or broad to include a clear perception of the total situation, aids in reducing anxiety. . . . No doubt the emphasis upon training for meeting emergencies is correct, but possibly for reasons other than the development of behavior patterns *per se*. The training may provide some stability in a situation that is otherwise perceptually unstructured.[62]

The more effective systems of warning and prophylaxis become, the less likely that an event will continue to be regarded as disastrous. As preparation and control continue to reduce anxiety and damage, the stressful event gradually becomes incorporated within the ambit of conventional, routinized living. In this manner, disasters of the past so diminish in surprise and consequences that they may eventually disappear altogether. Some, of course, are more easily and definitively dealt with than others. The great epidemics of the past are perhaps the clearest example of disaster events which disappeared once the means for control were at hand. History is a chronicle of changing patterns of disaster, a subject to which I want to return in chapter seven. Disasters remain disasters only so long as their incidence and effects lie beyond human control.

What happens when the onset of a disaster can be predicted but its effects cannot be controlled? In the first place, the information may lie so far outside accepted categories that it is not believed. This appears to have been the case in Europe just before the Black Death, when reports of epidemics in the Levant were dismissed.[63] It was certainly true of large numbers of Jews confronted by the Nazi extermination program.[64] The mere existence of information does not guarantee that it will be acted upon. Indeed, the more remote it is from common values and experience, the more likely that its dissonance may breed disbelief or repression. There is little disposition to believe the unbelievable, particularly when the suspect message foretells death and destruction. (An apparent exception to this—the case of rumors—will be examined in chapter five.)

Let us assume, however, that the message falls upon credulous ears. What then? The more specific it is, the more easily defensive action can be taken. Storm warnings which specify location, time, and intensity, and may even suggest specific countermeasures, are warnings of this type. In the degree to which predicted disasters are of this type, fore-knowledge is likely not only to mitigate the disaster effects but also make a millenarian reaction less probable. By making a potential disaster less destructive, such information deprives the event of its shock value and defends the environment against excessive disruption—both of which deprive millenarian movements of their reasons for existence.

But there is one kind of prediction which remains quite congenial to the growth of millenarianism, and that is a generalized, nonspecific sense of dread. It is quite possible for large numbers of people to believe that some fearful event is imminent, without knowing its type, specific time of occur-rence, or the kind of measures that may be taken against it. The sense of impending doom may have very little basis in fact. It may, on the other hand, serve in some subtle fashion as a self-fulfilling prophecy which drags in train the very dreaded events themselves. It is hard to know whether gloomy speculations about the apocalypse represent real fear of its occurrence or a kind of perverse fascination with it. George Steiner sees in the boredom and fantasy life of late nineteenth-century Europe a "great ennui" which fastened upon images of destruction: "Whether the psychic mecha-nisms involved were universal or historically localized, one thing is plain: by ca. 1900 there was a terrible readiness, indeed a thirst for what Yeats was to call the 'blood-dimmed tide.' " [65] Some periods seem to fantasize disasters more than others. At the same time that Europeans doted upon images of catastrophe, Americans, in the throes of industrialization, found in prophecies of doom a similar fascination. At a much earlier time, the imagination of the late Middle Ages was of a like tone. We may see, perhaps with slightly less assurance, that America in the last fifteen years has cultivated its own disaster imagination: nuclear holocaust, overpopulation, race war, ecological imbalance. The fashions may change, but the preoccupation with disaster remains. I have no desire to be flip in such matters, for the imagination of disaster reflects real stresses and risks. Yet all too often disaster prophecy becomes an end in itself, effectively separated from attempts to remove the imagined threat.

These prophecies may become self-fulfilling because they encourage a particular reading of events. Millenarians seek hopeful signs once a promise of salvation has been made. Earlier in the process, the existence of disaster itself may come from the connotations given to ambiguous events. The Haymarket Riot had the effects of a disaster, out of all proportion to its immediate, proximate consequences, because a tradition of apocalyptic watchfulness had led people to expect some event that fused violence, urbanism, and immigration. What might be passed off as of limited significance in one period becomes the ultimate concern in another. It helps also to explain the paradoxical fact that contemporary urban crime bulks as a far larger problem to farmers and small-town inhabitants, who know of it only through communications media, than to city dwellers themselves. It also helps to explain why, in the history of anti-Semitism, an intrinsically minor incident, such as the Dreyfus Case, can set up such fearful reverberations.

Disaster, then, is to some extent in the eye of the beholder. One must still not forget the reality of injury and disruption that less ambiguous catastrophic events produce. Unfortunately, the more ambiguous the event, the less we know about its consequences. Hence when the perception of disaster flows from a fertile and prepared imagination, we can only speculate about the reasons and results. One important element, however, in their self-fulfilling character may be the very sense of the inevitability of events. For when the mind dwells upon the likelihood of some cataclysm, thought tends to be diverted from efforts at defense and protection. If it must come, well, then it shall come. The consequences of any stress necessarily rise in proportion to the ill-preparedness of the victims. Inevitability and resignation, to the extent that they induce paralysis of will, serve to magnify the consequences. Damage rises by virtue of the inability of individuals to take measures on their own behalf.

It is at least arguable, then, that a small-scale event can have a catalytic effect when it is perceived within the context of disaster anticipations. It is similarly arguable that the disaster syndrome is as likely to result from imagined as from "real" fears. The temporary psychological consequences of Orson Welles's "War of the Worlds" broadcast came very close to what a "real disaster" ought to produce.[66] Even more strikingly, data on reactions to President Kennedy's assassination, summarized in the final chapter, show how much like a disaster the impact of a catalytic event can be. As media of communication become more and more important sources of information, as individuals become vicarious participants in far-off events, we may anticipate that the magnification of small events into communal disasters will become a more and more frequent occurrence.

Chapter Three

THE DISASTER-PRONE ENVIRONMENT

Disaster is prominent in the genesis of millenarian movements. One need only point to the eruption of European
chiliasm in the wake of the Black Death or the rise of the
Taiping Rebellion after a protracted period of flood, famine,
banditry, and invasion. At the same time it ought to be clear
that disaster, pure and simple, does not provide instant
explanation. It is a necessary rather than a sufficient condition, although I shall argue that it remains of primary
importance. The disaster concept must be refined and supple-
mented; otherwise, we will be overrun with anomalies and
contradictions.

Let us take two examples: Upstate New York in the early
and mid-nineteenth century was a breeding ground for all
manner of religious enthusiasms and millenarian fervor,[1] yet
we note two characteristics of this "Burned-Over District":
First, except for occasional financial panics of relatively slight
impact, the area did not suffer anything remotely resembling
disaster. It remained prosperous and relatively stable. The
second feature is the character of the millenarianism itself. It
was distinctly passive and subdued, as well as divorced from
issues of social protest. Except for the Millerites, who
anticipated the end of the world in 1844, millenarian themes
were projected into an indefinite future; or, as in the Oneida
community, expressed in insulated communitarian experiments. The major waves of religious revivalism centered upon
otherworldly salvation, not upon the dissolution of the
existing order. Those social issues that did emerge from the
welter of religious yearnings similarly did not threaten or
question the existing society. The abolitionist movement,
especially strong in upstate New York, drew sustenance from
religious enthusiasm but directed its attention principally to
anti-Southern agitation and the transportation of fugitive
slaves to Canada. Later, the temperance movement grew

from the same roots, but its highly focused reform program left the larger community very much as it found it.

The second example—very different—is Ireland at about the same time. The potato famine of 1845–49 was surely one of the major disasters of modern times. "In four years, 1,500,000 people had died, over one sixth of the population. A million had emigrated, and millions more were to emigrate over the coming decades until Ireland's population was cut in half." [2] Yet the curious thing about the famine was the apparent passivity with which it was borne. It left a legacy of anti-British bitterness alive to the present day, since the death toll was magnified many times by the callousness and ineptitude of British relief programs. But in the area of social movements, where we should expect a burst of activity, surprisingly little happened. The endemic military and para-military activity associated with Irish separatism emerged much later and, even when it did, was devoid of millenarian motifs.

Thus we have millenarianism without disaster and disaster without millenarianism. To be sure, in both cases factors come to mind to explain the disjunctions. In the New York case the population was made up heavily of New Englanders, heir to an even earlier millenarian-revivalist tradition. The Great Awakening (1730–45), for example, developed out of the crisis of Puritan theocracy caught in an increasingly commercial, cosmopolitan society.[3] It is perfectly plausible to speculate that revivalism, having been initiated as the genuine response to a genuine crisis, became institutionalized and tended to be carried along by migrants, to be reactivated in a different social setting. The Burned-Over District, having been populated by participants in the Great Awakening, simply became the arena in which a familiar form of religious excitation was played out. The absence of social content from the preaching is further evidence that the practice of periodic soul-cleansing campaigns no longer reflected deeper social or economic tensions.

Ireland, one place where we would most expect millenarian activity, offers in fact an unusually wide range of possible explanations for its absence. In the first place, the possibility of mass emigration served to empty the country of many of the most discontented and, presumably, the most able. Second, an unusually strong church may have provided an explanatory framework which even a catastrophe of this magnitude could not erode. Finally, those who survived did so at the very margin of physical existence, and it may well be that we see at work here the familiar principle that "when people toil from sunrise to sunset for a bare living, they nurse no grievances and dream no dreams." [4] Some disasters prove physically disabling for those who survive physically, as the relative apathy of slaves and prison camp inmates often demonstrates.

As these two examples have suggested, disaster by itself only begins to open the door on a full understanding of millenarianism. To do more we must add to it those elements essential to fulfill both necessary and sufficient conditions. The discussion which follows attempts to set these forth by, first, specifying those disaster conditions *unlikely* to produce millenarian activity; and second, specifying supplementary conditions which must be present. In order to specify the additional factors, we shall focus on four variables: agrarian versus urban society, single versus multiple disasters, the availability of millenarian doctrine, and the presence of a potential leader.

There are four kinds of disaster situations from which millenarian movements are *not* likely to emerge: those that leave a substantial portion of the perceived primary environment intact, those where the environmental damage is quickly repaired, those indefinitely prolonged within the same social unit, and those which occur in the absence of ideas of future change. The first two are characteristic of many community disasters: the tornado which destroys part of a neighborhood, the factory explosion, the mine cave-in. They may produce great loss of life and property; but the community as a whole emerges intact, and old routines quickly reassert themselves. The destruction may be physically limited; or, if it is widespread, as in a flood, the rapid mobilization of relief forces means that the damage is quickly repaired. The political system usually emerges unscathed. In one of the very few attempts to treat natural disaster as a political variable,

Abney and Hill found that Hurricane Betsy, which struck New Orleans at the beginning of the 1965 mayoralty campaign, did not adversely affect the incumbent.[5] Indeed, in some measure the situation provided an opportunity for the mayor to demonstrate his competence and concern.

When essentially the same conditions of deprivation affect successive generations, expectations may eventually move into line with capabilities.[6] Individuals come to anticipate less in the growing knowledge that their resources will never match their old level of aspiration. One cannot really regard constant deprivation either as a form of relative deprivation or as disaster. The essence of relative deprivation is the subjective interpretation the individual makes of his condition, and if he comes to see his condition as an immutable fact of nature, it is no longer deprivation—although, of course, it may remain *absolute* deprivation in the eyes of an outside observer. It cannot be considered disaster any longer, for it is neither sudden nor unanticipated, but simply "there." For example, silting deprived Bruges, Belgium, of its usual outlet to the North Sea, of which it was once the major port. While the initial change constituted a disaster for the economy of the city, its constant and irreversible character eventually made it a fact of life to which the eventual response was adaptation. In a somewhat different vein, the annual flooding of the Nile Valley ceased to be a disaster once its recurrence could be predicted; patterns of behavior incorporated this natural rhythm.

Two circumstances approach this situation but are sufficiently distinguishable to require special attention. Where continually depressed conditions combine with a continual influx of new people, the absence of millenarian movements can no longer be assured. This condition has been approximated in black ghettoes. While the conditions of absolute deprivation are more or less constant, the continual introduction of new persons turns them into disaster conditions. There is, for reasons indicated in chapter two, a time lag between in-migration and subjective disaster recognition. Until one has been, as it were, socialized to depressed life-conditions, they constitute a private disaster. Where large numbers of in-migrants are involved, these individual confrontations may aggregate into a social phenomenon. The effect is much the same as if the community experienced several consecutive disasters.

The second circumstance occurs where there are in fact multiple catastrophes. Since this case will be dealt with in detail below, it need only be said that where multiple catastrophes over an extended period are separated by periods of relative stability, and/or where multiple catastrophes are relatively unanticipated, the absence of millenarian movements can no longer be assured. Indeed, such oscillations between stability and upheaval may create a culture of millenarian expectation that is transmitted across generations.

Similarly, we shall shortly be dealing with the factor of ideas of future change. Suffice it to say now that the idea of future change is found in some form in most cultures. But where a linear view of time is strongly subordinated to, let us say, a cyclical one, millenarianism is correspondingly unlikely.

While millenarian movements have been widely distributed geographically, they by no means occur everywhere. They cluster in so-called backward areas, and this uneven distribution raises a major theoretical problem. Why are the movements so rarely urban? What explains their apparent affinity for rural areas? Yonina Talmon concludes that millenarian movements occur in "pre-political," "non-political," or "post-political" settings.[7] That is, they arise in societies that have not yet formed differentiated political institutions; among groups that lack access to political experience or influence; and in societies where the prior political system has collapsed. This classification assumes a narrowly Western conception of politics, ill-suited to cross-cultural application. Yet without accepting a culture-bound notion of the political, it remains true that millenarian movements have on the whole taken place in nonurban, nonindustrialized areas. The same conclusion can be arrived at whether one distinguishes agrarian from modern areas by spatial or temporal characteristics. Until fairly recently, the non-Western world, as a geographical expression, constituted the major agrarian segment of the globe. It was and to an extent remains the major locale of millenarianism: the Cargo Cults, Ghost Dance, Kimbangism, Hoa Hao and Cao Dai, Mahdism—the list is virtually endless. Similarly, if societies are viewed in developmental terms, millenarianism seems to disappear as industrialism, a market economy, and large cities consolidate themselves. Contemporary technological developments appear to severely qualify some of these observations, a point to which attention is directed in chapter six. For the moment, however, they may be accepted, if only on the grounds that almost all identifiable millenarian movements do in fact occur in agrarian societies.

In late medieval Europe, landless, displaced peasants formed a reservoir of millenarian adherents.[8] By the eighteenth century, however, the millenarian movement had begun to seem a thing of the past, particularly in countries such as England and France where industrialization, capitalism, and city life came relatively early.[9] Millenarianism continued into the nineteenth and twentieth centuries in Andalusia and southern Italy, precisely those areas which modern commercial-industrial society had just begun to impinge upon but had not yet transformed.[10]

In light of this evidence, it is easy to see why millenarian movements are so often called "prepolitical" or, to use E. J. Hobsbawm's term, "archaic." The modern age seems set against them. It is correspondingly easy to see why they have also—paradoxically—been viewed as a wave of the future. For, to the extent that in the non-Western world millenarianism prefigures nationalism, it may easily be seen as the beginning of a struggle for political liberation. Indeed, for Vittorio Lanternari it is the "religion of the oppressed, . . . the striving of subject peoples to become emancipated."[11] Maria Pereira de Queiroz speculates "that such movements are perhaps the specific forms of revolution and reform in traditional society."[12] Yet it is in the end unsatisfying to generalize from purely Western or purely non-Western experience, and even more unsatisfying to repair to explanation by definition. We learn nothing by simply declaring that millenarianism is the protest of traditional society, as if by so doing we neutralize all our unanswered questions. The definition serves only to beg the question: *Why* in traditional societies? What is it about the world of farms and villages, peasant, family, and tribe that so often gives us this volatile form of social protest?

Conventional wisdom on the matter asserts that discontent and collective violence rise with modernization and the displacement of large numbers of people from the countryside to the city. The city has never fared well in American political and social thought, and perhaps this insistent antiurban bias accounts for our readiness to ascribe violence to urbanization. Whatever the ultimate source, recent research on urbanization fails to confirm this bias for either America or Europe.[13] Charles Tilly argues that "in the short run, the growth of large cities and rapid migration from rural to urban areas in Western Europe probably acted as a damper on violent protest rather than a spur to it." [14] He ascribes this to two factors: First, urbanization drew the discontented from their home grounds, where they could organize for protest, and placed them in cities where they lacked a feeling of common identity and "the means to strike together." Second, there was a time lag between entry into the city and the point where an individual was sufficiently well assimilated to join with others in pursuit of a perceived common interest.

For our purposes, the significant differences extend beyond the temporary ability of men to organize better in one place than another. We have, after all, been talking in terms of disaster, and in terms of this variable there are additional significant distinctions to be drawn between city and country. In the first place, the disaster vulnerability of the two environments differs. Shocks and instabilities in rural and small-town life possess a greater potential for disruptive psychological effects than the same forces would in cities. For cities contain more heterogeneous populations and, to the extent that they frequently grow from in-migration, contain people less closely identified with their place of residence. The rural population is smaller, more homogeneous, and more closely identified with its place of residence. In his discussion of Spanish and Italian millenarianism, E. J. Hobsbawm observes: "In the 19th and 20th centuries such movements have been overwhelmingly agrarian, though there is no *a priori* reason why they should not be urban, and in the past they have sometimes been so." [15] I now wish to suggest that there may indeed be an a priori reason.

The rural–small-town milieu is, all other things being equal, likely to possess a population at once more stable and more homogeneous than that of a large city. The hallmark of the modern city is not only its sheer size but the diversity of its population and the flow of persons within it and between it and the countryside. A mobile, polyglot population is far less likely to be found where numbers are smaller, traditional communal identities are strong, and individuals are tied to the land and its rhythms. In this context, the concept of the "true society"—the individual's perceived primary environment—takes on new significance. For the agrarian resident, the true society and the actual place of residence coincide. When this occurs, stress is far more likely to assume collective, disaster proportions, with all of the concomitant social and psychological effects. Upheaval in a uniform, slow-changing agrarian environment is much more likely to destroy the true society. Migrants continue to internalize as their true society the locale they have left and hence continue to possess it internally in an idealized and stable form. It remains their area of primary identification even after they have left it. There is thus a disjunction between their locus of personal identity and their locus of physical existence. For those of fixed abode—the traditional rural inhabitant, for example—the loci of personal identity and actual life coincide. This person directly experiences upheavals in his perceived primary environment.

Agrarian life is much more likely to produce small, naturally "compacted" populations. Hence its society is correspondingly more vulnerable to the disintegrative effects of famine, epidemic, market fluctuations, invasion, and the like. In this we can see a clue to the prevalence of extreme decremental relative deprivation. There is a feeling that a way of life is being lost, that accustomed ways of doing things are under attack, and nothing will be as it once was. Objectively, present events are much more likely in this context to be *perceived* as disasters, and the disaster syndrome is much more likely to present itself. In short, the circumstances conducive to the growth of millenarian movements will be present.

Cities possess some buffering against these movements. The ebb and flow of population, the heterogeneity of interest, the presence of distractions and competing ideas, and the minimized opportunities for face-to-face interaction—all militate against the development of urban millenarian movements. In the city, one group's disaster may be another's windfall, save where the catastrophe is very great indeed; this in contrast to the tendency for agrarian residents to constitute a community of shared fate. Where the complexities of life produce many groups pursuing divergent interests, catastrophic change for a segment of the community is unlikely to greatly disturb the environment in which the majority functions; and the majority, in any case, offers a ready source of assistance. Even where urban millenarianism has managed to gain a foothold, the loyalties of members are difficult to maintain, for challenges and distractions lie on every side. Where each individual goes his own way, the opportunities for the reinforcement of new beliefs are few.[16] Groups under stress must rigorously control communications between themselves and the threatening environment,[17] and the city is a poor place to attempt such controls.

Traditions of close communal identification have begun to die out in the West, but they constituted deep attachments as recently as a hundred years ago. In America, for example, a sense of threat and imminent loss began to pervade small-town and rural life even before the Civil War. Agrarian, antiurban movements sought to preserve the rural idyll against immigrant, industrial encroachments, until by the mid-1880s a well-defined mood of impending cultural disaster had crystallized.[18] A century earlier in France, unrest and rumors of apocalyptic destruction spread from town to town through the countryside in a pattern that resembled the spread of an epidemic. The most dramatic "contagion" of this kind, the so-called *Grand Peur*, occurred in the mid-summer of 1789. Rudé attributes it to economic crisis, rural vagrancy, the dispersal of royal troops from Paris, and peasant habits of conspiracy thinking. The rumored aristocratic plots—all of which existed only in the imagination—kindled popular uprisings that continued for years after.[19] While the American case has a much more explicitly millenarian cast, both instances demonstrate the strength of local attachments, the potential vulnerability of traditional society, and the clearly localized reactions to threat. Apocalyptic movements are almost always highly localized, growing out of perceptions of local conditions, even where the same conditions exist over a wide area. There was not one Ghost Dance, but many tribal variants; not one Cargo Cult, but a succession of marginally differentiable cults. The sepoy mutiny in India in 1857, which Harold Gould argues was clearly millenarian,[20] did not take the form of a single anti-British campaign; rather, it broke into a series of parallel local movements.

The non-Western world, far less characterized by large urban centers, has preserved more cohesive traditions of local identity. When millenarianism has appeared, it has done so in the countryside. Melanesian Cargo Cults have been rural phenomena, occurring in areas with a moderate but not a very great degree of European contact.[21] American Indian movements were in a sense the natural outcome of both the pressures upon them and the closed, homogeneous character of reservation life. The Taiping rebels grew in a remote mountain area.[22] The Indian mutineers tended to come not from the coastal areas, already under substantial British influence, but from the backcountry. Indeed, as Gould remarks, paradoxically the clash of Indian and British cultures constituted a greater disaster in the backcountry, where most of traditional Hindu and Muslim life remained intact, than in the culturally polyglot area the British first penetrated:

> There was already a continuum of acculturation reaching up the Ganges that was in inverse ratio to the distance from [East India] Company headquarters. The farther inland you went, the less deeply changes had penetrated; for this very reason, the impact of changes which did come were the more profoundly felt and responded to. And, most significantly in this regard, the soldiers of the Bengal army were recruited mainly from the less acculturated upper Gangetic region and not from the more acculturated Bengal region.[23]

Since group memberships are better known and less ambiguous in rural than in urban areas,[24] disturbing events are more clearly shared by well-bounded communities. Along much the same lines, Tilly distinguishes between "communal" and "associational" bases of social organization. The communal is small-scale, localized, and traditional; while the associational produces "politics based on large-scale organizations formed to serve one well-defined interest." [25] The passage from communal to associational thus also marks the usual transition from millenarian to nonmillenarian thinking. Millenarianism, with its claims of total loyalty and a single authoritative world view, is incompatible with interest-group politics. Communalism, with its physical and social vulnerability, its homogeneity, and its well-defined local ties, is more likely to be the scene of a contagious atmosphere of anxiety and suggestibility.

Interest-group politics and the very idea of special-purpose associations are themselves products of specialized, relatively large scale societies. The agrarian milieu, resting upon a relatively simple agricultural economy, has neither the means nor the need for extensive specialization. The tendency for millenarian social protest to concentrate among the relatively less well off agrarians has led some social scientists—notably Seymour Lipset[26]—to incorrectly associate millenarianism directly with social class. In his view, it is the lower class, with its authoritarianism, political extremism, and emotional religiosity, which is the source of chiliastic revolt. To the extent that rural inhabitants do tend to be poor and low status in comparison to city dwellers, he is of course correct. But the millenarianism of the lower class is less a class phenomenon per se than it is a response to the peculiar conditions of rural life.

Disaster means damage—physical, social, and psychological. But environments differ in the degree to which that damage can be repaired and, more basic still, in their capacity to sustain high stress without simultaneously sustaining loss of life, self-esteem, wealth, or social cohesion. Societies differ in their disaster-proneness and disaster vulnerability. Until recently, for example, plagues simply moved over an area taking their toll; those who could fled, the majority endured as best it could. Plague has been largely eradicated only to be replaced by total war and the specter of ecological catastrophe.

The city, which now appears so vulnerable, until recently presented the best opportunity for disaster survival. This was due in part to peculiarities in family structure. The rural milieu was not as often characterized by extended families as is commonly assumed.[27] Where the extended family did exist—in the preindustrial city—it served as "an effective security agency," shielding its members from the disruptive effects of war, famine, plague, and other disasters. "Whereas the incapacity of one or two breadwinners can be disastrous to the small nuclear unit, the extended organization . . . can more readily adjust to adversity." [28] The extended family therefore served as one more buffer between preindustrial city dwellers and disaster. The decline of the preindustrial city and its family system was, of course, paralleled by the growth of technology, medicine, and public welfare agencies, which served many of the same security functions.

Our discussion of the millenarian propensities of agrarian areas would be easier to conclude were it not for the presence of a number of disturbing exceptions. There have been and are millenarian movements of an urban, modern character. Any attempt to explain chiliasm solely in terms of "agrarian-ness" must eventually take account of the anomalies and determine if indeed they are "mere" exceptions to an overwhelmingly valid rule. For the present I wish merely to indicate the kinds of exceptions I have in mind and leave to chapter six a detailed discussion of the place they occupy in the theoretical structure presented here.

Urban movements have existed in both the past and present. In earlier times, preindustrial, mercantile cities harbored some of the most famous movements. One need think only of John of Leyden's Münster or Savonarola's Florence. In modern times, the ghettoes of American cities have sheltered a flock of chiliastic black separatist groups, from Marcus Garvey to the Muslims. Outside the United States, millenarianism flourished in Tokyo (significantly enough, directly after the earthquake of 1923).[29] Despite the rarity of urban movements in Latin America, a relatively successful one did develop in the late 1940s in Rio de Janeiro, although by 1960 it had transplanted itself to the country-side.[30]

The major challenge, however, does not come from these scattered urban movements. Rather, it comes from one of the major political developments of modern times, totalitarianism. At one stroke, totalitarianism calls into question all we have said, for it is modern, large-scale, and successful. Far from being the creature of merely local discontents, nazism or communism under Stalin built technologically sophisticated systems of control on chiliastic ideological bases. Norman Cohn correctly grasped the connection between conventional conceptions of messianism and the totalitarian movements of the twentieth century. Totalitarianism, in its exploitation of technologically sophisticated modes of control, constitutes the modern political movement par excellence. Doctrinally, however, both nazism (to the extent that it possessed coherent doctrine) and communism present thinly secularized pictures of the coming millennium.

These notable exceptions apart, millenarian movements grow, as we have seen, from the compact, homogeneous, yet vulnerable environment of agrarian areas. We have seen that disasters are likely to strike heavier blows in these areas, and we move now to a more specific discussion of the characteristics of those disasters particularly likely to induce chiliastic reactions.

The principal distinction we shall draw is between single and multiple disasters. For example, let us look at the Brazilian *sertão*, an impoverished drought region in the northeastern part of the country. It manifests a pattern of virtually endemic millenarianism. The *sertão* also experienced major droughts in 1877–79, 1888–89, 1898, 1900, 1915, 1931–32, 1942–43, 1951, and 1958.[31] Andalusia, too, has been an area of frequent chiliastic activity and here we see famines in 1812, 1817, 1834–35, 1863, 1868, 1882, and 1905.[32] The Black Death in Europe during the mid-fourteenth century ushered in 350 years of intermittent epidemics; in England alone, epidemics occurred in 1348, 1361, 1368–69, 1371, 1375, 1390, and 1405.[33] Plague and famine represent, of course, only a few of the crisis-producing factors capable of inducing widespread collective disturbances. It would constitute a serious mistake to concentrate on them to the exclusion of other—frequently manmade—upheavals, such as war, inflation, depression, and colonization. For example, the succession of war, defeat, revolution, inflation, and depression in Germany from 1914 to 1933 presents an analogous set of hammerblows, delivered close together over two decades. The traumas of the American Plains Indians—military defeat, forced migration, destruction of the traditional food supply, and enclosure on reservations—constitute an even more vivid example of the combination of different disaster forms in the same area over a prolonged period of time.

When we speak of "multiple" or "successive" disasters, it must be borne in mind that distinctions among "separate" events are often difficult to make. Lines of possible causality cannot always be drawn or, more accurately, the present state of knowledge prohibits certain inferences. A depression followed by an earthquake must be reckoned as separate events, even though their consequences are cumulative. On the other hand, reversing the temporal ordering permits us to speculate that the earthquake might have had economic consequences, although, to be sure, other factors might have been necessary to produce the depression. Major disasters produce proximate consequences that can be easily identified—deaths, injuries, physical destruction. More subtle and long-term effects, harder to detect, may come to be recognized as disasters in their own right or as providing the requisite conditions for disaster. For example, war, colonization, or rapid urbanization may open an area to epidemic disease (the cholera epidemic of 1827–37 was diffused in part by marching armies)[34] or, by altering an area's ecology, make it more hospitable to epidemic disease.[35] Conquest and occupation often open the way for these unintended catastrophes. British control of Melanesia, site of the subsequent Cargo Cults, produced a total disruption of the indigenous status system.[36] The farther one seeks to trace disaster effects over time, the more difficult the task becomes.

Unfortunately, disaster-prone periods and regions are exceedingly difficult to study with any degree of rigor or with access to a full array of information. The exigencies of social research have meant that disaster situations subjected to study have been contemporaneous, localized, and of short duration. The historical record, for whatever light it might shed on disasters in the past, has been largely neglected.[37]

The studies of short-duration local disasters have little to say about the possible long-term consequences of long-enduring stress over a whole society, particularly one about which people can do little or nothing. The energy and rationality with which most people responded to tornado destruction, floods, even the massive bombing of cities in World War II, were a response to the presence of obvious actions that could be taken to relieve a temporary severe stress—people being buried in wreckage, suffering injuries requiring medical care, or requiring rescue from dangers of fire or rising waters.[38]

A society that has been hit by a disaster copes as best it can during the impact period and, if that period is short and the society's resources are sufficient, eventually returns to a new status quo. All of this is predicated on limits to the damage. Local disasters offer opportunities for the shift of stresses and functions to the larger environment, and we may view the mobilization of rescue and rehabilitation agencies in this light. For example, the Los Angeles earthquake of 1971 produced devastation at its epicenter, including the psychological effects associated with the disaster syndrome. Outside intervention, ranging from trucked-in drinking water to mental health clinics, held damage to a minimum. Yet this was a highly localized event, with only negligible consequences even in its own metropolitan area. The greater the magnitude of the disaster, the less likely that stresses and functions can be passed on to other subsystems, for the other subsystems will have fared just as badly.

A single disaster must be exceedingly intense in order to transcend the damage-control capabilities of a society. The East Pakistan cyclone in 1970 was a rare contemporary example. Most often, social organization is reconstructed after the first shock has passed. However, cumulative disasters necessarily hold down the ability of a social system to regenerate itself. Instead, each new disaster-increment falls upon a system less able to survive it. Put another way, new disasters need not be as strong as the prior ones to inflict the same amount of damage, presuming the inability of the society to fully repair itself in the intervals. By outrunning the capabilities of a society to shift stresses and pass functions to other units, multiple catastrophes create a situation peculiarly suited to the growth of three possible patterns of response.

The possibilities that lie open are: apathy and decay; defensive structuring; and millenarianism. The first response occurs when neither surviving resources nor cultural innovations suffice to return the society to a state of stable functioning. Societies which have in the past responded inadequately to challenge include the Minoans, Etruscans, and Mayans. The absence of millenarian activity may be due to the absence of future-oriented beliefs or to a leader endowed with charismatic qualities. There is, in any case, a level of stress so severe as to preclude any affirmative action; it serves only to numb.

Defensive structuring, in Bernard Siegel's phrase, means the establishment of mechanisms which in whole or in large part neutralize the effects of an external stress. It "is a strategy which occurs when protagonists have limited resources for direct and possibly violent confrontation with source[s] of frustration." [39] Certain forms of threat are obviously not amenable to this approach, which places emphasis on the maintenance of a boundary between the system and its environment. It can work only when it is possible to institute control of communications with other cultures, strong self-discipline, and authoritarian control. Defensive structuring thus is associated primarily with threats to cultural identity rather than to physical survival.

It will be immediately evident that the relationship between decay and defensive structuring, on the one hand, and millenarianism, on the other, is not one of mutual exclusivity. Societies in an advanced state of disorganization have given rise to millenarian movements only to lapse once again into a process of social decay, for example, the North American Indians. Defensive structuring often marks the conclusion of a millenarian movement, when its dynamism has begun to wane.[40] The routinization of millenarian activity maintains the boundaries and integrity of the community but no longer points toward an imminent transformation. Most ecclesiastical structures arise out of movements that initially sought massive, immediate change in the character of human life.[41] Christianity and Islam represent once-dynamic movements that have made their peace with the status quo. At the secular level, communism, by largely jettisoning its early belief in imminent world revolution, accomplished the same thing. To the extent that rapid growth eliminates minority status, expanding movements often reach a point where defensive structuring is unnecessary. The community of Jehovah's Witnesses comes much closer to an active millenarian sect transformed into a defensively structured community.

The defensively structured community, no less than the millenarian movement itself, grows out of protracted stress. "*Sporadic* stress encounters, however traumatic, will not lead to change either in the direction of defensive structuring or in any other direction away from the *status quo ante*." [42] One major disaster situation does not appear capable of generating either defensive structuring or millenarianism. Wherein, then, lies the difference between millenarian movements and defensive structuring? Defensive structuring represents a coming to terms with a threatening external world, where such coming to terms is in principle possible. *Shtetl* Jews, Mormons, Amish, and Pueblo Indians have all found it possible to so insulate themselves. The paradigmatic case of defensive structuring is the self-created ghetto, where the outside society is kept deliberately at arm's length so that the life within may continue to manifest its characteristic forms. This is of course very different from the activist stance of millenarian movements, to whom visions of a stabilized social order are abhorrent. The millenarian activist seeks change of the most radical and immediate sort and cuts himself off from the society at large only as a tactical expedient. While it seems to him necessary to escape the pervasive evil of society, he does so in the expectation that the evil will shortly disappear. Defensive structuring, on the other hand, signifies a long-term decision to seek a stable, continuing relationship —restricted though it is—with the world outside.

Why, given the disaster syndrome, do single disasters so rarely produce millenarianism? We should, after all, expect them to produce exactly the searching, anxious, suggestible populace required. In the first place, the more limited the disaster, the more likely that large segments of the environment remain untouched. The destructiveness of modern warfare as well as certain natural catastrophes (volcanic eruptions, severe earthquakes, and tidal waves, for example) qualify this observation. However, on balance a single disaster is, all other things being equal, less likely to dramatically alter the environment than a series of catastrophes. .

Second, and more significant, a single disaster is less likely to call existing modes of explanation into serious question, even though the disaster itself may be inexplicable in current cultural terms. Potential millenarians surrender their current beliefs only with the greatest reluctance, under the harsh pressure of events. All belief systems tend to be preserved as long as possible, even when alternative systems might yield a better understanding. Cultural systems possess an inertia of their own. Hence under the first impact of disaster, the victims almost instinctively seek to explain their predicament in terms of preexisting beliefs; just as we all seek to deal with unfamiliar stimuli by assimilating them to the nearest familiar category.[43]

As disasters and their consequences multiply, however, the inadequacies of traditional modes of explanation become patently obvious. Disasters have often been explained by recourse to religious categories. The Black Death was regarded as God's punishment and the most efficacious countermeasures, penance and supplication. Religious observances continued to be stressed long after it was clear that they accomplished nothing. There is an all too familiar tendency to seek alleviation of novel threats and stress by routine means. The nature of the relationship between cultural inertia and disconfirming events is consequently complex. As Dynes and Yutzy point out, there is no single religious interpretation of disaster. They suggest, rather, a typology of explanations of disaster events.[44]

There are, of course, naturalistic explanations for disaster, based upon imputed causal relationships in the physical world. While typically we associate these explanations with

modern science, they can occur wherever associations are
made between different phenomena. Such explanations, however, are more likely to prove attractive to those least affected
by a disaster, since they answer "how" but not "why."
Fatalistic explanations attribute disasters to random occurrence, the "powers that be," specifying neither supernatural
agencies nor causal laws. Supernaturalistic explanations are
themselves divisible. Where the deity is evil or angry, he must
be appeased. Where the universe is apportioned among two
or more good and evil forces, "good and evil are separated
and disasters are assigned to the evil forces in the universe."
Where the gods are indifferent, a rare situation, nothing may
be done. Often disasters are taken to represent God's
punishment, and "the idea of punishment seems strong
among certain religious groups who see disasters as indica-
tions of apocalyptic changes and millennialist hope.". We
shall return to this observation shortly. Where man is
conceived as good, and thus undeserving of punishment, the
faithful may only invoke "God's will," a supernaturalistic
version of fatalism. Dynes and Yutzy suggest that among
supernaturalistic explanations, the most common reaction to
disaster is a variant of the God's will explanation: "When a
disaster occurs, God is not assessed clear responsibility nor is
man guilty of provoking him. The causal agent is seen to be
natural forces. . . . In this interpretation, God is seen in a
similar role as the physician. He does not assume responsibility for the outbreak of the epidemic, but he deserves the
credit for mitigating its worst effects." [45]

Belief systems are, after all, forms of explanation for
recurring problems, and it is only natural that formerly
successful explanations should be preserved on the basis of
their past record. To the extent that disasters are relatively
infrequent and usually limited in spread and duration,
explanations that appear inadequate can survive many isolated "one-shot" disconfirmations. In this respect, the disaster
challenge bears a strong resemblance to the well-known
model of scientific change proposed by Thomas Kuhn. Kuhn
argues that the principal structures of scientific explanation
continue to be upheld even in the face of findings (which he
terms "anomalies") that they cannot adequately explain.

Only the accumulation of anomalies *and* the presence of an alternative explanation causes a revolution in scientific thought.[46] In fact, discrepant observations may well be put down to experimental error if their consequence would be the destruction of a useful theory.[47] The two requirements for change, then, are disconfirming evidence and an alternative explanation. In the present context, disaster provides the one and chiliastic beliefs the other.

Repetitive disaster events chip away, as it were, at conventional ways of ordering reality. The disconfirming, anomalous cases refuse to disappear. Where single disasters do severely shake existing conceptions of order, those conceptions were already under serious and protracted stress. Frederic Jaher, analyzing the rise of a belief in imminent catastrophe in late nineteenth-century America, asks why the sense of threat took so long to emerge. The key forces of urbanization, industrialization, immigration, and labor organization were well at work in the 1870s, but only in the 1880s were they perceived to have literally catastrophic significance. Jaher speculates that "the absence of a dramatic incident was the major cause. It often takes an electrifying event like the Haymarket Affair [1886] to bring fears to the surface and intensify them to the point of cataclysmic consciousness. The active presence of urbanized foreign anarchists amid a great strike attracted fearful attention to these characteristics of the new era—the apparent evidences of impending disasters." [48]

This idea of the dramatic, catalytic event serves as the most persuasive link between two conceptions of disaster, absolute and perceived. Disaster studies rarely address themselves to the problem, for most putative disaster events are similarly perceived both by the external observer and the victim. An earthquake, tornado, or mine explosion does not appear open to the question, Is it really a disaster? But what about changes in climate or access to the sea? Are these "disasters" only to the historian examining them in retrospect or were they also dread events for the participants? And what of social, political and economic events, monetary fluctuations, changes in commodity prices, differential access to markets, military defeat, alterations in the status system, introduction of new technologies? There is no reason to assume that the disaster syndrome is wholly dependent upon the presence of objective criteria. For the most part, of course, it is brought on by radical changes in the environment. Yet to a certain extent the very perception of these changes depends upon an individual's mental set. This is particularly apt to be the case where there has been a long, slow erosion of familiar patterns and institutions, changes which have gone largely unnoticed. In such circumstances, the catalytic event may appear relatively insignificant in itself, but it suddenly brings together in the mind of the perceiver a sense of the interconnectedness of previously discrete events and a concomitant sense of loss and dread. The Tokyo earthquake of 1923, one of the few single disasters to produce millenarian activity, followed a long period of very rapid modernization.

One of the great flowerings of millenarian activity in the West took place in England during the first half of the seventeenth century. It was also a period of protracted suffering and unrest:

> The years from 1620 to 1650 were bad; the 1640s were much the worst decade of the period. On top of the disruption caused by the civil war came a series of disastrous harvests. Between 1647 and 1650 food prices rose steeply above the pre-war level; money wages lagged badly behind, and the cost of living rose significantly. Taxation was unprecedentedly heavy. . . . These were the years when sales of church, crown and royalists' land were breaking traditional landlord/tenant relations, whilst disbanded soldiers were trying to pick up a living again.[49]

These specific developments occurred against a backdrop of long-term social, political, and economic stresses. Europe as a whole appears to have suffered major strains in the sixteenth and early seventeenth centuries, a period referred to by some historians as a "general crisis."[50] Indeed, traumatic effects once attributed to the Thirty Years' War (1618–48) may in fact derive from a much longer history of decline. The tendency to forget the long-term processes with which specific events occurred has obscured the extent to which these events may have been significantly reinforced by their context. The Puritan victory and the subsequent execution of the king became apocalyptic events read in the context of a long-decaying social order, by people ready to see in the events of the mid-seventeenth century the prelude to the millennium itself. The earlier belief in a physical world decayed, winding down, and dying was about to give way to millenarianism, which saw in social change a sign of imminent triumph.[51]

The cumulative damage done by multiple disasters is thus both material and ideological. That is, disasters destroy both the physical-social environment and the ability of commonly held ideas to explain the destruction. Physical damage includes the destruction of the material environment—homes, modes of transportation and communication, sources of economic productivity, and so on; while the social environment of loved ones, kin, friends, and traditional leaders also disappears. The radical disruption of the individual's life setting produces the disaster syndrome and in so doing throws the individual into a temporary but often acute state of anxiety. Where events have removed this environment by decrements, allowing a certain amount of piecemeal adaptation, a dramatic catalytic event may serve to bring home the enormity of change. It might be imagined that the time available for adaptive responses would mitigate the disaster effects, that a consciousness of disaster is incompatible with decremental destruction. Yet they are compatible precisely because each decrement constitutes a challenge to the existing ways in which social change is explained. Anthony Wallace stresses this slow transformation of an existing culture in his description of the transition from increasing individual stress to a period of "cultural distortion" which precedes "revitalization." [52] As individuals come under greater and greater stress, they seek new forms of stress relief, yet fear to abandon past modes of behavior and belief. Existing beliefs limit the range of adaptive responses, for certain forms of innovation are literally inconceivable. The result, which Wallace calls cultural distortion, combines regressive behavior and ineffectual piecemeal change. These forms of incremental adaptation in fact only make matters worse, for they continue to be based on the assumption that radically new challenges can be approached in essentially unaltered ways. Yet the distinguishing characteristic of a disaster situation is its dissimilarity to previous experience.

The ordinary landmarks and routines of life do not or cannot exist under disaster conditions. Equally, the culture may be hard pressed to offer an adequate explanation for the occurrence of the disaster and reasons for its unpredictability. As disasters multiply, it becomes more and more difficult to replace or explain the losses. Explanations grudgingly accepted at first ring more and more hollow each time they are invoked. Dynes and Yutzy's observation that millenarians frequently construe disasters as divine punishments indicates their desire to find meaning in the incomprehensible.

Millenarian movements do not attempt to reconstruct a disaster-ridden society. Instead, they turn their backs upon it, condemn it as evil and unredeemable, and concentrate on the development of an alternative. In this respect, the difference between millenarians and utopians is one of degree rather than of kind; indeed, in practice they often prove difficult to distinguish from one another.[53] The break with the present must be total. The individual, no longer left to his own devices in a social system which can do less and less for him, enters a new fellowship of believers, a completely enveloping substitute environment. In the process, he may expect all traditional beliefs to be turned upside down and his own identity to be transformed. In a sense, Eric Hoffer is correct in saying that the true believer seeks a movement because he wishes to shed his old identity and sense of self.[54] An examination of the catchword themes of millenarian ideology bear out the emphasis on a substitute environment: renunciation, rejection, defiance, inversion, fraternity, dedication, rebirth.[55] The adherent, having been enfolded in a new existence, is also provided with new beliefs. Whatever else the beliefs may do, they offer explanations for the problems of the present and predictions of their imminent solution. Just as scientific world views compete for individual and communal allegiance, one declining, another rising, so the explanatory systems of millenarian movements challenge and may supplant the faltering ideas of the traditional culture.

If multiple disasters represent one typical condition for the rise of millenarian movements, another and essential one is the presence of ideological "raw material." Ideas must already be present that, without too much distortion, can be interpreted in a salvationist manner. However creative the chiliastic prophet may appear, he can only work on those materials available to him, by emphasis on their novel restatement. The West has had a particularly rich store of doctrines that point toward an imminent future transformation. Indeed, the very richness of these ideas has led some writers—notably Worsley and Kedourie[56]—to claim that the occurrence of millenarianism elsewhere may be explained principally through the exportation of Western ideas. It is certainly true that Christian proselytizing unintentionally led to the wide diffusion of messianic ideas, and it is equally true that the secular counterpart to millenarianism—the idea of progress—filtered through from Western sources. The idea of utopia, closely bound up with millenarianism, also appears to be very largely a Western preoccupation.[57]

Nonetheless, virtually all cultures turn out on close examination to harbor motifs capable of a place in a new millenarian synthesis. This may even be true of Hindu India, with its cyclical view of time. Köbben argues that of all areas of the world, only aboriginal Australia and Hindu India lack mention of millenarianism.[58] More recently, Harold Gould's revisionist view of the sepoy mutinies of 1857 opens the possibility of genuine millenarian activity on the subcontinent.[59] However, the doctrinal content was vague and ill-defined: it amounted only to a fervent wish for the restoration of traditional Indian life as it was before the East India Company's invasion. Implicit in this case is the possibility that, where clear millenarian motifs are in short supply, millenarianism may nonetheless emerge through the clash of cultures. In other words, the juxtaposition of the indigenous culture and a despised importation gives to traditional forms an idealized character. As it becomes contaminated and suppressed, native, precontact culture comes to be regarded as a "paradise lost," infinitely better now than it ever seemed before. The past has thus been transformed into a favorite theme of millenarian literature, the lost golden age.

The rebellious Indian mercenaries forced the traditional princes to assume their old leadership roles. They were asked to function, not as messiahs, but simply as effective rulers, something they had not done in some time. Who then were the prophetic leaders? Gould can only fall back upon the assertion that the mutineers became "collective prophets." If that is the case, it renders the concept "prophet" largely metaphorical. It also explains the failure of the Bengal rebels to pose a serious challenge to the British. The princes took up their new roles under duress; and, while it is clear they eventually generated enthusiasm for the task, they had little conception of how to go about it. The rebels themselves, devoid of charismatic leadership, could only force into leadership roles individuals equally lacking in a clear conception of goals. The Indian situation suggests two important factors: First, Köbben is partially correct in his assertion that Hindu India lacks millenarianism.[60] There was certainly an absence of readily usable chiliastic motifs. The mutineers and the princes alike appear to have floundered about, desperately anxious to oppose British influence yet unable to find a set of ideas that would direct their efforts toward that end: it was millenarianism in a vacuum. Second, no individual(s) appeared with a doctrine around which the revolt could crystallize.

This example demonstrates the critical relationship between doctrine and leadership. Doctrine is not simply "in the air"; it must be fashioned by an individual, and where that individual is not present, the doctrine will not spontaneously appear. Why does a prophet-figure with a doctrine of hope and imminent rescue appear in times of doubt and unrest? The suggested answers fall into two categories. The easiest answer is that his appearance is fortuitous, the confluence of social needs and idiosyncratic personal traits. Such persons, were they to appear at a time of stability, might be ignored or regarded as threatening deviants. Their appearance at a time of collective receptivity must be thought a happy accident, but an accident nonetheless. The second answer, much more complex, argues that the availability of new identities at a time when they are required is neither accidental nor unrelated to the needs of the times.

In normal times, traditional leadership can be expected to

meet usual needs and, by virtue of adaptive capacities, occasionally meet extraordinary needs as well. Disaster not only creates extraordinary needs but often destroys the traditional leadership. Catastrophes break down existing groups, disperse leaders or render them impotent, and in their place ad hoc groupings grow with new leadership. When official leadership fails, the way lies open to emergent leaders.[61] While this may serve as a means of upward mobility,[62] its more significant function is as a mode of entry for charismatic leadership. With the failure or nonavailability of official leaders, and the presence of a perceived crisis, leadership is sought outside official recruitment channels.

Wallace argues that the same disaster circumstances that produce anxiety in many persons produce innovation in a few.[63] He posits an elaborate set of physiological changes brought on by chronic stress, which in some naturally susceptible individuals leads to rapid personality change and a dramatic reformulation of the existing cultural system.[64] In other words, the stress undergone by the entire group produces in some "a physicochemical milieu in which certain brains can perform a function of which they are normally incapable: a wholesale resynthesis." [65] One is tempted to accept Wallace's psychophysiological approach, if only for its audaciousness and for the precision it seems to afford. The appearance of charismatic leaders at propitious historical moments is a question of abiding interest, to the philosopher of history no less than to the social scientist. Yet at least insofar as millenarian movements are concerned, the appearance of the prophet and his message owes at least as much to cultural as to biological factors.

The temptation is to reduce poorly understood social processes to relatively well understood physiological processes. However, as Wallace concedes, the process of resynthesis is by no means limited to great and recognized leaders. The distinction between the latter and paranoid schizophrenics cannot be easily or lightly made.[66] We deal here not merely with the peculiar characteristics of an individual but with the interaction between his personality and the needs and receptivities of those about him. Much depends upon existing cultural norms. "When a society regards highly individuals

who are able to produce unusual psychological states, such
persons will appear." [67] The social distinction between the
incarcerated madman and the venerated prophet may be
made precisely on such grounds.

The prophetic leader has a better chance of appearing and
receiving a hearing where a charismatic tradition already
exists. Max Weber conceived the charismatic leader to be the
product of disaster. Charismatic leadership, he writes, arises
in moments of psychic, physical, economic, ethical, religious,
or political distress.[68] It is the product both of recognized gifts
and of extraordinary events. Paradoxically, despite the
uniqueness that this implies, its every appearance in a society
makes its reappearance more likely. It becomes a role,
although it is not always filled. Weber's discussion of
charisma is filled with unresolved ambiguities, sometimes
suggesting that routinization is the antithesis of charisma, at
other times asserting that charisma can be transformed "into
a capacity that, in principle, can be taught and learned." [69]
This ambiguity in Weber's own writings has been com-
pounded by the entry of *charisma* into everyday speech. Far
from being regarded as an extraordinary personal gift, it has
been converted into virtually a synonym for personal magne-
tism.[70]

An uncertain middle ground lies between the concept of
the absolutely unique charismatic leader and the merely
magnetic officeholder. In it we find societies where charismatic leadership has been known to occur but where its
occurrence is still sufficiently rare for it to mark a break with
traditional patterns of leadership. The prophetic traditions in
ancient Israel [71] and in tribal Africa[72] both balance the
uniqueness of personal gifts against the necessities of intermittently repeated social crises.

No matter how gifted an individual, his claim to charismatic leadership in the end rests upon the willingness of
others to accept it: charisma is not something one possesses,
but rather shorthand for extraordinary qualities which followers impute. Only if others see in an individual the fulfillment
of pressing desires will they choose to honor his qualities.
"Charisma is thus a function of recognition: the prophet
without honour cannot be a charismatic prophet. Charisma,

therefore, sociologically viewed, is a social relationship, not an attribute of individual personality or a mystical quality." [73] This simple observation, so often overlooked, establishes the vital link between leader and led. The personal decision to endow an individual with charisma, to see in him the exercise of extraordinary gifts, is not the product of careful calculation; it is precipitate and total. The suggestibility and value crisis produced by catastrophe help also to produce the audience without which charismatic gifts dissolve into personal eccentricities. The willingness to follow is surely as important as the desire to lead.

We shall return to the prophet-disciple nexus in the next chapter, in connection with the phenomenon of conversion. Suffice it to say for the present that disaster opens the need for alternative, emergency leadership. Ranger suggests that in East Africa the prophetic tradition, although usually submerged, constitutes an ever-available alternative should crisis occur. The predilection of the French in the nineteenth and twentieth centuries to seek out a military leader—a "man on horseback"—demonstrates that emergency leadership traditions are by no means confined to the non-Western world. The millenarian prophet-leader is distinguished not simply by unconventional recruitment but by his ability to formulate ideology. The reluctant prophet, by no means unknown, is occasionally accompanied by an ideologue, who, speaking in the prophet's name, produces the doctrine. The seventeenth-century Jewish false messiah, Sabbatai Zevi, was accompanied by just such a figure.

In summary, we began with the concept of disaster. We have seen that its impact falls far more heavily on rural than on urban areas. We must then expect millenarian movements to occur more frequently in agrarian environments. We have seen, too, that the attitudinal change and the loosening of existing commitments comes about more readily under the impact of multiple than single disasters. Consequently, we may expect that agrarian areas subject to repeated catastrophes, either natural or social, will constitute particularly likely breeding grounds for millenarianism. However, the final necessary ingredient is salvationist doctrine articulated by a prophetic figure. The doctrine without a charismatic leader cannot galvanize large masses of people—a point that will become more evident after the discussion of conversion in the next chapter. And where the doctrine is not obviously available, someone must synthesize and articulate it. As we have seen, while a charismatic figure may arise in virtually any unstable situation, his emergence is more likely where there exists a tradition of emergency, disaster leadership.

Chapter Four

CATASTROPHE AND CONVERSION

We have now seen the manner in which multiple disasters, existing millenarian ideas, and charismatic leadership converge to produce the millenarian movement. To be sure, we cannot predict with great certainty the occurrence of such a constellation. However, it should already be clear that some areas might well be predisposed to millenarian activity and that we should find such movements clustered according to the structural characteristics of regions. Consequently, let us begin this chapter with an outline of the typical millenarian-prone area. Having done so, we shall pass on to the mode of entry of members into these movements and the forces that determine a movement's survival or decay.

We have already seen that millenarian movements are overwhelmingly agrarian. This appears more natural when we consider that such movements create a microcosm, an insular social world with distinctive norms and goals.[1] This mutually supportive environment constitutes an alternative to a macrocosm perceived as evil, decaying, and doomed. This microcosm must be kept separate from its environment, and its activities must be directed toward individual commitment and group cohesion. Millenarian movements are not special-purpose organizations; they do not readily coexist with other, potentially conflicting group memberships.

The natural milieu for this kind of organization is one which already enjoys an insular existence, where common values prevail, and where opportunities for face-to-face contacts already abound. That is, of course, precisely the case in those remote areas where chiliasm has flourished, hinterlands of farmers, villagers, or tribesmen. In these settings, small size, homogeneous populations, and physical-cultural isolation create natural opportunities for the reinforcement of newly acquired beliefs. Just as many of the same characteristics accounted for the disaster-proneness of these areas, they now make clear why millenarian movements survive their

immediate disaster origins. By the same token, the relative
absence of outside interference, at least in the early stages,
allows a movement to consolidate.

As a result, most millenarian movements appear intimately
associated with well-defined population groups: culturally
homogeneous people inhabiting clearly bounded areas.
Wherever we look, localism is in evidence: The religiopolitical African separatist churches grew from small tribal nuclei.
The American Indian movements usually developed on a
tribe-specific basis—the Seneca, Comanche, and so on, each
giving rise to movements of its own. This is so even for the
final Ghost Dance movement, which swept the Western
Indian tribes. The cult took somewhat different forms among
different tribes, and only among the Sioux did it lead to
violence.[2] The Klamath, Nez Perce, Chippewa, Navaho,
Pueblo, and Apache were generally not affected.[3] Where the
dance took root, it apparently did so as a result of local
decisions, and there was certainly nothing approximating an
organization or church. Where it was adopted, it was usually
taken up by the entire tribe; it died out sporadically,
abandoned by a tribe at a time for quite separate reasons.[4]
The Melanesian Cargo Cults present an even more dramatic
picture of local development, with dozens of marginally
differentiable cults emerging throughout the South Pacific.[5]
The medieval European movements dot the central part of
the Continent. In retrospect, doctrinal similarities and their
sequential spread allow us to see large-scale movements—
"streams of heresy," as Ronald Knox refers to them[6]—but
any effort in this direction is an attempt to secure broad
understanding after the fact. We are dealing with small-scale
local eruptions, however much they may bear family resemblances to each other.

It is, of course, easy to argue that this attribution of
localism is circular, that movements in technologically under-
developed areas are necessarily small-scale and compact due
to poor communications. There is, to be sure, a measure of
truth in this. Chiliastic movements are associated with
cultures whose means of communications are poor by modern standards. Information could not be easily diffused over
large areas. Yet we must take care not to overstate the point.

Millenarian movements have frequently been smaller than the largest effective social units of their time and place. Students of primitive societies have concentrated on the ability of some movements to transcend local particularism and build larger social units.[7] Yet the cults have only rarely expanded to the point of maximum effective administration and communication. The medieval movements were puny compared with the administrative system of the Church. The Taiping Rebellion, very large by the standards of millenarian movements, nonetheless took in only a segment of the Chinese Empire.

What is required to control a hierarchical church or an empire is not sufficient to develop a chiliastic movement. The administrative systems of church and polity permit substantial delegation of power at the local level and make quite circumscribed claims over their subjects' total lives. By contrast, millenarian movements attempt to withdraw people from affiliations to which they have already been socialized and bring them into a community which asks total commitment. Clearly, a system which reaps the benefits of an established socialization process can afford to take commitment for granted. Millenarian movements, for which a transfer of primary allegiances is central, must regard the inculcation and maintenance of values with the greatest seriousness.

At the level of the local area, three factors may operate to foster deviant belief systems: family ties, occupation, and region. They quite commonly reinforce one another. For example, a family characterized by pronounced millenarian commitment may live in a region where millenarianism is endemic and pursue an occupation especially associated with radical dissent. In turn, those occupations associated with radical dissent occur in precisely the isolated regions which show up as seedbeds of millenarianism.

The family is a principal—often *the* principal—agent in transmitting political values to the growing generation.[8] However, a great gulf remains between an identification as nominal as that with a political party, and the unconventional character of millenarian beliefs, subject to abrupt disconfirmation and demanding high levels of commitment.

Millenarian movements in fact occur in predominantly
traditional, nonurban environments, where family commitments exercise uncommon influence.

Membership in Jewish messianic movements in the seventeenth and eighteenth centuries appears to have passed
through family lines with unbroken continuity for up to a
century and a half.[9] However, for the most part, the difficult
and tedious business of reconstructing family histories remains to be done, at least insofar as the history of millenarianism is concerned. The long preoccupation with leaders,
dictated in part by the greater availability of data, has left the
social characteristics of the followers vague and ill-defined.
Only tantalizing hints of the familial role emerge from time to
time. Thus H. G. Barnett, in his study of the millenarian
Shaker cult among Indians in the Puget Sound area, notes
that family units provide the key to understanding the
patterns of the religion's acceptance: "family nuclei of
converts rather than randomly distributed individuals have
. . . formed the spearhead of new growths in new areas." [10]
We are left to infer that studies over time would demonstrate
at least some survival of the conversion ideology within the
original family line.

It is also possible, although difficult to substantiate, that
families of millenarian activists socialize their children to a
subculture of messianic expectations. The assumption that
family socialization communicates only conventional, status
quo–oriented beliefs is clearly erroneous. While it may be
true for most families in contemporary America, there is no
reason to suppose that it is universally the case.[11] In order to
secure continuing political support, ongoing societies incul-
cate, and most persons internalize, a set of supportive values.
While this seems to be a requirement for long-run social
stability, there is nothing in either the family or the socialization process per se which compels it to function in this
manner. We shall return to the role of socialization at a later
point, since it holds profound implications for any explanation of millenarianism.

In societies where at least some division of labor exists,
students of radical dissent have long noted the apparently
pivotal role of certain occupational groups. In modern

industrial societies, political extremism has been associated
with those groups whose activities keep them apart from the
larger society: for example, sailors, miners, fishermen, lum-
bermen, sheepshearers, longshoremen, and farmers.[12] In the
Middle Ages, the isolated circumstances of weavers made
them a fertile source of heretical beliefs, so much so that as
late as the nineteenth century they were still regarded with
suspicion (as in *Silas Marner*).

An isolated work situation seems to have its political and
social consequences by cutting the individual off from
conflicting views. He sees only or primarily those who occupy
similar occupational roles, and the nature of the job generally
means that workers' families live in similarly homogeneous
circumstances, as in farming communities or mining towns.
Alternative views of the world rarely penetrate, while prevailing local opinions receive constant reinforcement. There
are immediate correspondences between the naturally existing circumstances of these workers and the homogeneous
microcosm which the millenarian movement intentionally
creates. Both cut the adherent off from dissonant stimuli
while buttressing conformist beliefs. The uniform, compacted
character of these occupational communities also makes them
singularly vulnerable to environment-destruction through
intense disasters. Indeed, we might speculate that the radicalism so often associated with, for example, miners, might be
attributed not only to isolation but to the disaster-proneness
of the work itself.

This is all part of a larger concept of isolation, whether
job-caused or not, as a source of extremist politics. "Wherever the social structure operates so as to isolate *naturally*
individuals or groups with the same political outlook from
contact with those who hold different views, the isolated
individuals or groups tend to back political extremists." [13]
Thus in the Middle Ages heresy was endemic in the mountain
fastnesses of the Alps and Pyrenees; indeed, in any areas
remote enough to serve as places of refuge.[14] Intense collective emotionality of the sort generated by millenarian movements is characteristic of culturally alienated areas.[15] Millenarian movements, as we have seen, have been
overwhelmingly rural phenomena. They have flourished in

such backcountry milieus as the Brazilian Northeast, Andalusia, and New Guinea.

We can now see that millenarian movements require a complex social ecology for nurturance, one in which cultural motifs, charismatic leadership, disaster vulnerability and occurrence, and isolation interact with one another. Familial ties, occupational separateness, and spatial-cultural isolation frequently coincide, reinforcing rather than neutralizing each other. It is equally true that modernization is the enemy of remote, homogeneous cultures. Urbanization, industrialization, role differentiation—all serve to attack and disintegrate the remaining backward or archaic enclaves. The elaborate kinship systems break down; patterns of residence show greater and greater dispersal; economies move from extraction to manufacturing; and diverse ideas are communicated over increasingly large areas. If isolation allows millenarian groups to flourish, then has not modernization made their days numbered?

Against this evidence of rising mobility and diversity, a number of additional factors must be entered. First, although millenarianism does develop in out-of-the-way locales, it does not, curiously, arise in the *most* remote areas. Just as the very poorest and most oppressed segments of a population rarely become revolutionaries, so the most cutoff and parochial regions do not seem to favor millenarian activity. Rather, millenarianism appears in regions which are still organized along traditional lines but which perceive threatening forces outside. These are not vacuums, totally sealed off from the external world. Instead, they are often bastions of traditionalism upon which the modern, nontraditional world has begun to impinge. It is this delicate position between stability and change which makes some backcountry areas such vulnerable and volatile sources of group activity.

Millenarianism, then, survives in areas with these characteristics: physical-cultural separateness; much communication within the area but little between it and other areas; relatively homogeneous population; preexisting salvationist ideas; potential charismatic leadership; and vulnerability to and frequent occurrence of environment-destroying disasters. Within this ecology of millenarianism, ideas that might be rapidly and effectively challenged elsewhere grow in a hothouse atmosphere of constant nourishment. Suspicion of dark forces outside and common interests and weaknesses within, well-articulated family structures and intermittent but unpredictable catastrophes—all serve to maintain adherence to ideas which in time of larger upheavals may spread rapidly outside.

Social scientists have long been aware of the difficulty in moving from a consideration of total communities to an examination of individual behavior. We cannot easily infer individual behavior from a knowledge of how men act or what characterizes them in the aggregate (the so-called ecological fallacy). Our attention up to this point has been primarily directed at the collectivity, the millenarian movement and the larger community from which it springs. We have attempted to specify that complex of conditions which produces a chiliastic movement. Even in doing so, however, the group and the individual could not remain apart. The concept of disaster as a causal factor involves simultaneous consideration of both communal and individual effects. The disaster syndrome is, after all, an individual phenomenon which grows out of a collective stress experience.

The individual aspects of millenarianism are not exhausted by a consideration of the disaster syndrome alone. Entry into a chiliastic movement constitutes a milestone in an individual's life and involves the abandonment of a lifetime's values and habits of mind. The initiate takes on a new existence, with new patterns of behavior and novel beliefs. How is this turning accomplished?

Our knowledge of conversion processes in social movements is remarkably sparse, considering the importance and inherent drama of the subject. On reflection, however, such systematic ignorance is not surprising, for the study of social movements has traditionally focused upon the person of the leader to the exclusion of the rank and file. Doubtless many factors have contributed to this bias, not the least of them the greater availability of information about leaders. But whatever the explanation, the motivations of followers have occupied a distinctly secondary position in most research.

One clearly does not join a millenarian movement as one would a fraternal organization, professional association, or political party. It is not an affiliation of convenience, nor are its demands partial or casual. Chiliasm deals in ultimate problems and ultimate solutions, and it is expected that adherents will assume their roles with the appropriate seriousness of purpose. If there is any ready counterpart to this attachment, it is that afforded by religious obligations, particularly those undertaken by recent converts. Indeed, whether millenarian movements themselves are regarded as religious, political, or social seems a judgment made in the eye of the beholder.

What does it mean to say that someone has undergone a *conversion?* From a theological standpoint, it means that an individual has deliberately moved from indifference or from a prior religious persuasion to a new form of piety, and that he has done so in the recognition that he is moving from error to truth.[16] Stripped of the theological vocabulary, conversion suggests a form of rapid attitude change that may occur in either a secular or religious context. It is characterized by abruptness, by the total nature of the reorientation, by the frequent surrender of beliefs once strongly held, and by the concomitant adoption of beliefs that once would have been rejected.[17] Nothing in the concept renders it nonpolitical except the cultural convention in American society that politics is not a matter of ultimates and that membership in a political organization is not so serious a matter. Were politics to be defined in apocalyptic terms—as even in America it occasionally is—conversion at once becomes an appropriate avenue of entry. It is both curious and revealing that we cannot even talk about the politics of ultimate commitments without falling back upon theological terms—*conversion, charisma, apocalypse, millennium, prophet.* In point of fact, there seems to be no essential difference between the conversion experiences of conventional religion and those of a "political religion" such as communism; both demonstrate phenomena of suddenness, totality of conviction, and reversal of past attitudes.[18]

Just as the conversion experience occurs in both the political and religious spheres, so it takes place in societies at all levels of complexity.[19] No special sophistication is required. Indeed, to the extent that modern societies tend to reward emotional control, such societies may inhibit conversion. In any case, there is certainly no reason to suppose that the manner in which revolutionaries take on value commitments differs in any significant ways from the processes that affect millenarians. The strength of commitment of, for example, the Mau Mau does not differ from that of Communists or Jacobins.

Since conversion is not a mode of entry into casual or temporary associations, it forms a convenient dividing line between different types of social organizations. Those that recruit heavily through conversion experiences may be expected to differ significantly from those that recruit by offering limited goals at the price of limited obligations. The latter may customarily be joined by such nominal acts as paying dues, registering as a member, voting in an election, or attending a meeting. Of course, mode of recruitment is an imperfect indicator of the nature of an organization. Movements which utilize conversion extensively may still attract many nominal followers, in the hope that they too will eventually undergo a profound change of heart. But as long as we talk of *characteristic* recruitment methods, conversion belongs to those movements which exact total loyalties and offer all-encompassing world views.

Many affiliations are not the product of conscious decision at all, but rather the outcome of the socialization process. The norm for political-party membership is entry in an only half-conscious manner as a result of communicated parental affiliation. Interest groups, on the other hand, utilize neither conversion nor socialization. One is unlikely, after all, to be socialized into membership in the Audubon Society or the National Association of Manufacturers, although to be sure certain childhood circumstances may predispose an individual to the one or the other.

Consequently, we may distinguish three forms of recruitment, together with the organizations which employ them. First, there is membership based upon a well-defined perception of interest. In this category fall special-purpose associations and interest groups, which exact limited demands from

new members and from which old members may depart with
minimal fuss. Second, there is the process of socialization.
The organizations whose membership is replenished in this
manner constitute a broad category. It may include organizations ranging from political parties to entire cultures. Membership in a specific culture involves a long process of
habituation to characteristic values and practices. One does
not experience a sudden transformation and find oneself, say,
a Trobriander or a Japanese. For this reason the lot of adult
immigrants is often so painful, for they must discard the
socialization of a lifetime and become resocialized at a stage
in life where such wholesale adaptations are increasingly
difficult. In contrast, political parties may be entered by
socialization or, occasionally, by later conscious decisions,
and exit from the organization is generally accomplished with
ease. Finally, there is conversion and those organizations
whose ranks are filled in this manner.

Established religions continue across generations through
the socialization process. But it has long been noted that the
early growth phase of religious denominations, which do not
have an established reservoir of member-families on which to
draw for new members, relies upon conversion. It is equally
true of nominally secular counterparts—for example, political
systems which make no distinction between the individual
and the state or between the public and private realms.
Millenarian movements, as might be expected, utilize conversion extensively, socialization less so. In this respect, they
differ from both long-lived religious communions and conventional politics. The reasons for the difference are not far to
seek. They involve the question of the longevity of millenarian movements. This is a complex problem, already encountered in the previous chapter and to be reexamined later in
this chapter. Suffice it to say for the present purpose that
areas may produce millenarian movements over long time
periods, but single movements possess relatively brief lives.
Hence, to the extent that socialization is used, it is socialization to a subculture of generalized millenarian expectation,
rather than to a specific sect or movement. That relationship,
the immediate product of later life rather than childhood

experience, depends upon confrontation with a charismatic prophet-figure.

The second major reason why millenarians are so often the products of conversion experiences is that the movements themselves are often social discontinuities. That is, they are set apart from culturally dominant modes of belief and action. Even when a subculture of messianic expectation develops in a particular area—as it has at various times in Melanesia or the Brazilian Northeast—it is precisely that, a subculture. Millenarian expectation always constitutes a repudiation of humdrum everyday existence, a protest against perceived inequities, a break with tradition. For that reason, it is so often pictured as an agency for innovation in traditional societies.[20] Millenarian ideologies ring changes on existing cultural themes, for example, the myth of a lost golden age. To this extent, socialization provides access to the cultural materials out of which the chiliastic doctrine can be fashioned. Socialization allows the potential convert to understand and react to the traditional elements of the new doctrine and places him in the proper state of knowledgeability. Beyond that, the novel emphases and recombinations lie outside traditional socialization and hence demand some additional leap of faith. Marxism, so intimately related to the Western idea of progress, falls on readied ears in Europe and America, yet even among those so prepared, the act of embracing communism has very often involved a sudden conversion experience. Millenarian adherence is in any case not simply a matter of doctrinal acceptance; it also demands repudiation of one's past life and a willingness to *act* in a manner which separates one from the traditionally oriented community. The combination of heterodox beliefs with noncomformist actions demands a reorientation of personality. The convert sees himself at a dividing point in his life, leaving one existence for another.

The initiate must sever conventional social, political, and economic relationships in anticipation of the millennium. E. J. Hobsbawm describes the self-imposed withdrawal of an Andalusian millenarian anarchist:

Everything that made the Andalusian of tradition was to be jettisoned. He would not pronounce the word God or have

anything to do with religion, he opposed bullfights, he
refused to drink or even to smoke . . . he disapproved of
sexual promiscuity though officially committed to free love.
Indeed, at times of strike or revolution there is even
evidence that he practised absolute chastity. . . . He was a
revolutionary in the most total sense conceivable to
Andalusian peasants, condemning *everything* about the
past.[21]

Such systematic isolation cannot simply be accomplished on
the basis of some calculus of self-interest; it is insufficient
merely to calculate the advantages to be obtained from
preservation as against those to be obtained from breach. The
inertial component in human life—the habit-following propensity of man in his social existence—militates against
sudden transformations. Under the limitations imposed by
habit and the desire for an ordered life, even compelling
calculations of personal advantage cannot alone swing the
usual individual onto untrodden paths. Tolerance for ambiguity and receptivity to innovation can carry us a certain
distance away from the familiar, but the demands of millenarianism are another matter. Indeed, all accounts of conversion emphasize how frequently transformations appear to
have been made in the absence of prior conscious reflection.[22]

What, then, causes an individual to convert? The major
sources of data on the conversion process are, on the one
hand, religious studies and, on the other, studies of what has
variously been called *brainwashing* or *thought reform.* These
terms refer to techniques employed in the Soviet Union,
Eastern Europe, and Communist China to induce confessions
of sin and wrongdoing and/or to induce a political conversion. There is at present no evidence that the coercive
character of these conversions in any significant way affects
the manner in which the process operates. Indeed, it is often
difficult to separate coercion and persuasion.[23]

This data suggests that the factors that facilitate conversion
can be grouped into two classes. The first concerns what we
might call *predispositional factors,* characteristics of individuals which discriminate likely from unlikely converts. The
second, *situational factors,* deals with forces in the environ-

ment which push an individual in the direction of rapid attitudinal change. The division is artificial in the sense that the result occurs because of the interaction of organism and environment, of predispositional and situational factors. Nonetheless, they constitute useful categories for exploring what is known about the conversion experience.

The assumption is almost universally made that individuals differ in their susceptibilities to zealotry. This idea has undoubtedly gained much of its present currency through the attention given Eric Hoffer's concept of the true believer. Hoffer himself ascribed the true believer's fervor to the "proclivities and responses indigenous to the frustrated mind." [24] From this one might make either of two inferences: that anyone might become a true believer if placed in a sufficiently frustrating environment; or that frustration as a formative influence might produce a personality type characterized by low frustration tolerance and consequent true belief later in life. While Hoffer clearly leans toward the former view, it is the latter that has become commonplace.

The most explicit attempt to classify men in terms of their "convertibility" has been made by the British psychiatrist William Sargant. Under the strong influence of Pavlov, Sargant reasons that conversion occurs as a result of stress, and that in individuals, as in Pavlov's laboratory animals, reactions to stress differ. Hence human subjects will react differently to different levels of stress, as well as to different balances between intellectual and emotional appeals. Sargant envisions a typology of personality types, disconcertingly parallel to those employed in the ancient theory of humors. All individuals are presumed to represent admixtures of these ideal types.[25] We are left to assume that differences between types—for example, between the "strong excitatory" and the "imperturbable"—must themselves be laid at the door of inherited temperaments. And, as Sargant is at pains to make clear, no individual, whatever his makeup, is unconvertible, so long as the stress is applied with sufficient persistence and intensity.

It is precisely the mixture of types in actual life which proves the limiting factor in Sargant's approach. Not only may the combinations be so complex as to vitiate any simple

typology, but in the end nothing clearly differentiates converts from nonconverts.[26] Individuals of all kinds may be
found among the converted. It may well be that the skilled
and ruthless interrogator in the closed world of the prison can
eventually induce anyone to subscribe to any set of ideas; the
test lies in the world outside.

Robert Jay Lifton, beginning with similar data, presents an
alternative. In dealing with conversion and resistance among
subjects of Chinese Communist thought reform, Lifton
suggests that susceptibility depends upon the individual's
"balance between flexibility and totalism." What then is
"totalism"? It is "a tendency toward all-or-nothing emotional
alignments." [27] Lifton adopts the term from Erik Erikson,
who conceives it as a counterpart to personal "wholeness." [28]
Wholeness for Erikson constitutes an organization of alternating states and attitudes—such as sleep and wakefulness,
dependence and independence, sociability and aloneness.
The integrated person consists of a number of such diverse,
shifting tendencies. Totalism, on the other hand, implies that
the individual abandons openness and diversity to align
himself with some closed and fixed set of attitudes. In so
doing, a sense of balance and adaptability has been lost.
There are many examples of the shift to totalism, including
both mental disturbance and religiopolitical conversion.[29]

An individual may be inclined to totalism (and hence to
conversion) through any of a number of elements in his
developmental history: "early lack of trust, extreme environmental chaos, total domination by a parent or parent-repre-
sentative, intolerable burdens of guilt, and severe crises of
identity." [30] Totalism serves as a problem solution in different
ways at different times. The problems of mistrust of the world
for the infant, of guilt for the child, and of unclear identity for
the youth may all yield to totalist solutions. Where the
proclivity for total solutions is linked to an unclear sense of
identity, conversion is particularly likely.[31] Given the sense of
rebirth, of becoming a new person, that conversion affords,
this seems wholly plausible.

Any population is likely to have persons within it either in
search of total commitments or anxious to exchange one such
commitment for another. It is tempting, consequently, to

think of millenarian movements as groups built around a totalist nucleus. Societies in upheaval are places where existing belief systems cannot easily be maintained; new events too often threaten old certainties. If some individuals require more in the way of certainty than others, then they must seek some comparably rigid alternative more in keeping with their present circumstances.

There are, in other words, situational factors of which we must take account, and it is to them that we now turn. We have already seen that some individuals tend not to do things by halves but rather take and maintain unequivocal positions. Such persons are, under normal circumstances, relatively uncommon. They exist in sufficiently manageable numbers to be absorbed by the occupational structure, religious sects and, occasionally, psychotherapeutic institutions. But of course millenarian movements do not appear under normal circumstances, but rather under disrupted ones, and hence it is worthwhile to explore the external factors associated with conversion to and between totalist positions. As we explore these factors, we shall see that the line between the predispositional and the situational grows less distinct. Obviously, an individual becomes predisposed to conversion and total belief through factors outside himself, at least so long as we are unwilling to postulate a genetic predisposition.

The principal situational factors involved in conversion are increased suggestibility, the breakdown of past and existing values, and the presence of a potential new identity. Under what circumstances do individuals become more amenable to suggestion? They become more suggestible when they lack the mental frame of reference that would permit them to critically analyze incoming stimuli.[32] Novelty or ambiguity, messages which cannot easily be set against existing standards, may be believed precisely because they are unfamiliar. This often proves to be the case in panic behavior, where the very unreasonableness of the belief seems to commend it to some people.[33]

When we speak of social change, we mean that array of situations which presents individuals with new problems and situations. Frameworks of experience cease to function effectively when confronted by problems they were not set up to explain. In Wallace's terms, the mazeway fails. We all hold beliefs concerning the operations of the physical and social world, beliefs transmitted to us from childhood on. However, the beliefs are meant to cover only such situations as have occurred in the past or are reasonably expected to occur in the future. Should these stereotypical events be supplanted by new and different ones, it is a fair surmise that the individual so confronted will prove unusually receptive to suggestion. His evaluative apparatus simply cannot function as well as it did. Since explanatory frameworks lag behind social change, in the initial period of change individuals must function as best they can with solutions designed for other problems.

Stress also increases suggestibility when it passes the point where it merely offers greater stimulation and acuteness. We are not concerned here with so-called functional stress, but rather with stress that produces nervous tension, anxiety, or physical debilitation. Under high stress, human information processing becomes less rapid and less dependable. Fear, anger, or excitement, when sufficiently prolonged, eventually produces a total collapse of normal intellectual functioning.[34] As mental efficiency diminishes, critical faculties necessarily cease to operate with their customary vigor, and suggestibility is enhanced. Moreover, the products of stress are to an extent self-perpetuating. For example, stress may produce anxiety, and the anxious person consequently for a time interprets ambiguous events in a way that confirms his own anxiety.[35]

When conversion occurs, it is customarily accompanied by substantial physical and/or psychological stress. Both the debilitation of the fasting supplicant and the vision of hellfire presented by the revivalist place the individual subject in a state where the acceptance of novel ideas is increased. Profound reversals of commitment have often followed lengthy periods of indecision, unsolved problems, and vague fears. While mild or brief stress enhances performance, insight, or creativity, severe prolonged stress makes a person more sensitive to stimuli, less able to learn complex tasks, less well equipped to make discriminations or solve new problems, and in general causes him to behave in a rigid and inflexible manner.[36] Stress as a cause of suggestibility renders the individual depressed and exhausted, altogether incapable of acting according to his original scheme of values. It has been a principal aim of proselytizers of all kinds to utilize stress in this manner, since by so doing they render the potential convert open to their message.

Thus the great revivalist, Charles Finney, advised that the sinner be unremittingly impressed with a sense of guilt and dread: "The sinner's guilt is much more deep and damning than he thinks and his danger is much greater than he thinks it is; and if he could see them as they probably are, he would not live one moment." [37] This stress is, of course, psychological, but it can be physical as well, a fact amply attested by the privations which have so often preceded transformations. This has been the case both for ascetics who have voluntarily denied their material needs and prisoners placed in a calculatedly debilitating environment.

Just as individuals may be made more suggestible and hence more receptive to new beliefs, so their old beliefs may appear less viable. What appears in retrospect to be a period of social change, usually turns out to be an era for which received beliefs seemed inadequate. The essence of the idea of progress is that the future is to be welcomed, since the values of the present are bound to be maximized in the period ahead. That kind of easy confidence in improvement is possible only for the person who possesses a system of beliefs that tie present and future together. For millenarians, a specifically future-oriented belief system bestows this confidence. Those whose inherited beliefs appear faulty, yet who possess no substitute, "confront the dark, inscrutable face of the future, not knowing what is to come." [38]

With the luxury of hindsight, one can pick out periods peculiarly characterized by a loss of purpose, a sense of inadequacy, and whose values were no longer regarded as valid. The late Middle Ages, so graphically described by Johan Huizinga, was one such era.[39] The late Roman Empire, too, fits this pattern.[40] America after the Civil War was a time of deep if transient disillusionment for significant segments of the population.[41] George Steiner argues that the entire Western world presently finds itself in a like predicament.[42] The feeling that things are not as they were and will never be so again may be expected to produce a search for a new certainty. There is an obvious interaction here between suggestibility and the decay of values, since a value crisis can constitute a form of stress productive of suggestibility.

But it is not enough merely that a person be more receptive to suggestion or that his prior beliefs be brought into question. Conversion is an impossibility without the presence of an alternative. And, indeed, no motif emerges more clearly from accounts of conversion than the feeling of sudden rebirth. The degree of voluntarism in the conversion seems to have little effect. Subjects of Chinese thought reform experienced the same feeling of renewal [43] as participants in religious revivals.

The historical record bears witness to the fact that a few individuals have always been able to forge new identities for themselves. They are capable, through some massive act of resynthesis, of totally reformulating their picture of the world.[44] This quality, held alike by psychotics and prophets, Wallace refers to as "mazeway resynthesis." It removes cultural innovation from the realm of incremental change and places it in the category of quantum leaps. Some resynthesizers come to be classified as "ill," while others found great movements. The difference between them is at most one of degree[45] and of the receptivities of potential converts. Resynthesis thus constitutes a kind of self-conversion. Since it depends upon a creativity of which most are incapable, the modal form of conversion is consequently to some external, preexisting belief system. Naturally, this prior system may itself be the product of prophetic self-conversion.

Conversion to a millenarian movement is frequently accompanied by dramatic physical signs. These phenomena of "enthusiasm," Margaret Mead notes, constitute symptoms of total conviction.[46] Muscle spasms and apparently unconscious actions appear here as they do in many conversion settings. Such phenomena suggest direct access to higher sources of truth, an implication particularly present in visionary experiences or speaking in tongues. Collapse into an unconscious or semiconscious state often signals conversion.[47]

Ecstatic behavior also serves an abreactive function. That is, it provides a means of releasing repressed emotions through the process of acting them out. These emotions may derive from either the disaster situation or the imminence of conversion, or both. In the first case, the emotionally unexpressive disaster victim has gone through experiences which he has no wish to repeat yet has not adequately worked through. They may involve grief through the loss of loved ones, guilt at being a survivor, shame at lowered social status, or fear that the disaster will return. Conversion to a millenarian sect adds a new dimension, for it demands of followers that they sever all loyalties to their past, a demand which cannot but be guilt producing. Ecstatic behavior effectively purges these emotions, whether through wild dancing, the response of crowds to oratory, or physical trembling.[48] The feeling of well-being and rebirth that often follows has led some observers to regard ritualized emotionalism as clearly therapeutic in effect, whatever may be its original intention.[49] We shall return to the subject of ecstatic behavior in the next chapter.

The intense emotions released in the conversion process cannot be evoked simply by a doctrine; rather, they require a human focus, in the person of a leader endowed with charismatic qualities. He may be perceived as the messiah himself, as was the case with Sabbatai Zevi. More often, he is the prophet-figure, who comes to announce and prepare for the final, culminating events of history. In either case, his presumed gifts set him apart both from his own followers and from traditional leaders. One of his principal functions is to facilitate conversion. In this he serves as a role model, having himself gone through a dramatic alteration of personality and values. He says in effect, "I, too, was once like you, but see what I have become." His message may indeed consist largely of an account of his own transformation. Hung gave the Taipings the substance of his 1837 visions. The Handsome Lake movement among the Seneca proceeded from Handsome Lake's visions, which occurred in two sets between 1799 and his death in 1815.[50] The content of the visions determined the belief system of the movement. One may speculate that charisma itself—the imputation of extraordinary gifts—occurs in part because of awe evoked by an individual's metamorphosis.

But such personal transformations do not always or even usually move others to imitation. Under normal circumstances, if the transformation produces culturally deviant behavior, the response is likely to be punitive or therapeutic rather than imitative. But of course the circumstances of millenarianism are not normal. The solutions offered in everyday life count for little in the disaster environment. Thus the manner in which an individual is classified—as charismatic leader, or eccentric, or psychotic—becomes a matter of context. As the context alters, so does the classification.[51]

Disaster provides a context in which, to borrow George Rosen's vivid phrase, some individuals reach "the wilder shores of sanity." [52] In the very instability of the situation, their metamorphosis strikes responsive chords in others. The significance of the metamorphosis is not only change qua change, but change that points toward the imminent transformation of the environment as well. In other words, for millenarians the individual's conversion and transformation prefigure the transformation about to take place in society at large, just as the microcosmic community of true believers prefigures the macrocosmic redeemed world that will soon emerge. The parallelism can be extended one step further: the disaster out of which the movement grew, and the disaster which will soon overtake the evil society outside, are repeated in the disasterlike conversion experiences of individuals, in which the old personality and values must be destroyed before the new ones can be implanted. Hence, it is to the disaster-conversion nexus that we now turn.

Millenarian movements draw in converts through the operation of situational factors: suggestibility, the breakdown of old values, and the availability of a new identity. As we have already noted, millenarian movements arise as consequences of disasters. Yet the correlation is at best only partial. We can point to the famines and violence in South China before the Taiping Rebellion, to the centrality of the Black Death for so much European millenarianism, and to the multiple upheavals caused by colonial penetration of the South Pacific before the Cargo Cults. Yet we have also seen that in the absence of additional enabling conditions—what we have called the ecology of millenarianism—very great disasters have not produced chiliastic movements.

Part of the reason why disaster does not always draw millenarianism in its train lies in the conversion process we have been discussing. There are those everywhere predisposed by past life histories to total affiliations. They form a natural reservoir of potential converts, small though it may be. To see the wellsprings of mass movements we must look primarily to situational factors, to those forces that make men more receptive to the new, that make the old more suspect, and that provide an as yet untested pattern for the future.

Suggestibility is enhanced in disaster, for disaster is a collective stress experience. A predictable event, even an objectively destructive one, is less likely to be perceived as a disaster than an unpredictable one. The loss must be perceived within a context of relative stability and security. During World War I, as many died from indirect causes—notably the influenza outbreak of 1918—as from the war itself;[53] yet it was the war and not the epidemic that was regarded as a disaster. In other words, the element of novelty is an important component of the disaster concept. Disaster is regarded as such, and has its own psychological consequences, because it is new and unfamiliar. As we have seen, suggestibility is increased in the face of new or ambiguous stimuli that fall outside existing mental frameworks. There is initially an attempt to assimilate the unfamiliar to the familiar, to understand the new in terms of the old.[54] Yet there always exists a point beyond which further reflection yields only increased bewilderment. "In the absence of reliable guides from past experience for perceiving or acting, suggestibility is heightened." [55]

The principal element in disaster is, however, unexpected stress. We have seen that stress is an important—perhaps the most important—factor in enhanced suggestibility, and nowhere outside the prison or laboratory does stress impinge upon people as it does in the disaster situation.

The psychological disorders of survivors have been ascribed, on the one hand, to sensory deprivation[56] and, on the other, to sensory overstimulation.[57] The survivor is the victim of sensory deprivation to the extent that disaster has destroyed his physical and social environment. Loved ones may have been killed or contact with them lost; normal social relationships can no longer be maintained; the very physical landscape may have been radically altered. On the other hand, new stimuli—those of the disaster itself—flood in upon the victim and challenge his received picture of the world. These new signals cannot be dispassionately examined, for there are too many of them and the dazed victim is in any event operating at diminished mental efficiency.

We can now see more clearly the parallel between disaster and conversion through brainwashing. Brainwashing, too, simultaneously deals in sensory impoverishment and the abrupt introduction of much that is new.[58] Although here the process occurs by design rather than by accident, the course of events is much the same. Interrogators remove the subject from everything that might allow him to form independent judgments and then expose him relentlessly to a new conception of the world. To a lesser extent, the same counterpoint of deprivation and overstimulation enters into religious conversion. Although it may be difficult to fully shield the proselyte from other communications, persistent mental excitation serves to keep "the mind tremblingly alive." [59]

The disaster syndrome is not unlike a transitory neurosis. Those so affected perceive and cognize less well than they did before. They are less capable of critical thinking and so are less resistant to appeals for change of belief. Well before the rise of systematic disaster research after World War II, Pitrim Sorokin had commented on the inability of victims to concentrate on anything unrelated to the disaster; on their decreasing personal autonomy; and on their intellectual dependence upon outside influences.[60] Subsequent research has both corroborated and amplified Sorokin's observations. The victim is seen to be docile, undemanding, emotionally dulled, suggestible, and passive. If he acts at all, it is likely to be through the ritualistic repetition of familiar but now irrelevant activities.[61]

The onset of a disaster reflects adversely upon a group's existing beliefs. The presence of disaster is proof that those beliefs have only a limited capacity to predict and alleviate stress. In short, disaster hastens the breakdown of old values associated with conversion. Many belief systems provide a built-in defense against this inadequacy by allowing for the occasional occurrence of unanticipated stress. Thus the medieval Church explained the Black Death through the conventional category of punishment for sins. The availability of scapegoats may also provide a temporary solution to the explanatory problem.[62] The Black Death was, at least in part, blamed on the Jews; wars are habitually blamed on the adversary; military defeat on enemies within; depressions on speculators; and so on. Eventually, however, these evasions can no longer be maintained, and the dominant belief system itself comes into question. Beliefs, after all, which can neither foresee harm nor prevent it are of distinctly limited validity and usefulness. The break with the past occasioned by disaster may in fact simply be the culmination of a long process of less conscious doubt and less dramatic failures.[63] As we saw in chapter three, a specific disaster event often becomes a catalyst, bringing together long-developing but previously unexpressed anxieties.

The occurrence of large-scale disaster provides needs and circumstances particularly conducive to the conversion experience. Short-lived and small-scale catastrophes—mine explosions, local unemployment, and the like—cannot be expected to produce these circumstances to the same degree, for opportunities for reconstruction or escape abound. When, however, a relatively self-contained society is buffeted by intense, protracted disasters, its members may be induced to rapidly abandon their old beliefs. They do so in the hope that the stresses may be quickly controlled.

We have seen that what religious proselytizing and brainwashing produce by design, disaster produces fortuitously. That is not to make a judgment of either, but simply to acknowledge that disaster accidentally creates conditions peculiarly fitted to the rapid alteration of belief systems. Inversely, individual conversion is a disaster-in-miniature, a process of extreme stress and relief experienced by any convert. The experience of abrupt transformation has been encouraged by some religions, political ideologies, and forms of psychotherapy. Millenarian movements depart from these

more common examples only in degrees: Here large numbers
of persons undergo similar personal transformations in a brief
time span, under the impact of the same stresses. What must
be artificially produced by an evangelical preacher, political
interrogator, or psychotherapist here occurs in a larger and
more spontaneous context.

Since the steadfastness of new members cannot be taken
for granted, social movements must develop patterned activities to maintain it. In some movements, the realization that
there is a relationship between these activities (dancing,
demonstrations, confessions, etc.) and the ultimate goal is
enough to stabilize attitudes. Millenarian movements are a bit
more complicated, since the original ends are never attained,
and it is often difficult to specify the relationship between
those goals and the round of organizational activities.

Reinforcement appears virtually a sine qua non for continued commitment. The induced conversions brought about
by Soviet and Chinese brainwashing and thought reform have
proven temporary. For all but a very few, removal from a
controlled environment produced a return to the attitudes
originally held.[64] Where the subject is returned to an environment containing consistent reinforcement, the induced conversion has enduring consequences. This no doubt accounts
for the much greater success attained by the Chinese with
Chinese than with Western subjects.[65] Less coercive movements, such as religious sects and political groups open to
voluntary membership, succeed to the extent that they can
supply steady support. Classes, study groups, discussion
groups, and public confession all serve to discourage the
waverer.[66] Utopian colonies closely resemble millenarian
movements in their goals and in their contempt for the
dominant culture outside. Here too members remain only
when the individual feels the constant support of his fellows.[67]

The millenarian must be reminded over and over that his
transformation is genuine and unshakable, that the unsettling
transfer of loyalties has been worth it. This places a responsibility on those already transformed to reassure the newly
converted. Yet it should not be forgotten that the relationship
is reciprocal. The individual who assures someone else that

his act was right also assures himself. And when he sees the effect of his reassurance on the other, he is again confirmed in the rightness of his own position. For this reason, the process of adding new members to a millenarian movement is more than a matter of simply increasing the movement's power or influence. The *plausibility* of a belief increases with the number who espouse it. Each new person won over provides supportive evidence for those won over earlier.

The urge to proselytize is especially great in millenarian movements, where the risk of disconfirmation of prophecies is so great. The existence of a community of believers is insurance against the traumatic effects of disconfirmed predictions, for within that community there are mutual sources of resassurance and rationalization. Festinger, Riecken, and Schachter argue that where a key prediction appears disconfirmed, one strategy for believers is to increase the number of people who believe in the falsified hypothesis: "*If more and more people can be persuaded that the system of belief is correct, then clearly it must, after all, be correct* . . . if everyone in the whole world believed something there would be no question at all as to the validity of this belief." [68] For this reason, millenarian movements contain a dynamic of growth. Growth serves as a means of validation.

Such emotional direction as the individual has must come from the prophet, the charismatic leader. His first function is to serve as a role model, since he has already accomplished the transformation, and its effects can be seen in him. The Seneca prophet, Handsome Lake, achieved influence both by the substance of his message and by the testimony of his own transformation from alcoholism and depression to a visionary tranquillity.[69] Hans Bohm, the so-called Drummer of Niklashausen, attempted a millenarian social revolution in and around Wurzberg in 1474; before that he was an unexceptional shepherd and part-time popular entertainer. Without warning he suddenly burned the drum with which he had often entertained and began to preach with astonishing eloquence.[70] Little appears to be known about Bohm before his appearance as a demagogic preacher. His very ordinariness, prior to the middle of Lent, 1474, doubtless accounts for the absence of biographical material.

Much more is known of the subsequent German millenarian, Thomas Müntzer, a subsidiary leader in the Peasants' Revolt. An exceedingly learned intellectual, Müntzer nonetheless had "a troubled soul, full of doubts about the truth of Christianity and even about the existence of God but obstinately struggling after certainty." After an initial contact with Luther, Müntzer came under the sway of an obscure Taborite preacher. He "changed his way of life, abandoning reading and the pursuit of learning . . . ceaselessly propagating his eschatological faith among the poor." [71] In all of these cases, the prophet is viewed by those around him as a new man, not simply in his social views but in his demeanor and style of life. He demonstrates to a yearning public that change is possible.

Conversion and acceptance into a millenarian community usually is marked by some distinctive ritual. The baptismal ceremony of the Taipings marked the movement from conventional life to a new identity. The *Parhundamdam* of Indonesia developed an elaborate ceremony of entrance that extended over eight days.[72] We can see in these initiation rites a mirror image of more traditional *rites de passage,* in which ongoing cultural systems induct youths into full membership. Not surprisingly, millenarian entrance rituals reverse many of the old values. Entrance into a chiliastic community constitutes repudiation of prevailing values, and initiation rites often fasten upon this repudiation. Thus there may be dramatic acts of norm-violation, which serve both to symbolize the transit from normality to millenarianism and to make that progression temporarily irreversible. Initiation rites, by dramatically violating traditional taboos, bring the new member into a community of common guilt, cut off from the conformism of the outside world. The best known such rituals of recent times have been the Mau Mau initiation rites. The rituals which accompanied the Mau Mau Warriors' Oath involved extreme violations of Kikuyu sexual taboos.[73]

While many entrance ceremonies occur only in the presence of those already initiated, they occasionally involve public acts, where their effect in marking the individual off from the rest of society is even more definitive. Thus the Tensho, a Japanese millenarian sect active in Hawaii, focuses upon the ingrained unwillingness of traditional Japanese to act conspicuously in front of others. The Tensho requires converts to perform free-form dances in public. This behavior serves to shame the converts in front of fellow Japanese, and many "recalled this confrontation as the peak of tension and conflict in their conversion experience." [74]

The prominence of guilt in conversion and in subsequent reinforcement emerges even more clearly from an examination of the role of rules in millenarian movements. The separateness of the movements, their need to maintain commitments, and their belief that they constitute the redeemed society in miniature combine to produce a complex system of behavioral rules. It is a counterlegal system, a set of very strict rules in the deliberate mirror image of the larger, official legal system outside. Utopian communities often require group confession, self-criticism, and the memorization of elaborate sets of rules.[75] The Melanesian Cargo Cults, in an attempt to capture the magic of European economic productivity, imitated Western judicial institutions and rigidly enforced an independent rule system of their own.[76] The most zealous revolutionaries commonly place the greatest emphasis upon asceticism, doctrinal and behavioral orthodoxy, discipline, and personal renunciation.[77] The world of extreme revolutionaries "is sharply divided into the pure and the impure, into the absolutely good and the absolutely evil." [78] Chiliasts reject the present order of things as tainted beyond hope of cleansing.

Commitment to the new order must be maintained, past allegiances severed, the world unambiguously divided into good and evil realms. A number of radical legal consequences flow from these desires: first, the construction of a new, competitive rule system; second, rejection of the incremental change associated with conventional rules systems; third, the search for a basis of legitimacy that does not share in the corruption of the old order.

The nexus of rules and commitment produces a strangely paradoxical complication, the frequent millenarian tendency toward antinomianism—the repudiation of law. Antinomianism in millenarian movements may be of two types. Commonly, it involves the ritualistic violation of previously accepted norms; we have already noted this in the context of initiation rites. In this selective antinomianism, the norms chosen for violation are usually those subject to the most deep-seated inhibitions—for example, those involving religious observance or sexual taboos. Alternatively, there sometimes exists a much more radical antinomianism, a rejection of law qua law, the belief that law is no longer necessary to assure an ordered society.

Both forms of antinomianism are in fact mechanisms for desocialization; that is, they force the individual out of his traditional value system through emotionally charged "bridge-burning" acts. Max Gluckman suggests that the Mau Mau revolt was made possible precisely because its members had participated in oath-taking ceremonies which involved the systematic violation of taboos. Thus united by shame and guilt, they were radically separated from traditional Kikuyu society.[79] Peter Worsley makes much the same point concerning Cargo Cult members. The cult "welds the devotees together in a fraternity of people who have deliberately flouted the most sacred rules of the old society. They are bound together by their sense of guilt and by the feeling of having cut themselves off irrevocably from the old life. . . . This most radical rejection of the past generates the most powerful emotional energy. . . . The ritual breaking of taboos is thus a most powerful mechanism of political integration." [80] The theme of the intentional commission of crimes for the purpose of separation from normal life recurs among the Nazis. Hannah Arendt argues that elite formations such as the SS functioned as a generator of mass guilt "by extending complicity . . . [to] make every party member aware that he has left the normal world which outlaws murder and that he will be held accountable for all crimes committed by the elite." [81]

The more comprehensive form of antinomianism, which rejects law as such, is far rarer; if only because, as a practical matter, its full attainment is impossible. Even an attempt in the direction of a lawless society appears a practical possibility only in the case of very small groups for short times. Even then, it is possible to dispense with legal institutions but not with rules themselves.[82] It is consistent with the millenarian ideal of immediate perfectability that law should be identified with all that is sinful, unredeemed, and imperfect in man. So long as one's conception of law is governed by the belief that only deviance makes it necessary, it is in principle subject to abolition the moment that a way can be found to eliminate past human weaknesses.

Millenarians, since they are committed to a belief in the abrupt eradication of evil, are particularly likely to regard law as dispensable. Late medieval heretical sects provide rich sources of antinomian doctrine and occasionally of practice as well. Joachim of Fiore (1145–1202) conceived an influential eschatological system based upon three successive ages of history: the Age of the Law, the Age of the Gospel, and the culminating Age of the Spirit. "The Age of the Spirit was to be the sabbath or resting-time of mankind. In it there would be no wealth or even property, for everyone would live in voluntary poverty; there would be no work, for human beings would possess only spiritual bodies and would need no food; there would be no institutional authority of any kind." [83] This became an influential source from which much subsequent Western antinomian thought flowed, although of course it became increasingly remote from the original theological roots. Fundamentally antilegal protest movements have never entirely died out, as nineteenth- and twentieth-century dissidence in southern Europe demonstrates.[84] The Spanish millenarian anarchists of the middle 1930s are among the most recent of European antinomians.

We have seen that the individual millenarian stands uneasily between a conventional past and a demanding and unconventional present. Having cut himself off from the past, he surrenders himself to a present and future fraught with instability. His conversion has been facilitated by the model of a charismatic leader, yet it is the nature of charisma to be unstable and problematic. He anticipates a future of unbounded promise, yet may at any moment be the prey of events that deny the promise.

Charismatic authority, Max Weber writes, "arises from collective excitement produced by extraordinary events and from surrender to heroism of any kind. This alone is sufficient to warrant the conclusion that the faith of the leader himself and of his disciples in his charisma . . . is undiminished, consistent and effective only *in statu nascendi,* just as is true of the faithful devotion to him and his mission on the part of those to whom he considers himself sent." [85] As soon as the original situation alters, the relationship between leader and followers is cast in doubt. Millenarian movements must fight against the gradual return to social stability, which is likely to bring with it more routinized forms of leadership. As disaster recedes, the environment, from the standpoint of organizational maintenance, becomes less and less hospitable.

The vulnerability of charismatic leadership is part of the larger dilemma of millenarian prophecy. Chiliastic movements inevitably become entangled in self-fulfilling prophecies, in prophecies that can neither be validated nor falsified, and in prophecies that are only too easily disconfirmed by events. The impact of predictions upon the charismatic leader and his followers can be profound, for it is of the essence of charisma that one who has it be seen to *perform*; he must prove himself in the eyes of his followers.[86]

All millenarian movements by definition look to the total transformation of society at some future time. So long as the movement makes only general kinds of predictions, "all events . . . are held to constitute fractional symbolic confirmations of the wider cosmic beliefs." [87] The world becomes filled with omens and portents, events ambiguous enough to support prophecies that are ambiguous in themselves.

But millenarian movements in their activist periods do not content themselves with mere vague expectations. Those that are most likely to run afoul of the political order, through either outright revolt or radical withdrawal, regard the coming transformation as imminent. These expectations lead them to make sweeping yet at the same time quite specific forecasts of future change. Such predictions are testable in a way that, for example, mere conspiracy assertions are not. It is difficult to falsify the assertion that some small group of individuals, operating secretly, is responsible for all the evil in the world. It is far easier to test the proposition that on a specified future date evil will disappear and good triumph.

The validation dilemma lies here, for leader and movement are expected either to produce the specific, imminent changes themselves or, at the very least, to possess detailed information concerning the time and manner of their occurrence. The millenarians' urge to proselytize, which we have already discussed, is a partial and often ineffectual response to disconfirmed prophecies, for each new person convinced provides confirmation to those already affiliated. The ideologies of millenarian movements, then, contain both testable and untestable elements.

The line dividing the testable from the untestable corresponds roughly to the division, respectively, between anticipations of future good and attributions of present evil. The former, because they so often result in time-specific predictions, lie open to empirical examination both inside and outside the movement. It is, of course, always possible to interpret existing events in a way which makes them appear to be signs of imminent transformation or even evidence of partial fulfillment.[88] On the whole, however, messianic movements remain peculiarly vulnerable to disconfirmation. When a prophecy has not been fulfilled, "most people, including members . . . are in touch with reality and cannot simply blot out their cognition of such an unequivocal and undeniable fact."[89]

We may choose to think of millenarian reality-constructs as delusions; or, conversely, of delusions as alternative reality-constructs. Millenarian movements appear to construct reality-pictures that are more vulnerable to disconfirmation than those of other groups. The disconfirmations may not always result in the dissolution of a movement but at the least provoke a major crisis. This is clear even in the case of Jehovah's Witnesses, which survived numerous disconfirmations of its end-of-the-world predictions, and the Sabbatians, the seventeenth-century Jewish messianists whose leader apostasized.[90] The common long-term strategy in such cases is to gradually reduce the specificity and imminence of the predictions, make one's peace with the world as it is, and assume a stance of relative passivity.

Thus the millenarian convert faces a potentially devastating contradiction. He has made a profound psychic investment in a set of beliefs and in the powers of a man, at the price of abandoning whatever satisfactions might still have been obtainable from his old life. Yet he is now prey to an environment which may at any moment render those beliefs false and absurd. The extremes of doctrinal interpretation and reinterpretation, exemplified not only in the Sabbatians but also in English millenarians during and after the Civil War,[91] testify to the lengths that chiliasts will go to rationalize away inconsistencies.

The wonder is that millenarianism has lasted so long. While individual movements appear to have brief life-spans, regions often harbor a string of movements over generations. People in some areas simply seem more receptive to millenarian appeals; they convert to chiliastic sects more readily. We have already seen something of the character of these areas in the earlier discussion of the ecology of millenarianism. It remains to relate these environmental characteristics to the process of recruitment we have been discussing.

Certain areas appear to produce socialization to messianic expectations, the transmission across generations of millenarian yearnings. In order to understand this process, we shall have to return to the concept of disaster and also look closely at the role of generational cohorts in political and social life.

True disasters are not predictable, at least not by their victims. Though some short-term warning is frequently available, the events themselves appear to take place at random intervals, even where an outside observer might be able to detect periodicity. A sufficient element of chance enters to render the events unusual and outside of normal routines. What is an unpredictable succession of disaster events likely to do to the socialization process? Writing of the social consequences of epidemics, William Langer observes: "It seems altogether plausible to suppose the children, having experienced the terror of their parents and the panic of the community, will react to succeeding crises in a similar but even more intense manner. In other words, the anxiety and fear are transmitted from one generation to another, constantly aggravated." [92] This provocative hypothesis contains the germ of a generational theory of politics. There is an intuitive plausibility to the suggestion that vivid events experienced early in life predispose individuals to uncharacteristically intense reaction patterns should similar events recur later.

We might suppose this to be a question upon which much light has already been shed in the social sciences. On the contrary, however, we know remarkably little of the later impact of events in early life, save from those relatively few social scientists influenced by psychoanalysis.[93] The reason for our relative ignorance is not far to seek. Any investigation of the socializing power of events requires a time span of no less than five years—from late adolescence to political majority. Ideally, the research should cover the whole period from early childhood to young adulthood. Longitudinal studies in social science rarely take their subjects even over the minimally adequate length of time. However, some recent work by demographically oriented political scientists and historians opens vistas on the problem.

Ronald Inglehart argues that significant political events witnessed during childhood political socialization leave their mark on later attitudes and behavior. His own research on attitudes toward European integration seems to bear out this proposition.[94] Important attitudinal differences emerge among cohorts socialized during World War I, during World War II, and during the postwar period. Attitudes on national versus international identification measured in 1963 appear to mirror attitudes prevalent during the childhood and early teen years. From this Inglehart infers the existence of a time lag between the acquisition of attitudes and their behavioral impact. Obviously, an outlook gained in late childhood will make itself felt in the political arena only when the individual moves to a position of political visibility and influence. Inglehart, for his purposes, sets ages six to twenty-one as the "zone of formation," twenty-one to forty-five as the period in which attitudes acquire political relevance, and forty-five to sixty-five as the "zone of maximum influence," the period in which individuals are likely to reach important decision-making posts. He stresses the critical socializing potential of major political events, such as World Wars I and II, the Depression, and the high tide of European integration during the early and mid-1950s. This emphasis upon events consti-tutes a major shift, for most socialization research concentrates on the continuity of the process, the absence of specific breakpoints, and the overriding impact of institutions (family, school, church, etc.).

Most attention until now has been centered upon the way in which society preserves itself by inculcating its values in successive waves of new members. Here, however, we have been discussing the discontinuities, the points in time where groups emerge with values and identifications that differentiate them from prior products of the socialization process. The initial occurrence of millenarianism in an area constitutes such a breakpoint, for it often heralds a lengthy period of millenarian identification.

Marvin Rintala suggests that communism and fascism drew disproportionately upon those whose formative years were characterized by an "especially disruptive set of historical experiences." [95] Close investigation of Nazi youth appears to bear this out. Peter Loewenberg's study of the German cohorts born between 1900 and 1915 builds upon the work of Inglehart and others to construct a demographic, psychoanalytic explanation of the growth of the Nazi party.[96] Loewenberg argues that these cohorts were exposed to the traumatic events of the years 1915–20: famine, fathers at war, mothers at work in defense industries, the return of the fathers in defeat, the social disorder that followed. By the time the Depression struck, these cohorts were from fourteen to twenty-nine years old, the age groups from which the Nazi party, Hitler Youth, SA, and SS drew so heavily. For Loewenberg, the fervor displayed by the young constitutes the regression and acting out of the World War I trauma in the context of the second disaster of 1929. Loewenberg's analysis is worth quoting in detail:

> A consideration of childhood certainly reveals much about the way people are programmed to respond in adulthood. Yet intensive experiences in later life, if they are of a massive traumatic nature, can supersede both earlier influences and individual predispositions. This means that a major catastrophe will have an impact on all ages who are subject to its blows. It will necessarily affect the very young most because their egos are the most fragile. But it will also

affect children in latency and adolescence and even adults, each according to his ego strength—that is, according to his ability to tolerate frustration, anxiety, and deprivation.[97]

We can see here the interwoven strands of disaster, socialization, and life history. Catastrophic events, which break abruptly into the usual pattern of generational renewal may, in Norman Ryder's words, "mark indelibly the 'naive eyes and virgin senses' of the cohort in the vanguard and change them into . . . a virtual community of thought and action." [98] Loewenberg suggests, first, that disasters differentially affect people of different ages and, second, that sequences of disasters differ in their effects from single catastrophes. The second point has occupied us earlier; the first, though implicit, now needs to be treated directly.

One need not adopt a psychoanalytic frame of reference to view the effects of disasters on behavior. Indeed, learning theory is quite consistent with many of Loewenberg's conclusions. However, the psychoanalytic constructs he uses sensitize him to the data of life histories, the points in time at which potentially shaping forces impinge upon the individual. What seems to matter is not simply the malleability of the personality but the vulnerability of the individual—what Loewenberg refers to as his ego strength. All other things being equal, the younger the person, the less frustration, anxiety, and deprivation he can deal with in an adaptive fashion. Thus it stands to reason that the young are more likely shaped by the disasters of childhood than the mature, whose personalities have already been formed in more tranquil times.

While populations generally reproduce themselves in a smooth process of death and birth, the association with particularly vivid events occasionally marks out some segments of the reproductive process so that they come to possess a sense of separateness. If so, we may expect that, over and above the immediate impact of a disaster, it may produce secondary consequences a decade or so later. By that time, those who experienced it in their youth have begun to reach an age of political participation. The manner in which these "aftershocks" show themselves will of course vary with the situation that exists at the time the disaster generation reaches its majority. If stability has been reestablished in the interim, the attitudes formed earlier will lead to incremental change rather than attempted radical upheaval. The Depression in the United States has left discernible political marks, but they manifest themselves in characteristic voting patterns rather than in revolutionary activity.[99] We might speculate, however, that intervening disaster experiences up to the point of emerging political influence would greatly intensify the character of the response. Indeed, Loewenberg argues in precisely this fashion to explain the enthusiasm of German youth for Hitler.

It has often been noted that revolution "is particularly a young man's affair." [100] The Bolshevik revolutionary leadership made its commitment to revolutionary action at an average age of seventeen, even though all were very much older by the time the revolution came to power.[101] The Nazi party, as already noted, was disproportionately a party of the young.[102] The relationship is not invariant. Surely the most dramatic counterinstance must be the supporters of the quasimillenarian Townsend Plan, almost all of whom were elderly.[103] But in general the young are more receptive to innovation,[104] and millenarian movements are profoundly innovative. Life becomes more and more a matter of habit with age.

Our discussion of disaster to this point has not dealt with the young. Rather, it has concentrated upon the immediate effects upon the adult population. Loewenberg argues that disaster effects fall upon all, though with less impact upon the old than upon the young. How might his observations be fitted into the earlier discussion of the disaster syndrome?

In the first place, the effects upon the young are not immediate; their political impact must await future events. Later disasters summon up the unresolved anxieties of earlier ones. The catastrophes that strike in late adolescence and young adulthood become particularly volatile when they strike those already, as it were, "prepared" by past events. Multiple disaster as a causal factor in the rise of millenarian movements acts in part because later events affect a population made peculiarly susceptible to their influence by earlier events. The famines of Andalusia or the Brazilian *sertão*, like the defeat-depression sequence in Germany, first predispose and then activate true disaster generations.

But catastrophe bears disproportionately upon the young only "all other things being equal"—which they rarely are. What of multiple disasters that strike the adult population, already socialized, conformist, and accepting of traditional values? We tend to think of socialization as a process that affects only the young, something from which one gradually emerges, such that by the late teens or early twenties it no longer figures as a significant life process. Yet adult socialization exists, even if it is uncommon. It occurs whenever there is an incentive for the comprehensive alteration of attitudes learned in childhood.

Experience with stable politics suggests that attitudes implanted early are a necessary and durable element contributing to political and social harmony. On the other hand, where old harmonies are under attack, the emphasis shifts to mechanisms which can effectively produce adult attitudinal change. Modernizing nations commonly produce an elaborate apparatus of parties, youth movements, schools, and military forces for precisely this purpose.[105] Resocialization can also occur within subgroups of a society, such as alcoholics or drug users, who may be motivated to create communities dedicated to adult socialization.

A sequence of disasters can serve a socializing function even for adults, for the following reason: The first in a series of catastrophes may well leave the basic attitudinal framework of the adult population intact. But each successive disaster-increment makes that framework less and less tenable, for each increment confronts the individual with more intense stress and more difficult problems of explanation. At the onset of each disaster event, traditional beliefs are just a bit shakier than they were before. Disaster thus is both socializing and "countersocializing." It works to subvert norms of stability normally communicated through family, school, and other institutions. A single disruptive event could easily be neutralized. Repetitive disaster events might, however, succeed in undoing much that the work of earlier socialization had achieved. At the same time, repetitive disasters socialize—or more accurately, "resocialize"—adults to a new climate of anxiety and uncertainty.

Thus we see two aspects of the disaster-socialization relationship. Among the young, sequential disasters produce anxiety in the early years that is "triggered" or reexperienced when it recurs in the disasters of later life. Among the adult population, disasters break down stable attitudes learned in childhood and only then induce anxiety and suggestibility. Thus, we can see that disasters must occur with greater frequency and/or intensity to have the same effect upon adults that they have on the young. In the case of lengthy series of disasters, however, the two socialization processes are, so to speak, collapsed. New generations are socialized to a milieu of anxiety, and hence there no longer remain significant attitudinal barriers to the outbreak of further millenarianism. The social environment supports rather than contradicts the yearnings for escape and transformation critical to messianic movements.

Thus areas like the southern Mediterranean, Melanesia, American black ghettoes, and southern Africa can support endemic millenarianism over long periods. Subcultures of messianic expectation arise. The doctrinal motifs and the generalized disposition to believe are already there. Any single new disaster, which might elsewhere be readily absorbed, triggers a new movement, falling as it does upon an already prepared population.

Multiple disasters serve to predispose individuals to millenarian conversion, either contributing to an atypical socialization or eroding conventional beliefs. Millenarian conversion and its subsequent reinforcement with the movement frequently manifest themselves in bizarre, ecstatic behavior, and it is to this aspect that we now turn.

Chapter Five

SOURCES AND FUNCTIONS OF
ECSTATIC BEHAVIOR

No aspect of millenarian movements attracts as much attention or spawns as much ill-considered analysis as their alleged psychopathology. A recent British medical journal speaks of "the epidemic spread of panic-stricken, fanatical, and hysterical behavior, the so-called 'madness of crowds'" and then goes on to characterize millenarian movements as "epidemics of zealotry." [1] This is, of course, very much in line with a firmly rooted nineteenth-century tradition. The very phrase "madness of crowds" comes out of the title of Charles Mackay's *Extraordinary Popular Delusions and the Madness of Crowds*, first published in 1841 and reprinted many times since. Mackay was concerned principally with hoaxes and sudden fashions, but he reflected a general disposition to view with suspicion any activity characterized by mass participation, high enthusiasm, and minimal organization. The pivotal work of scholarship in this tradition is Gustave LeBon's *The Crowd* (1895). With his typical pungency, LeBon asserts that "by the mere fact that he forms part of an organized crowd, a man descends several rungs in the ladder of civilization. Isolated, he may be a cultivated individual; in a crowd he is a barbarian—that is, a creature acting by instinct." [2] In this perspective, it is small wonder that millenarians were, and occasionally still are, regarded as essentially mentally ill individuals gathered together in a community of the deranged. We have already had occasion (in chapter two) to examine this allegation in a different context—that of the relationship between millenarianism and social change. We have seen that the charge falls far short of the reality. The evidence notwithstanding, old ideas die hard.

Two historical currents account for the linkage of millenarianism and madness. The first is specific to the English-speaking world. England before and during the Puritan Revolution was a veritable hothouse for the growth of millenarian sects.

Their political effect remains a subject of lively historical debate, but what is beyond debate is the conspicuousness of their presence in the early and mid-1600s. However, the Restoration and the Glorious Revolution of 1688 produced a turning point in sensibility, a move away from the "irrationalism" of the sects. "This emotional ambiance was characterized on the one hand by a preference for order, clarity, and balance in thought and behavior, and on the other by aversion to disorder, complexity, and irrationality. Associated with those psychological tendencies is a pronounced dislike of the eccentric, the peculiar, or the abnormal." [3] Any belief or movement which implied the ascendancy of emotion over reason was suspect. *Enthusiasm* —ecstatic religion—became a pejorative, and in the post-Puritan era "it became possible to regard certain aspects of enthusiastic conduct as psychopathological." [4] With the stigmatization of collective emotionality in religion, it was a small jump to the stigmatization of all large-scale emotionality. This was particularly easy, since the Puritan millenarian sects were themselves amalgams of politics, religion, and social protest.

The second source lay in the current of sociological thought epitomized by LeBon's *The Crowd.* This literature flourished in the last decade of the nineteenth century and betrays the political biases of the period.[5] It was, in the literal sense, illiberal and antidemocratic. The crowd was conceived to be evil because it implied an assault on the bastions of social and political privilege. These studies "appear to be aimed at discrediting not only the lower orders, with their claims for increased political power through the general franchise, but also in some cases the whole liberal scheme of parliamentarianism." [6] Its political premises camouflaged, the European sociology of the crowd made its entrance into American social science. The suspicion that observers of collective behavior often reserve for their subject is traceable to the prejudices of its first students.[7]

If academics originally recoiled from emotionality out of a feeling of sheer repugnance, their instinctual abhorrence has subsequently been reinforced from other quarters. To the extent that nineteenth-century students of society tended to hold antidemocratic political positions, they saw in the "crowd" a menacing force. To the extent that large-scale emotionalism occurs only infrequently and is of short duration, it is also automatically an uncongenial object of study. The data are usually sparse both as to numbers of incidents and to detail. Here, unlike so many areas, the public record has little to say, and the delphic character of what does appear is apt to put off the student in search of a neatly packaged subject.

The final bias comes from modern social science itself. Here the emphasis has been upon pattern rather than breaks in the pattern, upon the production of social order rather than the dissolution of social ties. In consequence, we know much about how social groups deal successfully with conflicts, much less about what happens when conventional devices fail to bring those conflicts under control. Social science has been hard pressed to formulate a general theory of social change. And to the extent that millenarian movements represent an extreme example of social change, they too have not been adequately explained.[8] Consequently, the tendency has been, with some noteworthy exceptions to be considered shortly, to regard ecstatic behavior and outbursts of apparent "irrationalism" as nasty interruptions, breaks in the pattern of functional behavior. The rationality problem may best be dealt with through a series of polarities that serve to at least partially expose the gap between initial appearances and participants' reality: inside versus outside views, expected change versus actual change, and short-term change versus long-term change.

As preceding chapters have tried to make clear, we rarely have the feeling of seeing millenarian movements through the eyes of their own members. Rather, the data almost always comes filtered through the consciousness of outsiders, be they administrators, clerics, travelers, or scholars. Thus to the extent that it is possible, we must insinuate ourselves into the consciousness of those involved. Events must appear to us contextually, as part of an ongoing process. Behavior that often scandalized nineteenth-century anthropologists, such as endemic physical violence, slowly became comprehensible with a greater understanding of the significance of kinship, corporate responsibility, the conflict tolerance of acephalous societies, and opportunities for mediation. In similar fashion, rationalist historians attributed the European witch craze to ignorance and superstition and let it go at that. Only quite recently has the phenomenon been related to the total fabric of village life, to the rise of natural science, and to the larger context of religious warfare. In neither of these cases is there any suggestion that modern scholarship morally condones what was once condemned; only that a sense of scandal is very different from a sense of having explained or understood a pattern of behavior. By attempting to view behavior from the inside, in a contextual fashion, it may be possible to suitably explain events which at present serve only to suggest anarchy, superstition, or "madness."

The second and third sets of polarities may be dealt with together, for expected versus actual change and short-term versus long-term change raise the basic question of the standards by which effectiveness should be judged. The conventional view has been that millenarian movements exist at the margins of political effectiveness—quite literally on the "lunatic fringe." It has been assumed that their small size and apparently brief duration give little leverage for securing large political and social changes. Our previous discussion of the persistence of millenarianism in certain areas (chapter four) already places this assessment very much in doubt. Beyond that, it also remains incontestably true that millenarian movements never achieve their stated goals. When one desires to change the world totally, disappointment is inevitable. Observers of millenarianism, having noted the sweep and totality of the objectives, have concluded that no rational person would set such extravagant goals. Since millenarians often participate in elaborate rituals and ecstatic behavior, observers further concluded that no rational person would adopt means so apparently ill-suited to the ends. In any case, it is in the interests of more conventional movements to portray millenarians in this light.[9]

Are millenarian movements, then, simply failures, the collective follies of individuals who cannot relate means and ends in a rational, instrumental way? Whatever the gap between professed aims and achievements, there *are* achievements. Millenarian movements supplant old leadership and make broader appeals than traditional sets of loyalties. They do instill a sense of larger identity that cuts across old parochialisms. No matter how this identity may be justified, it is supported behaviorally by the conversion dynamic discussed in the previous chapter. At the same time, it provides a new and broader organizational base, especially necessary in confronting a larger and better-organized adversary.[10] As a form of protest movement, millenarian sects usually fail to attain either the "pragmatic" objectives of power seizure or the transcendent goal of societal redemption. They may, however, introduce patterns of alliance that can subsequently be put in the service of later, more successful ventures. This is apt to come out most clearly where the history of sectarianism is joined to the larger study of protest, revolution, and nationalism. Where attempts of this kind have been made—for example, in studies of East Africa and the Philippines[11]—they have demonstrated not only that millenarian movements occur in the wake of larger protest movements, but that nationalism and revolution are very often dependent upon prior millenarian activity. I wish to deal with the character of this reciprocal relationship in detail in the next chapter and limit mention of it here. Its relevance to the present discussion lies in the fact that close historical analysis reveals that so-called rational and irrational movements cannot always be clearly separated from one another. Indeed, in the most extreme formulation of the relationship, Elie Kedourie argues that we cannot even conceive of nationalism apart from a chiliastic tradition: "The mainspring of nationalism in Asia and Africa is the same secular millennialism which had its rise and development in Europe." [12] That such an argument can even be constructed—we defer for the moment a closer analysis of it—indicates the intertwined character of conventional and unconventional protest movements.

If it is true that millenarianism so often coexists with nationalism, revolution, and other commonplace if violent modes of political activity, then we must exercise special caution in making a final evaluation of its impact. Movements which fall far short of their professed objectives may nonetheless crucially prepare for and determine major changes at a later time, and those preparatory functions and guiding forces must be entered into any calculation of overall effectiveness.

With all of these caveats in mind, let us now turn to the argument that millenarian movements harbor, encourage, or manifest aberrant forms of thought and behavior; that, try as we might to rationalize it away, millenarianism represents a form of collective psychopathology. Apart from the general cultural influences already discussed, the alleged psychopathological aspect of the movements has been argued from three separate perspectives, each of which will be examined in turn: as epidemic hysteria or behavioral contagion; as some form of paranoia; and as religious ecstasy. Having dealt with each, we shall then attempt to draw from them those observations that seem consonant with data on millenarianism and, finally, to relate ecstatic behavior to the nature of disaster experience.

Millenarianism is often distinguished by ecstatic behavior and by a sweeping contempt for the obligations and requirements of traditional social life. Both leaders and rank and file are said to behave in a manner strikingly similar to that of persons classified as mentally ill. On an individual basis that behavior denotes an inability to cope with the problems of everyday life. In the context of social movements, ecstatic and outwardly irrational behavior presents a different problem: Can mental illness take collective form?

George Rosen argues that under conditions of acute deprivation, large-scale attempts at escape and social revitalization are likely to occur.[13] This activity spreads with great rapidity and manifests the outward signs of ecstatic behavior: uncontrolled motor activity, trances, glossolalia, and fainting. Millenarian movements fall into this category, but so do demonic possession and ecstatic dancing. Yet Rosen is not quite willing to ascribe any of these to mass psychosis: "Mental illness as represented by the psychoses is hardly an important element in most of these group occurrences. On the other hand, the singing, drumming, dancing, and other means employed to achieve states of dissociation, trance, or hypnosis do involve psychopathology in a broad sense."[14]

The tendency to view millenarianism as psychopathological appears related to the tendency to view the spread of messianic movements as epidemiclike. The origin of the epidemic metaphor appears to lie with the nineteenth-century German physician-historian J. F. C. Hecker, who, in his study of the medieval dancing manias, speaks of a "nervous malady" communicated by "sympathy" and imitation.[15] Doubtless, the historical juxtaposition of the dancing manias with the Black Death facilitated the transfer of ideas. In any case, the metaphor was a vivid one and surfaces repeatedly in the collective behavior literature.

Metaphors can effectively evoke meanings, so long as they are not taken to be identical with the phenomena to which they are applied. L. S. Penrose, in one of the most original works ever written on crowd behavior, makes clear that he adopts the concepts of epidemiology for their explanatory value, not because the spread of ideas and behavior really "are" epidemics. Instead, he finds the notion congenial that epidemics follow a clearly traceable path over time, from latency to geometric growth, arithmetic growth, declining growth, and finally the return to equilibrium. Even Penrose, however, insists that he is dealing "with pathological idea[s], disruptive to the community in which [they] become . . . prevalent." [16]

The concept of the epidemic fitted in well with the LeBonist approach to crowds which we have already discussed. LeBon himself fell easily into the language of epidemiology: "[The] collective observations [of crowds] are as erroneous as possible, and . . . most often they represent the illusion of an individual who, by a process of contagion, has influenced his fellows." [17]

Yet we must also recognize that the epidemic metaphor has been reinforced from another source, medical research itself. Collective mental disturbance figures in a continuing set of clinical observations, generally grouped under the rubric of epidemic hysteria. These cases, though frequently reported in the nineteenth century, have grown sparse today.[18] This has been attributed by some to an actual decline in incidence,[19] but it seems more likely that a change in attitudes has made observers less likely to classify data under the epidemic heading. A medical-scientific culture sensitized to the possibility of "the madness of crowds" found its belief validated. A later mental set, which tends to ascribe behavior to organic causes, produces a corresponding decrease in the recorded incidence of hysterical epidemics. Thus the outbreak in 1955 of a poliolike disease at the Royal Free Hospital, London, was ascribed to organic causes at the time, although a careful reanalysis of the data fifteen years later attributed this and similar hospital outbreaks to psychological causes.[20]

It is tempting to say that the truth lies somewhere in between, but where one's conception of "truth" is so dependent upon categories of mind, the middle point is difficult to find. Suffice it to say that the sociology of knowledge operates in different periods to differentially organize sense perceptions. The nineteenth century was somewhat more willing than we to group certain instances of social behavior under psychiatric-epidemiological headings, whereas the dominant tendency today is either to demonstrate that the behavior is in fact rational (as social scientists tend to do) or to postulate an actual agent of physical infection (as clinicians tend to do).

Despite this change in emphasis, epidemic hysteria has proven to be a fairly resilient concept. This is all the more surprising, since those who use it seem unprepared to defend its clinical accuracy.

The term "hysteria" is not properly applicable to these epidemics, partly because the many uses of this term have blunted its meaning and partly because anxiety or panic appears to have been the central feature of most of the epidemic cases. Motivated, self-dramatizing, and importunate behavior, conversion symptoms, and dissociation of consciousness are inconsistent, often fleeting, and may be secondary to anxiety. The pejorative meaning that has come to be attached to "hysteria" adds to the reasons for the use of terms such as "epidemic hysteria" only when strictly justified.[21]

Yet the very frequency with which the term has been utilized in the past provides an explanation for the frequency with which it recurs. Two psychologists, Alan Kerckhoff and Kurt Back, are among the few nonphysicians to have studied the phenomenon closely. They call it "behavioral contagion," but in the end they too fall back upon "hysterical contagion." While they apply it as a term of art rather than as one of clinical science, it is difficult to separate their metaphorical application from all of the earlier meanings and overtones of meaning. They justify their choice on the grounds, first, that "hysteria" has a separate, well-understood commonsense meaning; second, that there are in fact observable similarities between so-called epidemic hysteria and more orthodox clinical manifestations; and, finally, and perhaps critically, the term already has been sanctified by usage. In the sense in which social scientists have used it, they have taken it to involve "the spread of physiological symptoms which are attributed to a fearfully mysterious and very threatening source." [22]

What in fact is the phenomenon? What if anything can it tell us about the outbreak of millenarian movements? Hysteria is a state characterized by dissociation, high susceptibility to auto-suggestion, and physical disorders of nervous origin. As the term has been applied to "epidemic" situations, it involves the very rapid spread within a population of symptoms for which no physical explanation can be found.[23] These symptoms may involve headache, "malaise," vomiting, fainting, and muscular spasms.[24] The question of precipitating circumstances has given rise to a wide variety of answers, none final or complete. The clinical accounts have variously ascribed epidemic hysteria to communication of symptoms by viewing; predisposition to hysteria; circumstances conducive to stress, fear, or guilt; high suggestibility; community isolation; and public announcement of similar outbreaks elsewhere.[25]

The behavior that suddenly spreads through a group may be completely imitative[26] but may also take somewhat different forms among different individuals, although all act unusually and in a presumptively irrational manner.[27] The Salem witch craze is often put forward as an example of epidemic hysteria. The explanatory problem here, as elsewhere is: Why do large numbers of outwardly conforming individuals suddenly begin to act in a new and bizarre manner? Why, when bizarre behavior occurs in one person, do others quickly repeat it or just as quickly adopt bizarre behavior patterns of their own? Most discussions finally come to rest upon a belief in the predisposition of the victims. They are somehow in a high state of readiness and await only a catalytic event. Taylor and Hunt call this state of susceptibility "pluralistic emotions, . . . uncommunicated feelings of the same kind in the individual members of the group." [28]

The notion of predisposition also figures in the many discussions which attempt to link epidemic hysteria with social change. This purported explanation, general to the point of triviality, was advanced in the cases of hysterical outbreaks in East Africa, which occurred in Tanganyikan and Ugandan schools near Lake Victoria in 1962–63. Ebrahim speculates that school children were particularly exposed to culture conflicts, with one life in the traditional village and another in the modern classroom.[29] Yet it is surely insufficient to simply say that "mental epidemics are likely to arise when times are unsettled and emotions are inflammable." [30] Apart from the imprecision of the terms themselves, we saw in chapter two that the alleged relationship between social change and mental health is far from simple or direct.

While these shortcomings predominate, some efforts have been made to deal with epidemic hysteria in a more systematic manner. It has, for example, been called a nonadaptive solution to problems for which no traditional adaptive solution exists.[31] This line of inquiry was pursued on a sustained basis by Kerckhoff and Back in their detailed examination of hysterical contagion in a Southern textile mill.[32] Dozens of mill workers complained of sickness, particularly fainting, as a result of having been bitten by an unidentified, probably nonexistent, insect. Meticulous subsequent examination demonstrated that those involved were likely to have been under many sorts of stress, arising from different sources. No traditional means existed for relieving the stresses. Those who first manifested symptoms turned out to be social isolates (this may relate to clinical observations that the outbreak of hospital hysteria tends to occur first among those with past histories of neurosis).[33] Eventually, the behavior moved from the relative isolates to those more socially integrated. At that point, the outbreak began to follow lines of social contact and influence. Eventually, so many people were affected in this manner that the very numbers came to validate general belief in the "June bug," and then the epidemic drew in even those outside the prior network of affected social contacts.

While this summary necessarily ignores much useful detail in the Kerckhoff-Back account, it does suggest the complex nature of the spread patterns. The authors speculate that the multiple stresses which affected so many workers in the small mill town, and the absence of satisfactory outlets, produced a situation in which (*a*) a form of stress relief was needed; and (*b*) a belief which would legitimate stress-relieving behavior was in fact quickly adopted.[34] I want to return to the Kerckhoff-Back model a bit later in the chapter. However, at this point some tentative conclusions may be drawn from it: First, the outbreak did in fact spread much like an epidemic.[35] Second, the individuals involved tended to be under multiple rather than single sources of stress. Third, the outbreak was triggered by notably atypical individuals. Fourth, it was necessary to have some belief which would explain and justify tension-relieving behavior, even though the persons involved were unaware that their symptoms constituted a tension-reduction mechanism. Finally, when the symptoms had become relatively common, their very frequency served to remove the doubts of many who had originally been skeptical.

The last point—social validation—suggests the ambiguous character of perceived reality. We test the adequacy of inner mental activity by comparing our perceptions with what is "out there." In carrying out the process of reality testing, we utilize the perceptions of others, for by bringing in new sources of information, we test the adequacy of information we already possess. If there were no method to disconfirm our own hypotheses about the world outside ourselves, we might subsist on nothing but delusions. Under normal circumstances, we have no reason to doubt the adequacy of the external checks. However, "if one is dependent on a psychotic person for a consensual discrimination of one's fantasies from reality, and if his delusions correspond with one's fantasies, one is likely to have difficulty or even is likely to make the wrong choice." [36] As this suggests, the categories of epidemic hysteria and paranoia, insofar as both may be involved in millenarianism, are linked together. Both involve us in the question of validation. We have already seen that epidemic hysteria may spread because with each additional adherent the plausibility of the sustaining belief becomes greater.

We shall shortly be examining the role of paranoid beliefs. For the present, let us turn to a form of behavior very much like epidemic hysteria, in which the validation problem is raised with particular acuteness: panic. In the narrowest sense, panic and epidemic hysteria differ. The former does not present the physical symptoms of illness. But the two are kin in the rapidity of their spread, the absence of reflection, and the uncritical attitude toward evidence. The rank and file of millenarian movements are often characterized as "panic-stricken." [37] In fact, however, panic is an infrequent occurrence, despite the ease with which the term is employed in everyday speech. Panic is usually thought to be typical of disaster situations, but its actual occurrence in disasters has been greatly exaggerated.[38] The social disorganization that disaster produces is often mistaken for panic. Behavior that "appears to be aimless, random, uncontrolled or conflicting" is taken by the observer to be evidence of panic.[39]

What then is panic? It is characterized by emotional agitation and uncontrolled physical flight. Two conditions must be met for panic to occur: there must be a perceived threat of immediate personal destruction and a feeling of imminent entrapment that appears to preclude any future possibility of escape. These conditions are most likely to be met at either of two points in the course of a catastrophe: they may occur while the physical impact is in progress and ways out are in process of being very rapidly exhausted.[40] More commonly, panic comes in advance of impact, when people believe the disaster is about to descend upon them.[41] This seems to be borne out by the best-documented cases of large-scale panic. Frequently, of course, no threat in fact "objectively" exists; impact never actually occurs. This was the case in the most extensively studied instance of modern mass panic, the product of Orson Welles's *Invasion from Mars* broadcast.[42] On the other hand, those who were able fled the cities of Europe during the Black Death, a case where panic, even though it did no good, was based on a realistic assessment of a real threat.[43]

Often, however, the less reasonable the threat appears, the more likely that it will produce panic.[44] The very improbability of an invasion from Mars made it acceptable to many. This may be because it is impossible to accommodate extreme rumors within conventional mental categories.[45] Even where the threat does not exist, the panic constitutes a self-fulfilling prophecy: "the crowd is infected with the idea of the imminence of disaster and the result may be a disaster—though of a different kind." [46] Note the epidemic metaphor and the dependence upon inaccurate consensual validation. The classic instance of a disaster-creating panic is a run on a bank, based on initially erroneous information, which becomes all too real as individuals withdraw their funds.

We can see in panic a form of collective behavior that is close both to millenarian movements and to hysterical epidemics. Panic moves with at least as much rapidity as epidemic hysteria, but the external threat is apt to be much more clearly focused. The "June bug" epidemic and the hysteria of the Salem witches at least possessed putative causes; many hospital epidemics lack even these vague but identifiable sources of contagion. Panic is distinguishable, too, because it attempts to cope with the threat, albeit only through the medium of escape. This more self-conscious perception of external sources of stress makes it more likely that a belief system will form. However, panics, like epidemic hysteria, are by nature unorganized. There may be instigators but not leaders. The life-span of a panic is necessarily short, limited by the availability of susceptible subjects and by the point at which correct information gradually overtakes rumor. Only where panic itself creates disaster can it begin to have a life of its own.

Fragmentary evidence suggests that millenarian leaders are often disordered individuals. The behavior of totalitarian leaders has shown strikingly paranoid aspects.[47] P. M. Yap argues that the leader of the Taiping Rebellion, Hung Hsiu-ch'üan, suffered an acute mental disturbance just before his critical visions and may have developed paranoid-schiz-ophrenic tendencies as the movement progressed.[48] In simi-lar fashion, Gershom Scholem argues that the seventeenth-century false messiah, Sabbatai Zevi, was a manic-de-pressive.[49] Such diagnoses from a distance are bound to remain speculative, yet it is also true that the documentary sources are often copious and detailed.[50]

A more significant reservation lies in the fact that a leader, no matter how charismatic and no matter what his mental state, is rarely the only source of information against which individuals may test their own perceptions. So long as scientific evidence, religious revelation, or other extrasocial standards remain, the individual possesses some recourse. He need not be wholly dependent upon the group as an arbiter of reality. Only where these external standards do not exist or no longer command their former respect does the validation of "reality" turn on consensus.

Millenarian movements do not accept the culturally trans-mitted conception of reality; they assemble sense data in new ways, because the old do not offer satisfactory explanations. Thus millenarian movements create and inhabit a distinctive reality of their own. It is quite possible that in some sense their pictures of reality are inferior to those more commonly utilized. Certainly circumstantial evidence points to this, in the frequency with which millenarians meet with political suppression or military defeat.

Millenarians work hard at the construction and mainte-nance of inclusive views of the world. Adherents are shielded from competing views, and this social and often physical separation significantly alters the validation basis. Validation comes from fellow-believers, from the leader, and from distinctive truth-gathering techniques, be they scientific, re-velatory, or oracular. The leader in turn receives his own confirmation from the rank and file. The movement resem-bles a closed information system, in which each component confirms the values of the others.

Is it not possible that this sense of closure and separateness is a product of psychological self-selection? That millenarian movements constitute the *folie à deux* writ large? Ernest Gruenberg suggests the possibility of socially shared psychopathology that extends to groups of very substantial size. These compact groups, whose views of the world cut them off from others, may not be mentally ill in the conventional sense: "the available evidence suggests that, rather than diagnostic groupings used in psychiatry, it is ideas, feelings, attitudes, defense mechanisms, and activities that are shared." [51]

The major problem involved in the hypothesis of self-selection must, however, be that of size. While in a purely a priori fashion one may imagine, as Gruenberg does, an entire nation that has lost contact with its old reality, the larger the group to which such alienation is imputed, the harder it is to explain. To be sure, every society possesses its share of misfits and eccentrics. It is natural to suppose that such persons gravitate toward social movements compatible with their own skewed view of the world. However, the available evidence suggests that the numbers of such individuals are sufficiently small so that millenarian movements cannot be regarded simply as instances of collective madness.

It does appear true that psychologically atypical individuals often gravitate toward leadership positions. The evidence on the point is necessarily fragmentary and inferential. However, such evidence as we presently have suggests that certain roles both attract and utilize the behavioral tendencies of aberrant individuals. For example, the shaman, for whom trance states are commonplace, may be recruited from such persons. "For these, the shamanistic role may well represent a precarious haven within which their eccentricities are tolerated and turned to advantage." [52] The prophetic role in general offers an acceptable niche to individuals who without it might be perceived as threatening deviants.[53]

In complex, modern societies similar observations have been made. At its broadest, this position, in the classic articulation of Harold Lasswell, sees political participation as "the projection of private affect onto public objects." [54] The political arena becomes the site in which unresolved inner conflicts receive expression. In more specific terms, political leaders have been disproportionately recruited from among manic-depressives and paranoid-schizophrenics. Brent Rutherford's research on participation within the internal political system of a mental hospital demonstrated the marked over-representation of both types, although he presents no direct evidence that the same is true in the world outside.[55]

If for purposes of argument we accept this thesis of the abnormality of leaders, we still must deal with their followers. Are they themselves "abnormal," "deviant," or easily induced to become so? Here the evidence is much more clear-cut. Millenarian movements, as well as other social movements of a related character, draw upon a strikingly representative cross section of the population. The close background studies of Hadley Cantril and George Rudé, for parts of Europe and America over two centuries, make it clear that both millenarian and nonmillenarian social movements attract such memberships.[56] None of the data suggest that members are either socially or psychologically atypical of the larger community. There is simply no evidence of psychological self-selection. Significantly, too, the manic-depressives and paranoid-schizophrenics in Rutherford's study led politically drab, conformist lives before hospitalization. Their rise to political ascendency within ward governments was in no way foreshadowed by any earlier adherence to "extremist" organizations. The only study which appears to bolster the self-selection theory in fact provides only partial confirmation. George Marcus, in a study of civil-rights workers, found them to be distinguishable from both black and white communities in terms of psychosomatic symptoms.[57] This would seem to indicate recruitment from the more troubled, yet there is no evidence of severe disorder, nor is it clear whether the nervous ills existed before organizational work began.

Perhaps, then, the normal follower might be made temporarily disordered by involvement with an aberrant leader. A reexamination of the concept of "socially shared psychopathology" shows this to be unlikely. "Groups are formed on this basis when a mentally disordered dominating person, most often affected with a psychosis, induces or provokes a delusional condition in one or more individuals who are relatively dependent and submissive." [58] The requirements are exacting, for this type of group formation requires not simply a severely disordered leadership figure but a symbiosis of the dominant and the submissive. Thus the rival hypothesis of inducement to psychopathology itself turns out to be a variant on the already rejected notion of self-selection. Those who select themselves, instead of being identified in terms of actual psychoneurosis, must all be submissives. Here, too, neither available evidence nor the actual size of millenarian groups makes this likely. The very wildfire, contagious growth of the movements, quickly involving everyone in an area, demonstrates a breadth of appeal that transcends personality differences.

So far we have found only a string of negatives: Millenarian movements are not easily explainable through any of the usual psychological rubrics. Epidemic hysteria, panic, demented leadership, and psychological self-selection all have had to be discarded. Only Kerckhoff and Back's embryonic model of contagious growth offered any hope of eventual utility. However, two possibilities still remain, both of which we shall find rather more helpful—the so-called paranoid style and religious ecstasy. Neither fits with complete comfort into conventional psychiatric categories, and it is perhaps this very incongruity with diagnostic concepts that makes them so much more useful for social situations.

Conspiracy thinking—or, in Richard Hofstadter's phrase, "the paranoid style"—bears strong surface resemblances to panic. Panics often do occur as a result of belief in the machinations of an evil conspiracy. However, in order to induce panic, the belief that is transmitted must be exceedingly simple.[59] Conspiracy theories may be simplistic but they are rarely sufficiently elemental to be rapidly transmitted from person to person. Their simplicity lies in the range of effects imputed to a single, malevolent cause rather than in the ease and brevity with which the idea can be expressed. Then, too, many conspiracy beliefs last for very long periods of time and rarely induce true panics; the Jewish conspiracy presented in *The Protocols of the Elders of Zion* is a case in point.[60]

Hofstadter's formulation of the paranoid style grew out of his work on American nativism, and his description of the syndrome is worth quoting at some length:

In the paranoid style, as I conceive it, the feeling of persecution is central, and it is indeed systematized in grandiose theories of conspiracy. But there is a vital difference between the paranoid spokesman in politics and the clinical paranoiac: although they both tend to be overheated, oversuspicious, overaggressive, grandiose, and apocalyptic in expression, the clinical paranoid sees the hostile and conspiratorial world in which he feels himself to be living as directed specifically *against him*; whereas the spokesman of the paranoid style finds it directed against a nation, a culture, a way of life whose fate affects not himself alone but millions of others.[61]

Hofstadter recognized in European millenarianism a social phenomenon which "closely resembles what I have been considering." [62] These sects, too, as Norman Cohn puts it, engage in the demonization of outgroups.[63]

Millenarian movements cannot help but fall into conspiracy thinking, for they rigorously divide the world into the good and evil, the saved and the damned. Evil constitutes an ever-present threat. Only the final consummation of history will remove it. In the meantime, the evil cabal—whether of capitalists, landowners, Communists, Jews, Papists, or colonizers—will exercise its powers to the utmost in order to eliminate those who know the path to salvation.

Hofstadter remains vague concerning causal mechanisms. He goes only so far as to suggest that every society may possess a minority psychologically predisposed to think in paranoid terms. Actual or anticipated disaster serves to bring their predisposition into full flower.[64] Much light is shed on cause and effect relationships, however, by a controversial essay of H. R. Trevor-Roper's. Trevor-Roper's concern is for the manner in which social tensions are discharged. The occasion for his speculations is an investigation into the European witch craze of the sixteenth and seventeenth centuries.[65] He observes that the belief in witches and the Devil's kingdom was shared by both the inquisitors and by many of their victims. The confessions, far from having been extracted only under torture, were often made voluntarily and in elaborate detail. This apparent collaboration poses the same kind of problem that we have already examined in seeking a link between the demented leader and his followers.

What manner of symbiosis can account for it, especially during the witch craze, where the interests of persecuted and persecutors could hardly have been farther apart?

Trevor-Roper argues for the existence of "social stereotypes," beliefs which may appear unusual when first articulated but which upon repetition come to be widely accepted within a culture. Prominent social stereotypes include the attribution of an unusual propensity for evil to small, distinct social groups. In European history, these have included witches, Jews, Jacobins, Papists, and Communists. Trevor-Roper postulates that at all times members of any society share common fears and anxieties, not from epidemic psychopathology but simply as a result of the tensions of everyday life. In times of social change, the scope and intensity of anxieties increase. These fears are, in turn, discharged upon stereotypical institutions, groups, or individuals who have become identified with manifest social evils. In the sixteenth and seventeenth centuries, "the mythology of Satan's kingdom . . . [became] the standard form in which the otherwise undefined fears of society became crystallized." The personification of evil in the person of "Satan" or "Antichrist" conforms to the rigorous Manicheanism of both the millenarian doctrine and the paranoid style; figures of ultimate malevolence simplify a world that has become increasingly complex and out of joint.[66]

The relationship between persecutor and persecuted became reciprocal, for "just as psychopathic individuals, in those years, centered their separate fantasies . . . on the Devil, and thus gave an apparent objective identity to their subjective experiences, so societies in fear articulated their collective neuroses about the same obsessive figure, and found a scapegoat for their fears in his agents, the witches." [67] "Collective neurosis," as we have seen, may be far too strong a term. Nonetheless, there are "ages of anxiety" in human history, in which established patterns and values come into question and the future suddenly confronts us with the possibility of new and utterly unforeseen possibilities.[68]

Messianism becomes for Trevor-Roper, like panic, simply another form of collective emotion centered upon a prevalent, fear-discharging stereotype. These symbols for the

expression of discontents change slowly and may persist for
centuries with only minor modifications. The fact that a
particular symbol fades from view is not always evidence for
its permanent obsolescence. The witch craze, too, had its ebbs
and flows. It crested in the 1560s as a consequence of
religious war, and precisely in those frontier areas where
religions impinged upon each other.[69] When there was reason
to believe that a social unit was under threat, the complex of
ideas associated with the Devil suddenly moved from obscurity to political prominence. On each return, it became clearer
that the preceding calm consisted simply of a time when the
beliefs performed little function for most people.

Here too the correspondence with millenarianism is striking. We saw in the last chapter that messianic movements
possess a tenacious ability to survive underground; their
periods of open growth represent the continuing dialogue
between environmental upheaval and a subterranean tradition of radical transformation. This surely corresponds to
"the common stock of European social mythology," of which
Norman Cohn writes.[70] There exist in any society complexes
of ideas to explain individual and group anxieties. They lie at
hand for periods of widespread unease and are superseded by
new fear-discharging symbols only when the metaphysical
assumptions behind them lose acceptance. By the mid-seventeenth century, the witch craze died out abruptly for this
reason. "Then the medieval synthesis, which Reformation
and Counter-Reformation had artificially prolonged, was at
last broken, and through the cracked crust the filthy pool
drained away. Thereafter society might persecute its dissidents as Huguenots or as Jews. It might discover a new
stereotype, the "Jacobin," the "Red." But the stereotype of
the witch had gone." [71]

Under what circumstances can social stereotypes be acti-
vated? If Trevor-Roper is correct, both millenarian movements and panic can grow from the same ideological base.
What kinds of beliefs can initiate panic? We have seen that
they must be simple; complex systems of ideas rarely lend
themselves to it, although the far more compressed symbols
implied by social stereotypes fit the bill admirably. There
must be belief in an imminent threat and in the impossibility

of future escape. Finally, there is some reason to suppose that the idea must appear extreme and unconventional; its very unthinkability is what compels people to take precipitate action.

The social stereotype is available as a focus for diffuse tensions and anxieties, the idiom, as it were, in which perceived discontent and unease become objectified.[72] The collective behavior that may result can possess varying degrees of structure, from the relative anarchy of panic to the communalism of millenarian movements. The statement of the belief, too, can differ, ranging from the convoluted speculations of the political paranoid to the slogans and catchphrases that animate panic. What accounts for the range of organizational and ideological manifestations? The principal reason is that Trevor-Roper's "social stereotypes" must be viewed in two quite distinct ways. These stereotypes are symbols, but they can function differently for different people in different situations.

They may function as either referential symbols or condensation symbols.[73] Both constitute forms of mental shorthand. The referential symbol refers to an aspect or relationship in the environment outside of the individual who employs it. It functions as an aid to understanding, reasoning, and logical manipulation and is presumably retained only to the extent that the outside world confirms its reality and utility. The condensation symbol does not point to portions of objective reality; rather, it evokes emotions. The function of the condensation symbol lies in its ability to draw forth feelings in a situation, whether of pride, hate, or exaltation.

We have been operating at the margins of millenarianism, where panic, political paranoia, witchcraft, and related phenomena blend with the apocalyptic and transformative thrust of messianism. In so doing, we have seen that stereotypical beliefs figure prominently as explanations for present evil and uncertainty. Where they function as referential symbols, they serve as the basis for complex theoretical constructions. These constitute the working out of elaborate conspiracy beliefs. Richard Hofstadter draws our attention to the pedantry so common to the paranoid style: "The typical procedure of the higher paranoid scholarship is to start with

. . . defensible assumptions and with a careful accumulation
of facts, or at least of what appear to be facts, and to marshal
these facts toward an overwhelming "proof" of the particular
conspiracy that is to be established. . . . It is, if not wholly
rational, at least intensely rationalistic." [74] Witch-finders'
handbooks, *The Protocols of the Elders of Zion* and its
commentaries, and the anti-Catholic tracts of American
nativists all manifest this fusion of scholarly apparatus with
fantastic, conspiratorial conclusions. The stereotype of *witch,
Jew,* or *Papist* certainly evokes strong emotions from the
political paranoid, and thus acts as a condensation symbol.
But it is at least as important in its referential capacity. For
the theorist of demonic power, the *Devil* is not simply a
slogan or the object onto which one projects one's fears: it is
a palpable reality, a fit subject of intellectual inquiry.

Referential symbols are generally meant to point toward
elements of the "objective" world. The ideologies of conspiracy theorists, which are normally thought of as fantasies or
delusions, hardly fall comfortably within this category.
Suffice it to say for the present that the individuals who
construct and accept conspiracy theories regard them as true
pictures of the real world and utilize them accordingly. When
social stereotypes are employed as referential symbols, the
result is the spinning of conspiracy theories, rationalistic
explanations of evil and change. But when they are employed
as condensation symbols, as triggers for immediate emotional
response, the result is more likely to be the short, sharp one of
panic. Social stereotypes can be turned to either purpose.
They may be the center of quasitheological pedantry or the
catalysts of immediate emotional responses.

These two levels of symbolic utilization can coexist within
the same person or the same society. The paranoid theorist
may be motivated by the emotional charge of his key
concepts; the panic victim may, in more tranquil moments,
nod approvingly at the intellectualization of his slogans. A
single society can simultaneously accommodate what Hofstadter refers to as "the higher paranoid scholarship" along
with a popular culture filled with the nebulous dark forces of
Norman Cohn's "social mythology."

How is it that social stereotypes can be expanded into

intellectual constructions? How is it that they can be used referentially, if in fact the things to which they refer are "nonexistent"? In the first place, as the social stereotype becomes embodied in cohesive behavior, the potential increases for what we may call its double utilization. More directly put, the particular belief involved becomes the focus of a social movement and thus relieves the anxieties of those who subscribe to it. That constitutes the first use to which the belief is put. However, the mere existence of such a movement itself evokes responses from the larger society. It too becomes the focus of suspicions and discontents. What the larger environment is to the movement, the movement may become for the larger environment. Each sees the other as a threat and source of evil, in a mirroring relationship. Each confirms the worst suspicions of the other.

In concrete terms, medieval European chiliasts organized themselves around preexisting eschatological beliefs. Once a movement had been organized, however, its very existence made it in turn a potential target. Just as members of the movement discharged their tensions upon the corrupt society outside, so that society saw in millenarians an opportunity to give vent to its own frustrations. Available categories, such as "witch," "heretic," and "Antichrist," offered both sides a suitable armory of invective.

In the West, both sides possessed the same vocabulary, though they often understood the same term in very different ways. The non-Western world presents millenarian movements in a two-culture situation, where indigenous protest movements confront European adversaries. Occasionally, categories may be shared even here, for Western religious and political rhetoric has been widely diffused. However, even where hatred of the other is expressed by each in different terms, the mirroring relationship still takes place. Each side interprets the words and actions of the other as fulfillments of its own dire predictions.

This peculiar version of the self-fulfilling prophecy suggests the development of patterns of behavior that serve to confirm initial conspiracy fears. The movement believes the outside world is evil and withdraws; the withdrawal is interpreted as evidence of hostility, and the society acts against the group;

the group finds its initial beliefs verified; and so on. This
process provides some explanation for the recurrent references to paranoid behavior. Paranoid beliefs are also often
self-fulfilling prophecies, for the paranoid individual acts
toward others in a manner which evokes hostility and thus
confirms his own delusions.[75] By and large, social scientists
who utilize terms such as *paranoid beliefs* make clear that they
are not doing so in a strictly clinical sense.[76] But even as a
term of art, the *paranoid style* reflects some striking characteristics of the syndrome from which it is drawn.

Paranoid delusions are not only self-fulfilling prophecies,
they are virtually nonfalsifiable. Those who hold them prove
immune to argument, and the beliefs themselves possess a
high degree of internal consistency and surface plausibility.[77]
Here is yet another reason why conspiracy theories may be
constructed of and function as referential symbols while
having nothing in the objective world to which they actually
refer. Belief in a malevolent, virtually omnipotent conspiracy
has the advantages, first, that it explains everything requiring
explanation through a single factor; and, second, that all
apparently disconfirming information may be dismissed as
snares and delusions fabricated by the conspiracy itself. Hans
Toch suggests that when conflicting information from the
environment becomes too difficult to explain away by simply
imputing evil or defect to others, the paranoid fastens upon
the idea of conspiracy as a final, irrefutable explanation.[78]

Millenarian movements, for whose members the outside
world is corrupt and evil, do in fact see that evil embodied in
and directed by a sinister individual, group, or institution. To
that extent, all millenarian movements are instances of the
paranoid style. What is equally important, all instances of the
paranoid style are *not* millenarian. As we saw in the preceding
chapter, millenarian movements suffer from a unique validation problem, stemming from the fact that they so often make
specific, testable predictions of transformation in the immediate future. These predictions subject them to the virtual
certainty of radical disconfirmation. On the other hand, the
manner in which they explain existing evil, while in principal
testable, is, as we have seen, in practice unverifiable. One can

establish whether the messiah appeared and destroyed evil on a certain date, but one cannot so definitively establish that a small, secret, all-powerful group has caused the reign of evil in the first place.

The line between present and future, between existing evil and anticipated salvation, divides the untestable from the testable. It also divides nonmillenarian paranoid movements from millenarian ones. Paranoid movements which concentrate solely upon investigating and attempting to unseat a conspiracy make no claims concerning the date at which it will be accomplished. They limit themselves to minutely describing the workings of the conspiracy and attempting to alert others to it. They thus free themselves from the disconfirmation problem. Only when conspiratorial beliefs are joined to a vision of imminent salvation do we have genuine millenarianism.

In addition, the nonmillenarian paranoid style centers its view of the future upon an anticipated disaster. Without specifying the time of its occurrence, the "political paranoid" sees the future in cataclysmic terms. But where millenarians view the coming disaster as necessary for the destruction of evil, more conventional representatives of political paranoia take a decidedly grimmer view. The disaster is conceived less as the inauguration of the good society than as the triumph of the hated conspiracy. As a result, the future is oriented toward preventing the catastrophe from occurring, not welcoming it. "The apocalypticism of the paranoid style runs dangerously near to hopeless pessimism, but usually stops short of it. Apocalyptic warnings arouse passion and militancy. . . . Properly expressed, such warnings serve somewhat the same function as a description of the horrible consequences of sin in a revivalist sermon." [79] It is the distinction between almost inevitable doom and absolutely inevitable salvation that finally distinguishes between the otherwise similar natures of the paranoid style and its millenarian variant. Pure conspiracy theories in the end possess a rather greater durability. It is, after all, one thing when salvation fails to arrive, quite another when doom does not materialize. Conspiracy theories, devoid of salvationist promises, thus possess a built-in, though surely ironic, capacity for success: the signs of defeat persist, but the righteous always receive one more reprieve.

Thus millenarianism emerges as larger and more complex than categories transplanted from psychiatry might suggest. The individuals involved are neither hysterics nor paranoids. However, to say what they are not is not to tell us what they are; that remains to be done. The balance of this chapter will be given over to an explanation of ecstatic behavior and of apparently contagious growth.

Descriptions of millenarian movements are filled with references to ecstatic behavior. We have already dealt with many of these phenomena: feelings of persecution and conspiracy, in the discussion just ended; dependence on the leader and feelings of rebirth and transformation, in the preceding chapter on conversion; abandonment of normal routines, in the sections on disaster in chapters two and three. However, ecstasy itself, as manifested in dancing, hallucinations, glossolalia, tremors, and so forth, has not been directly confronted.

The behavior of millenarians often demonstrates profound emotional upheavals. We have seen that this agitation cannot be explained simply by classifying those involved as mentally ill. Emotional agitation also occurs too frequently, in too many different cultural settings, to be dismissed as purely local, idiosyncratic manifestations. The phenomenon is too common to be explained in terms of independent ecstatic patterns, each one of which simply happens to exist naturally in a particular culture. Thus we find the Sioux Ghost Dancers dancing to physical and mental exhaustion;[80] the Cargo Cultists twitching compulsively;[81] the initiates of the Free Spirit indulging in ritualistic eroticism; and the Flagellants engaged in relentless self-destruction.[82] European dancing manias from the tenth to the seventeenth centuries sprang up at the margins of millenarianism.[83]

Such diverse examples cannot easily be made to yield to some common cause. The causes may indeed be multiple but not necessarily divided along geographical or even cultural lines. In any case, some initial qualifications are in order.

First of all, there is evidence that among the Cargo Cults, the more recent the cult, the less likely that it will show special physiological features. Cochrane argues that this is due to the distance between recent cults and traditional religion, from which he assumes the enthusiastic behavior originally stemmed.[84] However, since the physical "aberrations" appear jointly with the repudiation of old norms, it seems at least as reasonable to attribute the behavior to tensions caused by rejection of the past rather than to the carry-over of traditional practices.[85] We shall return to this point shortly. The apparent "normalization" of behavior becomes explicable in terms of the metamorphosis of millenarian movements into more conventional interest groups. Then, too, as we have already seen, great care must be exercised in attributing pathological or quasipathological significance to acts which in their indigenous setting might seem quite normal—for example, hallucinations.[86] The key lies in the significance the act has in its natural setting, whether it is common or uncommon, rewarding or stigmatizing; and the functions the act serves for the individual and his group.

What are the outward, physical indicators of ecstasy? George Rosen's description is worth quoting at length:

An extraordinary inner tension seizes the individual, and he experiences irresistible and perhaps incomprehensible emotions. As if under the compulsion of some force acting upon him, the individual feels constrained to speak or to act. In this state, he may also feel fear and resist the apparent invasion of his personality. At the same time he may experience pains and seem to lose his strength and breath. These internal developments are associated with external bodily changes. The individual's features are altered, and he begins to act as if he had lost control of his motor system. Trembling, lassitude and drowsiness may precede the period of convulsive agitation. Then, the limbs become agitated, the gestures wild and excited, the voice changes, and what is uttered seems to be the expression of another personality. Violent trembling, frenzied leaps, spasmodic convulsions and other forms of motor hyperexcitement occur for varying periods, and are followed finally by prostration and unconsciousness. While in trance, the possessed or ecstatic person has hallucinatory experiences such as visions, auditions (voices), as well as other distortions of sensation. To be sure, these aspects are not all present in every instance.[87]

Such behavior may well already exist in a society. Millenarian movements are associated not so much with its sudden first appearance but with the rapid diffusion of it to uncommonly large numbers of people.

In examining the nature of ecstatic behavior, we shall look first at its causes, next at its modes of transmission and growth, and finally at the functions it serves.

Mass ecstasy—or, to use the terminology of historians of religion, *enthusiasm*—stems from two principal causes: radical changes in sensory stimulation and situations which create extraordinary degrees of tension and anxiety. Both circumstances relate in a direct and striking manner to the conditions of disaster and social cataclysm which we have already discussed.

The same disaster effects that induce individuals to conversion help trigger ecstatic reactions. Indeed, we shall see that conversion and ecstasy are in fact closely related phenomena. Ecstatic behavior often accompanies conversion, and subsequent ecstatic experiences confirm the convert in his new faith. William Sargant notes that the acquisition of a new faith may be brought about through two strategies of sensory manipulation—overstimulation and deprivation.[88] Extreme excitation, through dancing, music, mass chanting, and related techniques, can produce enthusiasm, but so can solitude and meditation. Mystics have utilized both to good effect. The apparent prevalence of overexcitation in millenarian movements is easily explained: ecstasy as a group experience grows more readily out of joint participation than out of numerous experiences of individual isolation.

The repertoire of ecstasy-inducing techniques is large and expanding. It also seems to have very little to do with the past mental health of the individual concerned. "As is well known, trance states can be readily induced in most normal people by a wide range of stimuli." [89] To traditional techniques of music and dancing, which have already been mentioned, we may add alcoholic spirits, hypnotic suggestion, hyperventilation, and drugs.[90] Large numbers of perfectly normal, conventional people in any cultural setting can experience states of ecstasy as individuals or as members of a group.

Disaster inadvertently produces many of the same effects as intentional ecstatic techniques. Unlike other natural occurrences, however, disasters manage to combine both strategies of ecstatic attainment. That is to say, disasters produce sensory deprivation by destroying the old environment and overstimulation by creating a new one. The bewilderment of disaster victims reflects the whipsaw effect of alternating deprivation and stimulation. The same suggestibility that induces individuals to take up new beliefs can alter their behavior patterns as well. The convert and the ecstatic are one in responding emotionally to radical changes in their sensory loads. Millenarian movements combine the time-tested techniques of the religious enthusiast with the peculiarly conducive situation of the disaster environment.

It need hardly be added that many, perhaps most, instances of group enthusiasm have not been millenarian. Indeed, many have encouraged the individual to turn inward, in apparent avoidance of contact with others. For example, large movements of affective mysticism existed in Christian Europe from the eleventh to the eighteenth century. However, they lacked any components of direct social protest or millenarian expectation and instead concentrated on the cultivation of individual ecstatic states. Largely centered around religious orders, such examples as Bernardine and Carmelite mysticism utilized conventional techniques yet were essentially passive. In their predominant appeal to women, Herbert Moller argues, they were essentially reactions to the out-migration of men from the areas of Europe in which they flourished and the unavailability of direct outlets for sexual expression.[91] Social change left numerous women in a problematic position, yet there was no general disaster condition that might have broadened the base of the movements or directed their attentions outward.

Enthusiastic movements also flourished in upstate New York during the first half of the nineteenth century without

giving birth to substantial social disruption.[92] The waves of
ecstatic religion that broke over the so-called Burned-Over
District did not (with the notable exception of the Millerites)
anticipate either an imminent apocalypse or a messianic age.
They operated out of an already old tradition of periodic
ecstasy, which they brought with them from New England.[93]
Here, too, an ecstatic tradition in the absence of disaster
found expression in a basically passive manner. Disaster
consequently operates as a facilitator of ecstatic expression.
Catastrophe may accentuate tendencies already present in a
culture and open up to greater numbers of people the
possibility of ecstatic experience.

The other causal element lies in the demands made by
millenarian doctrine. The call is for rejection and separation,
for repudiation of the old and adoption of the new. The old
has failed both to prevent disaster and to explain it; indeed,
to the extent that the old is synonymous with the evil and
corrupt, the traditional culture may itself be seen as a direct
cause of the catastrophe. But however besmirched traditional
culture may be, it is not an easy thing from which to break
away. We have already seen that conversion is a painful
process. It calls for the severing of previously valued loyalties.
We have seen, too, that it is often accompanied by rituals of
initiation that incorporate extreme and exaggerated acts of
defiance. The ritualistic antinomianism so often in evidence
bespeaks the tensions of rejection, the sense of betrayal;
hence the defiant way in which movements embrace the
forbidden. These are the "bridge-burning" acts that irrevocably sever the individual from his past.[94] The act of separation
demands decision and the mobilization of resources. Ecstasy
is often simply the outward manifestation of this mobilization
process. The break with the past shows itself in the emotional
agitation of the ecstatic.

Disaster makes a break with the past appear necessary and
desirable, for the old life has been seen to fail. At the same
time, disaster facilitates the conversion to millenarianism by
predisposing the individual to ecstasy and conversion. How
then do patterns of ecstatic behavior spread? Here the germ
of a growth model already exists in the work of Kerckhoff
and Back on behavioral contagion. They suggest that an

adequate explanation depends upon the fusion of three hitherto separately conceived models. The *social isolation* model asserts that outcasts are more easily influenced than individuals who are well integrated. The *group-influence* model tells us that contagion should follow interpersonal ties. The *crowd response* model depends upon a concept of unstructured, spontaneous contagion in a compact group.[95]

No one of these models proves sufficient by itself. The three must be used in conjunction with one another. Thus the social isolate provides the starting point. Such persons, by reason of their isolation, are less affected by group pressures for conformity. They may also possess looser ties to traditional values. They are more easily drawn to bizarre behavior and toward innovation because their threshold of acceptance is lower. This is in effect a variant on the "marginal man" hypothesis. Lack of strong ties to the rest of the community means less resistance to change. It is perhaps also true that individuals with a history of mental disorder tend to fall into this category. This, in turn, may partially explain the prevalence of disordered individuals among millenarian leaders. Imperfectly integrated into the community, cut off from group pressures, such persons may be more likely to achieve what Wallace calls "mazeway resynthesis," creative leaps which eventually take a society into a reformulated cultural pattern.

In any case, the social isolates constitute the catalyst. The major, and in part inexplicable, step is taken when the jump is made from social isolates to group influence, from the atypical few to the well-integrated, mutually reinforcing many. How does this jump occur? To know this in a positive way would be to know the secret of human change and innovation. We can only imperfectly grasp the character of the process, as it seems to occur among millenarians.

Disaster is a leveler. It reduces much of the disparity between the social isolates and the rest of the community. The conformism of the majority gives way to anxiety, suggestibility, doubt, and questioning. Disasters are the great shakers-up of human society. They give to the isolates a newly receptive audience. Once the leap has been made, information travels along lines of social contact and influence. As it does so, the rate of growth and spread increases. The message, since it confronts newly recognized needs, travels quickly from person to person.

Now the crowd response model comes into play. "As larger and larger numbers of people exhibit the behavior, the sheer size of the affected category makes the credibility of the phenomenon greater." [96] The behavior validates itself, for if so many people say it is so, can things really be otherwise? Hence the phenomenon of crowd contagion that many writers see as the entire explanation for the growth of social movements turns out to be but the final stage of a much longer and less conspicuous process. In the final stage, the doubters are at last swept in. Ecstasy is less easily resisted when it constitutes one's whole immediate reality. Ecstasy appears to spread in a snowballing manner, from the few, to many, to virtually all. When it ends, it is apt to do so abruptly. Thus the metaphor of epidemic growth does fit, but only as a metaphor. [97] The growth pattern is analogous, but the actual process of transmission is reproduced only in the group-influence stage, where, like germs, ideas and behavior follow lines of contact. [98]

What functions does ecstatic behavior perform? In the first place, it facilitates the break with the past. As Worsley observes, millenarian movements generate and manipulate guilt. "In the end it is the fount of the marked hysteria and emotionality which we have so often found. This most radical rejection of the past generates the most powerful emotional energy." [99] People must, in effect, be desocialized from one set of values and resocialized to another;[100] a process of years must be compressed into days, weeks, or months. Through ecstatic experiences they mobilize energy for personal transformation. The experiences themselves, to the extent that they also violate conventional norms, constitute the most vivid kind of release from former values and obligations. To the extent that participants are bound together by common experiences and common guilt, they rapidly become socialized to a new kind of community.

It is frequently difficult to distinguish millenarian antinomianism from ecstatic experience. The initiation rites of the Mau Mau or the ritualistic sexuality of the Free Spirit,

Sabbatians, and Frankists simultaneously draw the initiate away from the old and toward the new in the most emotionally compelling manner. In Takie Lebra's study of the Tensho, a contemporary Japanese cult in Hawaii, she demonstrates the nexus of ecstasy and socialization. The central ritual for converts consists of public religious dancing. "A bizarre dancer or singer, the convert confronted himself with spectators who looked shocked, amused, disgusted, or in the case of a 'fellow-Japanese,' ashamed. . . . After overcoming the extreme sense of shame by 'jumping' into the dancing group, they became free, they said, of the problem of 'face.' . . . Freedom from shame was acquired as a result of experiencing a condensed form of shame." [101]

If ecstasy is a critical way into a movement, it is also bound up with a movement's survival. Ecstasy helps create the new community; but later, after the community's confrontation with its environment, ecstasy may be equally necessary. As we have seen, millenarian movements face critical problems of testing and validation. The world fails to conform to expectations. While the contradiction can be partially resolved by the favorable interpretation of ambiguous events, the cognitive dissonance dilemma cannot be entirely escaped.

Ecstasy maintains commitment, and it insulates against a sense of worldly failure. As I. M. Lewis remarks, ecstasy and success are inversely related.[102] The movement that cannot change the world finds in continued enthusiasm a refuge from failure. The movement that continues to grow and mold its environment suppresses ecstatic experience. The suppression of ecstasy is not simply a by-product of growing organizational rigidity, it is an intended tactic. The centralization of power and authority within a movement requires the elimination of any means by which those not in positions of authority might gain access to it. Ecstasy destroys the monopoly of knowledge vested in those at the center. It is commonplace that ecstatic religions often drain away social and political discontent.[103] This function has long been ascribed to black fundamentalist churches in the United States. Ecstasy becomes a surrogate for the attainment of tangible goals and serves an essentially cathartic function for members of a failed movement. The experience is therapeutic·

and abreactive: "repressed urges and desires, the idiosyncratic as well as the socially conditioned, are given full public rein." [104]

The millennium sometimes recedes as a consequence of worldly success. Total transformation is hardly necessary for a movement which, like communism, has solidly established itself. But the millennium can also recede as a consequence of failure. In the former case, its adherents abandon it; in the latter, the millennium, as it were, abandons those who have pursued it. For those whom the millennium abandons, it is natural that ritual activity should begin to appear as a substitute for environmental change. Ritual is, after all, a "motor activity that involves its participants symbolically in a common enterprise, calling their attention to their relatedness and joint interests in a compelling way. . . . Men instinctively try to find meaning and order when placed in a confusing or ambiguous situation." [105] The essence of ritual is reassurance, confirmation that one's values and hopes have not died. Thus, while it is a source of solidarity in success, it is also a consolation in failure—or, rather, a way of guarding against the recognition of failure.

Max Gluckman has directed our attention to "rituals of rebellion," in which protests occur in stylized, rule-governed form.[106] No matter how violent the appearance, there is never any real danger of fundamental change. Everyone plays out his part. The conflict never exceeds certain culturally defined, mutually understood limits. In at least a metaphorical sense, ecstatic experience can be understood as a variant of the ritual of rebellion.[107] The continued performance of antinomian acts, the claim to independent access to sources of knowledge and authority, the use of ecstasy as a means of proving the degree of one's contact with higher powers— these all constitute modes of protest, however passive, against the established order.

The preoccupation of established, well-organized movements with heresy demonstrates the degree to which outwardly innocuous behavior may be construed by both sides as acts of protest. Indeed, the history of medieval millenarianism can largely be written in terms of the history of heresy. This is equally so for their latter-day, secular successors.

Modern totalitarianism is a chronicle of purge and deviation, of the continuing battle between orthodoxy and heresy. As protest behavior itself ceases to produce the anticipated results, as predictions of outside intervention fail to materialize, an inward-turning preoccupation with ritual blunts the sharp sense of hopelessness.

Rituals of rebellion and transformation point to a future that may never be but which cannot be abandoned; they also, significantly, point back toward a past recalled with nostalgia. Millenarian movements are born out of disasters. One of the curious ambiguities of disaster is that, while it is by definition a form of intense deprivation, it produces feelings of well-being that sometimes verge on euphoria.[108] This is often referred to as the *disaster utopia*. It occurs in the postimpact situation, when there is a "great up-surge of goodwill among the survivors and on the part of outsiders who come to their aid." [109] The dominant feelings are apt to be ones of generosity and unusual friendliness.

Disasters alter the social structure of a community and introduce a temporary sense of common purpose. Earlier social conflicts appear muted or absent.[110] Invidious social distinctions disappear under the impact of disaster. In this suddenly opened and democratized atmosphere, individuals who led formerly separate lives identify with each other. It may be an exaggeration to suggest, as some students of disaster have, that the disaster utopia is positively therapeutic in its effects;[111] but unquestionably catastrophes are often, perhaps with the luxury of hindsight, perceived in oddly favorable terms. After disasters are over, it is not unusual for survivors to remark that strangers talked to one another then and, "Why can't people always be so friendly and helpful?" In addition, like a play, the sudden onslaught of disaster introduces the unusual and dramatic into lives that may have seemed bland and commonplace.[112]

The disaster utopia, transient though it may be, possesses direct links with millenarian thought. Beliefs in the millennium, too, often anticipate great disasters which must precede the final consummation—the period of upheaval referred to by medieval Jewish messianists as "the birth-pangs of the Messiah." The wave of fellow feeling seems itself to presage a fundamental transformation in social behavior. "In the time immediately after the disaster, when generous feelings are in the ascendant, there may be a sense of the millennium having arrived. . . . The demonstrations of help and good will which the disaster victim receives may conceivably be construed in terms of an anticipated millennium. He overestimates them and is also unprepared for their dwindling away." [113] Disasters, consequently, engender ambivalent feelings for those subjected to them. The pain inflicted may be offset by the belief that surely an event of such magnitude cannot be without significance. The sense of community proves transient, but by offering intimations of a different kind of society it too turns the disaster into a harbinger of better things. We can also see an interaction here between the event itself and the way in which a culture prepares people for it. Myths of necessary disaster structure the subsequent perception of the actual event. The victim may be unable to explain the event or his own suffering in an adequate manner, but he may well possess culturally transmitted beliefs about some unprecedented cataclysm.

Of course, the disaster utopia is in reality only a brief, transitory episode. Human relationships gradually return to "normal." As a community proceeds with reconstruction, some losses are made good. A measure of predictability and familiarity return. Loved ones who have been killed cannot be restored; but, insofar as resources allow it, some effort is made to repair and rebuild. Generally, these efforts are welcomed. In only one respect are they unwelcome: the closer one comes to a restoration of the status quo, the farther one moves from the disaster utopia. The old exaltation seems infinitely precious, and it is now unrecoverable—or so things seem at first.

Millenarian movements in fact work diligently to recapture the disaster utopia. They do so in the most obvious way simply by anticipating and attempting to bring about a permanently utopian state. In a less obvious manner, millenarian ritual attempts to engender the same euphoric emotions. The communal sharing of moments of intense feeling suggests the use of artifice to reproduce states of consciousness once brought about naturally. Ecstatic states involve artificially produced high stress situations, with which mille-narians hope to recapture the sense of purpose and harmony once brought about by the high stress of a natural situation.

The perpetuation of ecstasy is thus, in the final analysis, motivated by nostalgia. Whatever other functions it performs, its final service is to transport the individual back in time to critical past events which can, if not be reexperienced, at least be simulated with a reasonable degree of faithfulness. Thus ecstasy does not appear as the outward manifestation of mental illness but as the attempt to control and freeze an unrecoverable moment.

Chapter Six

MILLENARIANISM IN
THE MODERN WORLD

Our discussion thus far strongly suggests that millenarianism is an anachronistic fringe phenomenon, politically, sociologically, and intellectually at the margins of modern society. The point has been made—most strongly in chapter four—that millenarian movements flourish in a relatively isolated agrarian milieu. I have argued that the relationships between this milieu and disaster make millenarianism a predominantly rural form of unrest, ill-suited to the polyglot character of city life. If that is true, an obvious corollary should be that millenarian movements are eventually destined to disappear. As urban, industrial—indeed, as some would have it, postindustrial—society expands, such archaisms as chiliastic sects are bound to constitute early casualties. E. J. Hobsbawm and others argue that the apparent upthrust of such groups in recent times represents only the dying paroxysms of agrarian society. The city, which as recently as the turn of the century had been overwhelmingly a Western social form, very rapidly diffused into the non-Western world. "In 1900 . . . there were fourteen cities with a population of one million or more, and of these six . . . were in Europe, three in Asia, three in North America, and two in South America. By 1960, when the total had risen to sixty-nine, the distribution had changed radically. No less than twenty-six (i.e. more than thirty-seven per cent) were in Asia." [1] Examples might be multiplied, but the major point should be clear enough: a major transformation has steadily reduced the size and importance of the reservoirs from which millenarian movements have traditionally drawn their adherents.

Are the movements of our own time, then, mere sputterings, the last volatile by-products of an irreversible process of change? That argument can certainly be advanced for some, such as the Melanesian Cargo Cults. But if we come full circle, back to the discussion in chapter one, we shall see that millenarianism cannot be disposed of so easily. I said there that the larger implications of millenarianism lay in four directions: in their bearing on major revolutionary upheavals; in the continuing presence of messianic themes even where movements are absent; in the millenarian character of so many modern social movements; and, finally, in its hypothesized influence on the rise of modern totalitarianism. Ideological survivals, divorced from their original social context, offer no conclusive evidence of future vitality. But the actual presence of modern movements does, particularly where they occur not in the backcountry but in the heart of urban areas.

That is precisely the case, and it is to the enigma of millenarian activity in a modern setting that this and the concluding chapters will be directed. The anomalies fall into three more or less distinguishable categories: In the first place, there are what one might call "classical" millenarian movements; that is, those that conform in almost all particulars with the predominant rural movements, except that they occur in urban settings. These deviant cases include such conspicuous historical instances as Savonarola's Florence, Bockelson's Münster, and the Fifth Monarchy Men in London, as well as contemporary examples, such as the Black Muslims or the Jamaican Ras Tafari. Second, there is messianic nationalism, the so-called pan- movements so influential in Europe in the nineteenth century as well as the newer, mission-conscious nationalisms of twentieth-century Asia and Africa. Finally, the most dramatic instances of all, we must confront the totalitarian movements of the twentieth century. Nazism, Soviet communism, and Chinese communism have all built great political systems upon millenarian foundations.

The urban anomalies force us to reexamine the character of the city, its vulnerability, and its relationship to a rural hinterland. Is there a species of millenarian movement peculiarly urban in character? What accounts for the rise of millenarianism in the twentieth century? Is the United States, as Peter Farb speculates,[2] on the brink of a wave of millenarian fervor?

Let us begin by examining the two most famous historical cases of urban millenarianism, Münster during the reign of the Anabaptists and Florence under Savonarola. In the first place, both were preindustrial cities. The preindustrial city, lacking inanimate sources of energy, was small and socially rigid. The historical reputation such cities have acquired turns out to be a poor index of their size:

> Preindustrial cities of more than 100,000 have been sparse, at least until the late nineteenth and early twentieth centuries, when they came to be subsidized by industrial societies. Even preindustrial centers with populations between 25,000 and 100,000 have been relatively uncommon. Numerous preindustrial cities of consequence have undoubtedly sheltered little more than 10,000 and perhaps only 5,000 persons. Size alone is never an index of a city's historic role.[3]

To the extent that we employ the term *city* in an undifferentiated way, we superimpose upon historic cases a misleadingly contemporary stereotype. To call Münster and Florence cities in the same sense that we might use the word for contemporary Tokyo or London is to distort reality.

Münster was a member of the Hanseatic League, located just southeast of the Netherlands-Germany border. When the Reformation reached Münster, in 1531, three years before the millenarian phase, the town had a population of about 15,000.[4] Even this figure represented almost double the population of the preceding century.[5] Though small, Münster possessed an unusually influential and cohesive set of guilds. Their rivalry with the town's ecclesiastical rulers constitutes the dominant motif in Münster's history from the latter part of the fifteenth century. The monasteries, free from the regulations which hampered the economic life of the laity, stood as both political and commercial adversaries of the artisans and burghers.[6]

In addition to internal factors, the life of Münster in this period was further complicated by a series of catastrophes which served only to exacerbate social and economic tensions. The attack of the guilds upon the monasteries during the Peasants' War ultimately failed, and the reestablishment of ecclesiastical government in 1530, after a brief period of lay ascendancy, further aggravated social tensions. Unforeseen occurrences made the economic situation worse: A late outbreak of the Black Death in the region and a crop failure, both in 1529, drove up the price of grain for two consecutive years. In 1530 the tax burden rose due to an extraordinary levy to support military action against the westward-driving Turkish Empire.[7] As a relatively well off mercantile town, Münster thus was required to bear a number of unanticipated and uncommonly heavy burdens in the early 1500s.

Heavy though Münster's burdens might have been at this time, they provide only a partial explanation for the massive millenarian upheavals of 1534–35. The missing parts—ideology and the social mechanism for its transmission—also set the town apart from the rest of northwest Germany. The times were bad, too, in the adjacent Netherlands. All manner of disaster—plague, flood, famine, war, and blockade—occurred from 1528–36.[8] The events found their prophet in the person of Melchior Hoffmann, who in 1530 took the leadership of a chiliastic Anabaptist movement. Hoffmann predicted the Second Coming for 1533, although, as luck would have it, he died in prison before the predicted day.[9]

The Reformation finally arrived in Münster with the sudden ascendancy in 1531–33 of a young Lutheran preacher, Bernt Rothmann. His rise, together with unstable conditions in the Netherlands, acted as a magnet upon Melchior Hoffman's Anabaptists. Leaders and followers, the latter artisans from the textile industry, converged on Münster.[10] Rothmann, the darling of the guilds, infused Münster with a fervor which appeared to constitute proof of the Melchiorite prophecy.[11] Thus the activist Anabaptism of Hoffmann came more and more to center upon the town of Münster, in what Ronald Knox has called "a fatal policy of concentration." [12] It is unclear how many millenarians streamed into Münster. Given that some 3,000 Anabaptists were preparing to depart from Amsterdam as the military defeat of Münster drew near,[13] it is fair to assume that the newcomers caused a significant demographic shift. Coupled with converts made within the town, the immigrants turned Münster into an unnatural concentration of revolutionary Anabaptism. By the time the guilds saw the shift toward social radicalism occurring, it was too late to halt.

Münster consequently appears as a town wracked by disaster, small and peculiarly concentrated in population, and host to a powerful chiliastic doctrine. It lacks the heterogeneity that produces diversion and challenge to millenarians in larger urban centers, nor does it possess sufficient resources to buffer against catastrophe. Like many preindustrial cities, it is subject to sudden demographic fluctuations caused by disasters elsewhere.[14] Upheavals in the Netherlands brought to it a restless and suggestible new population. The tightly knit family structure of the preindustrial city was of little consequence in the face of this in-migration.

What, then, of Florence? Certainly, Florence was in every way a much more substantial place, next to which Münster was indeed little more than a large village. The population of Florence during the period of Savonarolan chiliasm (1494–98) appears to have been very near the upper limits for a preindustrial city. The city and suburbs contained between 80,000 and 100,000 people.[15] It had long been a wealthy, powerful, and influential city. Along with the Papacy and a number of other city-states, it dominated Italian politics. However, Florence, like Münster, fell upon difficult times.

Piero de Medici incurred the wrath of Charles VIII of France, who invaded Italy in 1494. When Charles arrived at the Tuscan border, Piero, instead of fighting, bought peace through the surrender of a number of Florentine fortresses and seaports. The infuriated Florentine notables deposed Piero and, in a far from ideal bargaining position, managed to come to their own agreement with Charles.[16] This in itself may appear to be a trivial espisode, yet its impact must be measured against the peculiar corporate self-image of the Florentines.

Florence viewed itself through an image of civic chosenness, both more intense and more clearly articulated than the pride that is commonplace among cities; indeed, Donald Weinstein speaks of it as "the myth of Florence." [17] "In both

popular and sophisticated expression we find not one but two
central themes of civic destiny—the idea of Florence as the
daughter of Rome and the idea of Florence as the center of
rebirth and Christian renewal." [18] The myth of a special
Florentine destiny had received currency since the thirteenth
century, and it gave to the capitulation before the French a
special anguish. The French approach was accordingly read
in the context of a line of prophecies which saw France as an
instrument of divine retribution for Florence's sins.[19]

Belief in a great historical mission undoubtedly gave the
Florentines a sense of separateness and corporate identity
beyond the usual attachments to city and region. The myth
conferred purpose and uniqueness. It legitimized achievements, infused meaning into distress, and offered hope for
eventual vindication. "Apocalyptic prophetism was an available model, and one they [the Florentines] would be likely to
turn to in . . . a time of anguish." [20]

The civic myth functioned in an open, thoroughly respectable, and approved manner. It did, however, have a less
public and far less legitimate aspect. That was the equally
ancient tradition of heresy. From the twelfth century through
the Savonarolan period Florence harbored and occasionally
supported heretics.[21] Such sects as the Fraticelli drew upon
the influential millenarian prophecies of Joachim of Fiore.[22]
The stream of revolutionary messianism that surfaced in
northern Europe before and during the Reformation put
down early and apparently deep roots in Florence, even
though its potential for social and political disruption and
renewal was not immediately apparent.

Why was it that Florence, a relatively populous and
sophisticated commercial center, maintained this identification with heretical belief? Heretical beliefs were originally
and predominantly rural, as we should expect. From the
isolated hinterland, the beliefs of Cathars and Fraticelli,
Waldensians and Adamites, moved gradually to the cities.
There, however, the reception was usually inhospitable. The
machinery of repression, such as the Inquisition, quickly
made heterodoxy unwelcome, and heresy migrated once
again, this time back to remote areas where it might be free

from effective challenge.[23] To the extent that a millenarian
tradition remained alive, it did so, as we have already seen, in
rural areas.

Florence appears to have constituted a strong, somewhat
puzzling exception. The reasons are necessarily speculative
and inadequate: the ineffectiveness of the Inquisition; the
political power of secular commercial groups; and the
proximity to a rural refuge, the March of Ancona.[24] It may
also have been that the very transmutation of millenarian
heterodoxy into a venerated civic myth made the related
heresies more respectable. "In fourteenth- and fifteenth-cen-
tury Florence, a debased Joachimism was the common
property of heretics and of orthodox alike, just as it was the
single common property shared by different heretics." [25] As
"the cult of Florentine greatness" developed, particularly in
the fourteenth century, it drew in more and more of the
eschatological prophecies associated with Christian heresies.

Savonarola, like many millenarian leaders, was less a
creator than a brilliant synthesizer. Working with a vast,
accepted body of doctrine concerning the role Florence was
to play in history, he was able to construct "a single
millenarian vision that was also a program for action." [26] His
message fell upon ears long prepared to hear it.[27]

Is Florence, then, a true exception, proof that millenarianism can gain a powerful following in an urban center? The
answer must be more equivocal than in the case of Münster.
Florence exemplifies both the rule and its possible exceptions.
The city was, by modern standards, small and homogeneous.
Its unusual self-image must have made it appear to its
inhabitants much more an immense village than a cosmopolitan metropolis. Certainly, it drew in millenarian beliefs with a
facility that is perhaps unmatched by other urban centers.
The question why heresy should have been so popular in the
first place and why the civic myth developed lies buried in
unique, multiple historical circumstances. That Florence had
so different a view of itself than other cities is powerful
evidence that the growth of millenarianism within it in
1494–95 was rather a fluke, revealing much about the appeals
Florentines wanted to hear but little about larger urban

receptivities. Florence was still a preindustrial city, small-scale and homogeneous, for all its prominence.

Münster and Florence loom large as the two great examples of cities overtaken by chiliastic expectations. Yet it is instructive to remember that the two sets of events occurred only some forty years apart, in an era unusually given to beliefs in total transformation. Indeed, we should be surprised that urban millenarianism did not occur more often at this time, given the compactness of cities and the prevalence of doctrine. As cities changed character, becoming larger, with mobile, polyglot populations, the possibilities for messianic movements suffered a corresponding decrease.

We should not leave the premodern period, however, without at least some brief consideration of yet a third example: the Fifth Monarchy Men, which flourished briefly in England after the execution of Charles in 1649. The Fifth Monarchists are worth a glance, first, because they were predominantly urban[28] and, second, because the special circumstances of their growth and demise are instructive. The growth of the movement stemmed from a number of factors: Millenarian beliefs were both current and respectable in England up to mid-century. It is noteworthy in this regard that, although the Fifth Monarchists came to be regarded as dangerous revolutionaries by the 1660s, Oliver Cromwell himself remained a "fellow traveler" of the movement until 1653.[29] The millennium was "in the air." In addition, the political success of the Puritan cause raised intense hopes of imminent perfection. Although the Fifth Monarchists lived in cities, principally London, a common source of recruits was the New Model Army. The army provided an extraordinary concentration of the radical and the disaffected; it was in effect a large town without the latter's social and intellectual diversity.[30] The general climate permitted the Fifth Monarchy Men to establish themselves, but it is also important to be aware of the movement's essentially elitist character: it did not seek a mass following and remained quite small.[31] But by the late 1660s the movement had begun to dissolve. After 1649, the millennium did not in fact arrive, and there was the problem, already familiar to us, of prophetic disconfirmation.

By the time Fifth Monarchism had begun, the days of greatest unrest were already over. Fifth Monarchism came after the larger millenarian crest had passed,[32] and, as a result, the Fifth Monarchists were exposed in the 1660s to the quite effective attacks of a more settled society.

One factor preserved the possibility of urban millenarianism into the modern era. That factor was the very incompleteness with which urbanization took place, even within the nominal confines of cities. The quintessential industrial city counts among its chief characteristics a fluid, achievement-oriented class system, diffused social power, the conjugal family, complex division of labor, highly trained specialists, mass literacy, and permissive norms.[33] Yet how rarely have these traits come close to being maximized. Anomalies have persisted, and millenarianism has occasionally sprung up in these enclaves of contradiction.

The chief manner in which a totally mobile, polyglot urban-industrial society has been thwarted has been through compulsory or voluntary ghettoization. The concentration of homogeneous populations has produced virtual urban villages. Sometimes by force, sometimes by voluntary association, individuals of like backgrounds have formed well-bounded enclaves within more heterogeneous cities. Urban millenarianism, where it has occurred at all, has originated here.

The Ras Tafari sect clings to a particularly wretched bit of land on the outskirts of Kingston, Jamaica.[34] The slums of Rio de Janeiro have appeared to breed relatively successful movements, although significantly the most successful left the city for the countryside around 1960.[35] But the most sustained tradition of urban millenarianism in the twentieth century has taken place in the black ghettoes of the United States. Sects have come and gone since World War I. Two in particular—the movements organized around Marcus Garvey and Elijah Muhammed—have reached high levels of public visibility.

There is evidence of a messianic tradition reaching far back into the history of the American black community. The conception of a black messianic leader begins in the nineteenth century, and such early black resistance leaders as Denmark Vessey and Nat Turner were aware of it.[36] At a later point what Essien-Udom calls "the Nationalist tradition" [37] passed to the cities, where in recent times its leaders have included Garvey, Noble Drew Ali, and Muhammed. The recent history of millenarian activity among American blacks manifests curious and interesting connections between the American separatist movements and millenarianism in the West Indies. Garvey, Stokely Carmichael, and Malcolm X came either from the West Indies or from households of West Indian heritage.[38] Millenarian movements began among Jamaican blacks in the late eighteenth century.[39] Indeed, the lines of influence were if anything reciprocal. Not only may Jamaican movements have molded American black leaders, but in at least one conspicuous case a single leader created movements in both. The Jamaican Ras Tafari movement was an offshoot of the Universal Negro Improvement Association, the back-to-Africa organization built by Marcus Garvey in 1914–25.[40] The American Garveyites combined nationalist aspirations with economic organization. Garvey grafted a strong emphasis on organization to his original vision of "uniting all the Negro peoples of the world into one great body to establish a country and Government absolutely their own . . . a new world of black men, not peons, serfs, dogs and slaves, but a nation of sturdy men making their impress upon civilization and causing a new light to dawn upon the human race." [41] The Ras Tafari movement itself began in 1930. Its return-to-Africa theme, however, took a far more exotic form than that adopted by Garvey and his American followers. The Ras Tafarians of West Kingston see the agency of redemption not in modern economic organization but in the emperor of Ethiopia, whom they believe will one day miraculously transport them back to Africa.[42] The movement continues, and in 1960, under the influence of black separatists from the United States, a group of Ras Tafarians made an abortive attempt to seize power through an armed insurrection.[43]

There are, then, contemporary exceptions to the rule of strictly rural millenarianism. The ghetto or culturally distinctive enclave can breed messianic dreams of its own. But by any indicator urban movements are indeed the exception. The city has remained basically hostile, and it may be well at this point to return once more to the structural reasons for this.

It is a commonplace to think of interdependency as a form of social fragility. Stress is often assumed to have more serious consequences where a unit that bears the stress is dependent upon others. In the early twentieth century, for example, a world war was regarded as inconceivable because the interdependence of nations had so broadened interests and vulnerabilities. Interdependence can be viewed as the distribution of risks; but, as in insurance, pooled risks can also diminish costs. This is a matter of particular importance within the context of disaster and its consequences. The more complex a social system, the greater the interdependence among its members. This interdependence has two consequences: In the first place, it does force individuals and groups to become parties to the catastrophes of others. Disaster can have a spillover effect. The problem with the 1929 stock market crash was precisely that it proved to be impossible to segregate. Pollution, precisely because it affects such public goods as air and water, crosses functional and political boundaries. Interdependence involves the involuntary sharing of fates; the troubles of each are transmitted along lines of contact and influences to others not immediately involved. This side of interdependence has been the one most noted, but a second aspect exists—the more complex a social system, the less vulnerable it is to stresses that attack its parts. A complex society builds in enough redundancy so that vital functions can be transferred to undamaged units. The more complex the relationships of interdependence, the less dependent single units or the whole community may be on any other parts. Thus, while consequences may be rapidly diffused, they are also diluted. Family tragedies that might deeply affect a kinship-oriented village, corporate bankruptcies that could destroy a company town, price fluctuations that could cripple a one-crop economy—these are the sorts of potential disasters against which urban-industrial society provides buffers. Size, complexity, and diversity provide alternative resources and, while linking each to all, diminish the degree to which any single link can jeopardize the entire community.

Urban millenarianism can take place when incomplete urbanization leaves some groups relatively more vulnerable than others, cut off in homogeneous enclaves from both external stresses and supports. There are of course many groups whose life in the modern city has been characterized by separateness, yet which have not been vulnerable to disaster. Indeed, the wealthy and privileged are at least as likely to live separate lives as the downtrodden. Immigrant groups, too, have maintained uniform residence patterns for cultural reasons. The poor, among whom millenarianism is most common, have not been the sole occupants of ghettoes, broadly defined.

Millenarianism has been so uncommon among more privileged groups, even where they have separated themselves, simply because their resources have been so much greater. Isolation entails the acceptance of greater, not lesser, risks, but those risks are sometimes willingly assumed where there is a high degree of wealth, skills, organization, or stress tolerance. The wealthy Manhattan urbanite can hardly be more separated in his high-rise than the black ghetto dweller. The black's isolation in an impoverished ghetto renders him vulnerable to a multiplying series of personal and communal disasters: unemployment, disease, malnutrition, drugs, crime, familial dissolution. The wealthy white is just as isolated but can afford whatever goods and services are necessary to keep the stresses at bay, whether it is the ability to purchase the same foods when prices go up or the ability to hire doormen and guards to perform social control functions.

Where cultural differences form the basis for residential patterning, a culturally self-conscious group often builds up and institutionalizes the division. This we have referred to earlier through the use of Bernard Siegel's term *defensive structuring*. Here a group deliberately turns inward and carefully regulates its transactions with the outside world. This kind of existence, exemplified by the Amish or the *shtetl* Jews, is an uncertain one. It is a strategy engaged in by those who lack the means for a direct confrontation with the environment and who draw into themselves sufficiently so that they can maintain cultural autonomy at the sufferance of that environment.[44] It should not be surprising that groups

that practice defensive structuring either do so in rural areas
(e.g. the Amish and Pueblo Indians); in the artificial environments of large institutions (e.g. the Black Muslims in pris-
ons); or in well-defined urban ghettoes (again, the Black
Muslims are the leading example). Nor should it be surprising
that urban groups often either dissolve under urban pressures
(e.g. the Haight-Ashbury hippie groups) or flee the city (e.g.
hippies who establish rural communes or the New York
Hasidic Jews who have increasingly begun to establish
separate new towns). The same pressures that militate against
the formation and survival of millenarian groups press
against all separatist experiments.

The city is a bulwark against disaster. Only upheavals of
very great magnitude seriously disrupt the functioning of a
large city. Those who wish or are compelled to lead a
ghettoized existence become prey to more limited forms of
stress. The city at large somehow manages to tolerate flood,
pollution, recession, and disease. The old urban terrors,
plague and fire, no longer menace. Total war and (perhaps)
pollution have taken their place, but in the running competi-
tion between new threats and even newer forms of defense,
only total nuclear war really seems able to definitely breach
urban defenses. Thus as the city has extended itself and either
assimilated, forced out, or segregated those who wished to
live separate lives, the prospect of urban millenarianism has
grown correspondingly dim.

The wave of urbanization which so marks this century
seems to have made millenarianism a casualty of the age. The
city, insofar as it constitutes a bulwark against disaster,
protects the great mass of individuals from precisely that state
of doubt and suggestibility in which chiliasm flourishes. The
individual, in the normal round of daily life, to be sure
remains prey to all manner of tragedies—disease, the death of
loved ones, unemployment, and mortality itself. But these
remain personal disasters, distributed more or less at random
through the population, and hence they do not become the
flash points for communal upheaval. Only as desires and
circumstances place coherent groups apart does the potential
for urban millenarianism remain. And, as we have seen, these
conditions constitute the exception, for only rarely do all

these factors coincide: disaster vulnerability, population homogeneity and compactness, insulation from the environment, millenarian ideology, the occasion for disaster, and a leader. The rarity of this concatenation helps to explain why millenarianism has remained so largely rural.

Millenarianism has not swept cities since the preindustrial age. The Münsters and Florences lie in the past. The city intermittently shelters millenarian dreams only to the extent that it also shelters quasi-villages within itself. Yet if the city as such has failed to provide nurturance for millenarianism, can we say the same about nations as a whole? It seems to me impossible to make the claim that the locus of millenarianism has shifted from countryside to city. But can one not make the claim that its scale has been radically altered, that in the twentieth century it has ceased to be the eccentricity of the backlands and become a great force which sweeps up entire nations? This is essentially the claim made by Kedourie that messianism is the root of nationalism and by Talmon and Cohn that it is at the root of totalitarianism.

Such claims raise notoriously difficult questions of causation. How seriously ought we to take ideology as a cause of behavior? Inasmuch as both hypotheses imply a kind of ongoing "millenarian underground," do they not come to resemble the conspiracy theories of millenarians themselves? An equally serious question concerns the rural-urban distinction we have been discussing. If cities have proven so resistant to millenarianism, why should entire industrialized, urbanized societies prove any more receptive? Can we affirm the latter without invalidating the former?

In any case, there is always the danger that we are the victims of our own metaphors. Nationalism may be very much *like* millenarianism in some respects, but that does not necessarily mean the two are identical. Some millenarian sects do in retrospect appear to prefigure totalitarianism, so much do the two resemble each other, but that does not provide any basis for asserting that the one caused the other. It is always a cruel dilemma to intuitively recognize a connection yet be unable to fully articulate the linkage to those who fail to share the intuition. Granted that millenarianism seems to stimulate insights into the origins of large-scale political transformations, it remains to bring these insights to the level of conscious, reasoned discourse.

Let us begin at what seems to be a relatively nonproblematical starting point: There is substantial and increasing evidence of a temporal continuity in Western millenarian thought. One can trace its turnings and surfacings with a fair degree of accuracy over a span of centuries. The ideas themselves appear and reappear in books, pamphlets, and speeches; and it has fallen to historians of ideas to try and piece together coherent accounts of their development. It ought to be clear at once that a major roadblock in the way of a proper evaluation of millenarian ideas is the fact that we know much too little about the link between ideas and actions. It is one thing to know the existence of a particular book at a particular time, even to know that it was widely read, and quite another thing to know whether and what effect it had on human behavior. For example, the principal locus of Western millenarian ideas, at least until the nineteenth century, lay in Judeo-Christian religious traditions. Since these traditions flowed with unbroken continuity through Western history, it may be said that millenarianism too has always been present. At a very general level this of course is true; these ideas always found some expression, however nominal. Yet in the terms in which this inquiry has been cast, the merely nominal expression of vague chiliastic hopes counts for very little. The incorporation of messianic longings into the liturgy or into the exegesis of sacred writings need not give rise to millenarian social movements, nor shake the social order. Indeed, the nominal expression of millenarian hopes can actually buttress existing institutions. To the extent that a ruler can associate his own power with traditional hopes for salvation, he possesses a strong bulwark against opponents. Up until 1641 the British monarchy was able to exploit millenarianism to support its own claims. The king was the "Godly Prince" that had been promised in the Book of Revelation.[45]

Consequently, millenarian ideas per se lend themselves to manifold, often contradictory uses. At least in the West, they have always been in the air, more prominent in some periods than in others, but never wholly absent. The appearance of millenarian movements requires some ideology as a necessary condition, but, as we have seen, ideas alone are not sufficient. Some kind of millenarianism always existed in the West, simply by virtue of the pervasive character of Christian theological categories. What did not always exist was an interpretation of traditional beliefs as promising imminent, this-worldly, collective transformation. These attributes have informed all of the movements we have considered, and they are among the key identifying features employed by students of millenarian movements. There is nothing nominal or conventional about this conception of the millennium; indeed, it was often associated with outright heresy. It lived a subterranean existence with periods of suppression punctuated by spasmodic uprisings.

What then has been the relationship between these two forms of millenarianism, the one bound up with respectable forms of belief and placing change in some supramundane future, the other heterodox and looking to an immediate terrestrial transformation? In the first place, the former provided the raw material for the latter. Millenarian prophecy, again limited to the West, after all grew out of a set of almost universally accepted canonical writings. The twists of interpretation, not the sources themselves, led millenarianism into disrepute. Second, the tradition of millenarian revolution was often transmuted back into something acceptable and widespread. We saw this happen in the case of Florence, where Joachimism became a building block for the civic mythology. On a much broader scale, the very idea of progress itself can be traced back, as Ernest Tuveson has done,[46] to slightly disreputable millenarian antecedents. Third, in times of multiplying disasters the old ways of seeing the world prove less and less adequate, and the messianic leader has strong incentives for modifying and embellishing conventional ideas. Indeed, the prophet is a synthesizer who takes ideas that already have currency and shapes them to meet the exigencies of social and cultural crisis.

While revolutionary messianism maintained this fluctuating relationship with more widely accepted doctrines, its survival depended upon more uncertain social factors. "Respectable" millenarianism always had some adherents; in any case, it was too much a part of orthodox beliefs to disappear, even when doctrinal tendencies of the moment caused it to be de-emphasized. Revolutionary messianism, hounded as it was by those who saw themselves threatened by it, dependent for support upon unpredictable catastrophes, survived only among small groups of believers. These had to be sufficiently steadfast to see it through the drought periods of social stability and prosperity, the times when no messiah was required. This kind of transmission, dependent upon people we would ordinarily regard as cranks, was obviously an uncertain enterprise.

Peter Worsley refers to these nuclei of believers as "coteries," which suggests something a good deal smaller and less organized than "movements." [47] Because they were few, because they were eccentric, and because they feared suppression, we know very little about millenarian coteries. Nor was there much disposition to find out, since they hardly constituted the accepted stuff of history. We return here again to a motif mentioned many times previously, the fact that millenarianism stands outside the mainstream of accepted history-worthy events. Christopher Hill, in his study of belief in Antichrist, has occasion to quote Dean Inge, to the effect that "the historian . . . is a natural snob." [48] In any case, conceptions of what was interesting at an early time need not conform to the interests of a later generation. "What seems to us a blind alley in human thought was for a hundred and fifty years after the Reformation—and for most of the fifteen hundred years before it . . . —full of life and significance." [49] Whether the subject is Antichrist, apocalypse, or millennium, we find it difficult to see what might be worth studying in matters so removed from contemporary interests.

The matter of tracing the line of millenarian agitation, whether in the form of coteries or large-scale movements, is obviously a venture far beyond the scope of this study. Others have already taken some large steps: Jeffrey Burton Russell and Norman Cohn for the Middle Ages; William Lamont, Christopher Hill, and Ernest Tuveson for the seventeenth century; George Rosen, J. L. Talmon, and E. J. Hobsbawm for the eighteenth and nineteenth centuries. The task is neither easy nor complete. The process of socialization to millenarianism across generations, described in chapter four, lacks public visibility and must often be inferred from the tedious business of examining family histories.

In addition, beginning in roughly the seventeenth century, the terms of reference shifted. The language of political and social dissent became, along with the rest of society, increasingly secular. It ceased to be necessary to convey hopes for sudden transformation in exclusively religious terms. The religious origins of millenarian doctrine make it easy to trace their path as long as these origins continue to be manifested. When, however, the concept of the millennium is transmuted into nonreligious terms, it is often regarded as having disappeared entirely. Thus, Peter Worsley, otherwise most insightful, is clearly in error when he asserts that "after the Reformation . . . with the defeat of the activist left wing, millenarism became more and more passive, no longer supported by the most forward-looking elements of society, but becoming more and more associated with the most backward elements." [50] What Worsley means is that the religious idiom was increasingly confined to the unsecularized elements of society, while those most in tune with advancing industry, science, and technology adopted a nonreligious language.

We are now very much at the crux of the matter, the point of intersection of a number of themes already touched upon separately: the rural locus, the religious-secular division, the growth of nationalism, the continuity of millenarian traditions, and the allegedly "prepolitical" or "archaic" character of chiliastic movements. Worsley and Tilley regard millenarian movements simply as way stations on the road to more rational forms of political protest—nationalist movements for the former, interest groups and political parties for the latter.[51] According to them, a society outgrows chiliasm as it might, in its maturity, slough off magic or animal sacrifice. There is, to be sure, a large measure of truth in this. Everything we have said up to this point concerning rural origins points to the manner in which urban-industrial society has left these movements behind. They seem to be both a product and a casualty of modernization and growth. But before adopting Worsley's position wholesale, we must first face the fact that millenarian doctrines need not be expressed in exclusively religious terms. That is the major complication. The idea of total, sudden, imminent, mundane transformation which will abruptly place man in an ideal society is not the property solely of religious thinkers. It is closely related to the secular tradition of utopian speculation as well.[52] It lies at the heart of all revolutions, at least for that inner circle of zealots whom Crane Brinton calls "the extremists." [53]

Let me now attempt to sort matters out a bit more clearly: We have seen that millenarian ideas gradually become secularized and diffused through society. The notion of divine intervention in history gradually became the redemption of man's condition through science and technology, in a word, *progress*. Another aspect of millenarianism which became secularized and diffused was its social vision, the disappearance of want and hierarchy, the leveling of distinctions, the elevation of the downtrodden ("the last shall be first"). Elie Kedourie argues that social agitation in support of these ideals came to the fore with the French Revolution, a position consistent with that of J. L. Talmon.[54]

> The disreputable political style of medieval millennialism erupted, before the French Revolution, only in rare, albeit notable, episodes; it was generally suppressed into the obscure world of heretical sects. But from the French Revolution onward this style has become increasingly respectable, has indeed shared its respectability with the secular idea of progress, and what we may call *sans-cullotisme* has become a striking element in the European political tradition. . . .
> . . . the mainspring of nationalism in Asia and Africa is the same secular millennialism which had its rise and development in Europe.[55]

Like any ideas that are broadly transmitted, currency produces dilution and corruption. The more widely secular counterparts of religious millenarianism were known and accepted, the more they lost in purity and rigor. Inevitable human progress came to mean the gradual amelioration of social and physical ills, whose final conquest was reserved for an unknown time in the distant future. In like manner, concepts of revolution and national mission came to signify developments of considerably less finality and inclusiveness than the total visions from which each sprang. Revolution ceased to be a once-and-for-all event and came to be taken as a lengthy process, its culmination reserved for a veiled future.[56] From there, by metaphorical extension, *revolution* was attached to any change thought sufficiently noteworthy to require special mention. National mission, too, was diluted to include any aspiration for autonomy; far different from Dostoevski's assertion in 1880 that "to become . . . truly Russian means to provide the solution of European contradictions . . . to receive with brotherly love all brothers into his Russian soul, and perhaps even finally to be able to utter the word of universal great harmony." [57]

The more widely millenarian beliefs are known, the less likely that they will either retain their original characteristics or become the bases for action. We have seen the distortions that can take place, all in the direction of reducing the emphasis upon sudden, dramatic change. The problem is akin to that which faces movements themselves. A choice must be made between small numbers of the highly committed or large numbers of nominal adherents. *Destiny, fate,* or *mission,* when they become common property, connote a general upward movement of the historical curve, not a cause that demands total sacrifice and commitment.

Eschatological terminology has pervaded statements of American foreign policy since the early days of the Republic. But the sense of the unique American world mission was often as nominal for Americans as the Second Coming for many Christians. It has had to survive in a competitive intellectual atmosphere, where antithetical tendencies strive for dominance. The redemptive role of the United States in world affairs, while of venerable origins, has been counterbalanced, indeed usually overbalanced, by a tendency toward isolationism and withdrawal. Millenarian themes have been able to assert themselves only on rare occasions. "The generally less powerful idea, it would seem, was that of active messianism; yet, like a recessive gene, in the right situation it could become dominant. In the years immediately preceding

American entry into each of the great wars, there was a period of passionate non-involvement." [58]

The true millenarian movement is distinguished by the totality of its members' commitment. Competing tendencies are banished; there is an identity of beliefs, a common cutting off from the old life. This is no mere rhetorical enterprise. The rhetoric of the millennium keeps the idea alive and makes it possible for movements to coalesce around it. But the translation of ideas into organization and action demand, as we have seen, the rare environment of multiple disaster.

If we look at the origins of millenarianism in politics, we can see this in operation. The great revolutions do indeed articulate and frequently act upon messianic ideas. But that is precisely because they arise out of disordered societies. When a revolution takes power, the millenarian rhetoric survives, just as, on the religious level, millenarian doctrines survive the transition from sect to church. We have had occasion to touch upon this process in chapter four, in the context of disconfirmed prophecies, and it is part of the larger problem of adjusting expectations to realities. The inhibitions against totally abandoning old aspirations are apparently sufficiently great so that ritual deference to those aspirations survives long after changed circumstances have rendered them irrelevant.

Norman Cohn has asserted that two great revolutions, nazism and Soviet communism, were in fact active millenarian movements. He regards them as lineal descendants of the medieval-Reformation tradition which he chronicles in *The Pursuit of the Millennium*. To view it with any kind of completeness would require an effort far more extensive than the one here. But I do want to try and demonstrate, first, that Cohn's intuition stands upon a solid foundation and, second, that much the same approach might be taken with non-Western revolutions (e.g. the Chinese Civil War).

If we probe the Cohn hypothesis in the light of earlier chapters, we find, first, that bolshevism, nazism, and Chinese communism reached power only after lengthy disaster prologues. All three societies underwent prolonged stress experiences of the kind earlier discussed in the section on multiple disasters (chapter three). Second, in each, prominent millenarian motifs were already available. Third, each was led by a charismatic prophet-figure capable of molding existing doctrine to the needs of the moment.

Where one places the onset of disaster for Russia is an arguable point: as early as the assassination of Alexander II in 1881 or as late as the beginning of the Russo-Japanese War in 1904. In any case, by 1904–05 a staggering series of upheavals and deprivations began, which continued with only brief respites until the February Revolution. The period started with a humiliating military defeat in 1905 and an abortive revolt. Crop failures occurred in 1906–07. Systematic terror in the cities followed the 1905 revolution. Governmental administration decayed. The onset of World War I in 1914, with its attendant inflation, pushed administration to and beyond the point of breakdown.[59] The unusually bitter winter of 1916–17, when food was rationed,[60] and the collapse of the Russian counterattack in late 1916 left the Czarist regime crippled beyond repair.

As we shall see shortly, the impact of these events did not lie solely in the material deprivations they inflicted. Rather, they must be gauged in terms of traditional Russian conceptions of world role and mission. The years between 1904 and 1917 were filled with evidence that history was not prepared to validate the messianic pretensions of the old regime. Indeed, any analysis of Russian history in millenarian terms is complicated by the fact that the rise of one millenarian movement—Soviet communism—follows directly upon the demise of a society only slightly less chiliastic in its view of history. The old regime is itself a kind of failed millenarian movement, its prophecies of the Third Rome undermined by events. Communism can be seen as a successor movement, substituting a new but compatible set of prophetic expectations.

The disaster prologue in Germany is, if anything, even clearer. World War I in its later phases inflicted great hardships upon the civilian population. Military defeat was followed, of course, by the whiplash effects first of inflation, then of depression. From the time that the Allied blockade began to be felt, in 1916,[61] to the accession of the Nazis to power in 1933, German society underwent a series of upheavals comparable to those in Russia from 1904 to 1917.

We see the concept of nostalgia for the disaster utopia operative in the composition of the Nazi party itself. Almost half of the "political leaders of the National Socialist party took active part in warfare during the period 1914–21." [62] What were taken from the war years were not recollections of rigidity or hierarchy: "What remained was a memory of heroism and comradeship under the most dangerous conditions. A yearning for the comradeship of the trenches and the commonly experienced dangers of the war and of post-war battles of the private armies prompted many former soldiers and those who sought soldierly life to join the National Socialist party." [63]

The economic dislocations of the interwar period were greatly exacerbated by demographic trends. The German population grew progressively younger in composition from about 1880 and reached its peak of youthfulness in the early 1930s. By the time the Depression struck, the labor market was glutted with young people, who made up the largest potential work force in German history.[64]

In Germany, too, events cannot be separated from the interpretations made of them. Here, as well, existing millenarian beliefs made the realities of defeat and poverty all the more galling. Traditional expectations of future greatness left little room for adaptation to the rigors of the present.

Disaster is no stranger to the history of China. Indeed, by one count, in the period between 206 B.C. and 1936 China suffered 1,035 droughts and 1,037 floods.[65] What set the twentieth century apart from the general run of natural calamities? In the first place, we have seen that events need not qualify as "acts of God" to be counted as disasters; men make them almost as often. In the second place, revolutionary activity in the twentieth century stands at the end of a process of upheaval and disintegration immense even by Chinese standards.

There is no need to recapitulate the events connected with the Western penetration of China in the nineteenth and twentieth centuries. Whatever might have occurred in the past could be assimilated to a view of the cosmos in which even floods and droughts had their place. The political ascendancy of barbarians was somewhat more difficult to deal with. The Manchus, much like the Romanoffs, did not suffer defeat at the hands of insurrectionists as much as they collapsed of their own weight.

The rise of the Chinese Republic in 1912 did not, however, produce stability, growth, or improvement. During the era of warlordism, from 1916 to 1928, "the multitudinous alliances, counteralliances, struggles, and open wars among these factions ravaged China, year in and year out, almost without interruption." [66] While the country as a whole passed through the turmoil of endemic conflict, famine, and, later, Japanese occupation, the Chinese Communists suffered a uniquely separate disaster of their own. That disaster was the Long March (1934–36) to take them out of reach of the Nationalists. Even more than the Nazis, the Chinese Communists have looked back upon the Long March for the stuff of legend, the disaster utopia of total community.

Russia, Germany, and China thus experienced prolonged periods of multiple disasters which preceded the full emergence of revolutionary messianism. Preexisting splinter groups—Worsley's "coteries"—could only claim a mass following under the impact of such catastrophic events. But, as we have seen, disaster alone is insufficient, for a message of imminent salvation must fall upon ears already prepared to hear and understand it. Thus we must now turn to the climate of ideas in which each revolution developed.

Cohn's hypothesis asserts that the messianic character of Soviet communism derives from the millenarian character of Marx's thought and the ready availability of millenarian ideas in Marx's society. There is a good measure of truth to this. The early Marx, up to 1848, utilized a distinctly prophetic style to envision an imminent and perfected future. The environment in which he wrote was, following on the promise of the French Revolution, fully supportive of such prophecies of transformation. "No period before or after has experienced so luxurious a flowering of Utopian schemes purporting to offer a coherent, complete and final solution to the problem of social evil." [67]

The old concept of a slow, smooth flow of historical time

had been shattered in 1789. The sense of stability, continuity, and predictability had been altered. As George Steiner comments: "We lack histories of the internal time-sense, of the changing beat in men's experience of the rhythms of perception. But we do have reliable evidence that those who lived through the 1790s and the first decade and a half of the nineteenth century, and who could recall the tenor of life under the old dispensation, felt that time itself and the whole enterprise of consciousness had formidably accelerated." [68] It is no wonder that in such a cultural milieu it became commonplace to conceive history as disjointed and thus capable of great jumps, away from a now meaningless status quo toward a moment of final human fulfillment. Belief in a "religion of History" [69] became possible.

In time, belief in salvation through history migrated eastward from France. "The original ideology of political Messianism wandered eastwards, and away from its homeland spread as the creed of alien and distant civilizations, sharing thus the fate of other great religions, Christianity and Buddhism, which failed to be accepted by their begetters, yet won dominance over vast continents outside the countries of their birth." [70] The idea is simple and appealing: Marxism, as a millenarian ideology, is nurtured in France and Germany during the nineteenth century, fails to achieve political success in either, but is at last adopted in the East by the least likely of potential converts.

Appealing though this may be, other factors were at work in Russia itself. They suggest, first, that Marxism was not brought into an alien situation and, second, that its acceptance and modification owe much to indigenous millenarian ideas. At the most visible level, Russian Orthodox and Slavophil thought already attributed to Russia a preeminent world role: it was through Russia, in some form, that humanity would achieve fulfillment.[71] The Orthodox church, under monastic leadership, gave definitive form to a belief in Holy Russia as the Third and Final Rome.[72] At this point, theological dogma and Russian nationalism are inextricably interwoven.

Yet there was a pre-Bolshevik millenarianism in Russia even richer and more complex than that suggested by the doctrine of the Third Rome. The problem of *how* the Russian role was to be fulfilled created a line of heterodox, often millenarian movements at the margins of the Orthodox church, in much the same manner as millenarian heresies flourished at the edges of Catholicism and Protestantism in the West. They began in the seventeenth century, in opposition to Patriarch Nikon's reforms, and continued into the twentieth. The so-called Raskolniki schismatics, made up of many sects, sought to recover and intensify messianic leadership, where the church itself appeared irretrievably corrupted.[73]

To the extent that church and tsar were fused, religious and political dissent were inseparable. A threat to one institution jeopardized the other. The heretics of the seventeenth and eighteenth centuries laid the foundations for the revolutionary messianists of the nineteenth. The perceived corruption of the church yielded to the greater corruption when Westernizing Czars destroyed native Russian institutions. Thus come the early revolutionary and anarchist groups: Dekabristi, Zapadniki, Slavophili, Pocveniki, Vostocniki, Narodniki.[74] Each sought to revivify the Russian messianic mission, to redirect energies toward a concept of salvation grown formalized.

Marxism, as articulated by the Bolsheviks, was but another proposed solution for a very old problem. Under the impact of the early twentieth-century disasters already referred to, this new, secularized concept of communal salvation took hold. It did so not simply by virtue of its Marxist utopianism, but because it was Marxism at once Russified and implanted in a situation where salvationist visions were known and accepted responses to crisis. Thus a convergence occurred between Marxism and traditional Russian messianic expectations. In this convergence process, charismatic leadership, first of Lenin and later of Stalin, played an essential mediating function. The role of Supreme Leader and the acceptance of Russian nationalism represent end results of this adaptation to indigenous institutions and values.[75] The rise of the Soviet regime, far from appearing as an importation, struck roots among a people habituated to chiliastic thought. That Marx's millenarian vision itself derived from the culture of Western Europe was simply an additional complexity; it neither determined bolshevism's success, nor was it the sole source of its eschatology. The revolution was both a definitive break with tradition and tradition's culmination:

> To most of the sectarians, after hundreds of years of fervent praying, longing and struggling for, the radical and violent destruction of the corrupt state church and Antichrist's rulership, stubbornly prophesied by many charismatic virtuosi, appeared to be finally actualized. Their basic religious doctrinal tenets seemed to be put in practice by the new rulership. Even if their practice seemed anti-religious, this had happened many times before when the newly radicalized messianism accused the old of failure, betrayal of messianic purposes or inability to deliver the messianic promise. . . . Diffused through several centuries the religious expectations of the millennial kingdom . . . helped at least in part to facilitate the initial success and legitimacy of the new power structure in 1917.[76]

The situation in Germany was at once similar and far more complex. The millenarian legacy was there as well, but the absence of a central institutional focus comparable to the Orthodox church makes its historical development much more difficult to trace. The Nazi symbolism itself reproduces with astonishing fidelity the idiom of late medieval messianism: The "Thousand Year Reich" is the literal millennium itself. The "Third Reich" echoes Joachim of Fiore's Third Age. The phrase was popularized in the book of the same name by Arthur Moeller van den Bruck (1923), first entitled *The Third Way*.[77] Van den Bruck sought explicitly to revive the concept of the new age expressed centuries earlier in German millenarianism.[78] The concept of an evil Jewish conspiracy was also a staple of medieval millenarians, from the Flagellants to Emico of Leiningen and the Master of Hungary.[79]

Yet where are the connecting links to span the medieval and modern periods? In the first place, there was a good deal of conscious medievalism in the Nazi movement. Like so many millenarians, the National Socialists looked back upon a golden age, in this case the mythical world of the medieval German town apotheosized in Hitler's favorite opera, *Die Meistersinger*. There was nothing unique in this idealization, for it had already been fully expressed by Riehl and Lagarde in the nineteenth century.[80] However distorted the resulting conception of history, this conscious reversion to a romanticized past brought renewed contact with the obscure world of medieval chiliasm.

It might be added parenthetically that the Soviet and Chinese revolutions, too, have involved complex new attitudes toward the past. Marxists have maintained an ambivalent relationship with older millenarian revolutions. There has been a natural tendency to seek political and doctrinal forebears as evidence of an inevitable historical process. At the same time, care must be taken to distinguish past from present, lest similarity diminish the necessary uniqueness of *the* Revolution. European socialists, notably Engels and Kautsky, were absorbed in the restudy of Thomas Muntzer, the Münster Anabaptists, and the Taborites. In the same manner, Chinese Communist historians look back with mixed feelings to the Taipings.[81]

There is little need to deal at length with the apocalyptic character of Nazi thought, particularly the fixation upon a Jewish conspiracy. The endemic character of European anti-Semitism meant that essentially the same ideas current in the Middle Ages were transmitted intact to the modern period, as Norman Cohn demonstrates in his history of *The Protocols of the Elders of Zion*.[82] Folklore, works of art, religious beliefs, and patterns of speech made the "diabolization" of the Jew a virtually continuous theme in Western thought. By the 1870s this cultural predisposition was finally converted into political anti-Semitism, affecting political rhetoric and party structures in France, Germany, and Austria.[83]

Thus a number of tendencies in nineteenth-century German thought pointed toward an essentially millenarian conception of the world; divided between good and evil forces, between a perfect past and a blemished present, awaiting only some unknown catalyst in order for the perfection of the past to be dramatically inserted into the present. Indeed, German

social and political life from the 1880s on may be viewed as a
search for the organizational form that might accomplish this
objective. A number were tried and discarded: the youth
movements, utopian colonies, pan-German organizations.
The Nazi party, bureaucratically organized yet charismati-
cally led, served as the final point of fusion for these trends.

Nazi political and social doctrines were presented in a
sufficiently unsystematic form so that it is easy to think of the
movement as devoid of ideology. The only work with any
claim to providing a systematic statement, Alfred Rosenberg's *The Myth of the Twentieth Century* (1930), was not even
read by Hitler himself.[84] The doctrines arose out of an
ephemeral world of crank pedantry and pamphleteering.
Hitler appears to have owed his anti-Semitic views as much to
the pamphlets of the former monk, Lanz von Liebenfels, as to
Richard Wagner or Houston Stewart Chamberlain.[85] Here,
too, we can see the charismatic figure able to bring together
ideas which already have wide currency, but doing so in a
novel and compelling manner. There was little that Hitler
said that had not already been said many times before. The
intellectual origins of nazism provide such fertile ground for
historians of ideas precisely because the components of
nazism were themselves so strikingly unoriginal. The conceptions of a mission for the German *volk,* of a Jewish
conspiracy, and of a glorious past to be recovered were there
already.

One cannot speak of a strong indigenous Chinese millenarian tradition. Rebellions were common in China, but they
were precisely that: rebellions, not revolutions. The basic
framework of institutions and the view of the cosmos
continued to be accepted by rebels themselves, at least until
the Taipings. Yet by the middle of the nineteenth century the
pattern had begun to change. The so-called Taiping Rebellion was the clearest indicator.[86] In terms of purely internal
developments, the grievances of the peasantry mounted, the
elite of literati competed for the limited posts in a corrupt
system, and administrative efficiency declined.[87] On the
external side, Western penetration posed a radical challenge
which traditional Confucian doctrines could not meet. There

was simply no adequate explanation for the Western presence and its power:

> The "evil" wrought by foreign encroachment, by imperialism if you will, was to present a permanent threat to the Chinese political equilibrium that could not be overcome within the parameters of the traditional society. Compounding the increasingly difficult internal task of squaring existing institutions with basic social values . . . external foreign pressure introduced two additional disequilibrating elements. It induced a questioning of the values themselves, of the viability of the traditional society as a whole, and it brought in its train new uncompromising ideologies whose irresoluble conflict resulted in a prolonged and fatal instability.[88]

This is part and parcel of the nineteenth- and twentieth-century cycle of disasters already referred to. But the crisis of the mid-nineteenth century was not fatal to traditional Chinese culture. Beginning about 1860—that is, contemporaneous with the Taiping Rebellion—traditional values made one final attempt to reassert themselves, in the so-called T'ung-chih Restoration.[89] Finally, all but inevitable decay was thus held back another half century.

Though the Taiping Rebellion failed to dislodge the Manchu Dynasty, its bloody consequences and its force of example made it a common point of reference for both incumbents and insurgents thereafter. The rebels served as an example and inspiration for Sun Yat-sen.[90] Subsequently, the Kuomintang regarded itself initially as the Taipings' heir. But by 1932 Chiang Kai-shek had reversed himself: it was the Restoration leaders he desired to emulate, not their Taiping adversaries.[91] Now in power and faced with more radical opponents, the Kuomintang identified with the goals and tactics of the anti-Taiping forces. For the Communists, particularly after they gained power, the Taipings were a source of endless fascination. They prefigure the present and, by virtue of their failure, also provide a measure of edification.

Traditional Chinese history moved in cycles of disaster–rebellion–new dynasty–decay–disaster–rebellion. As a dynasty became corrupt and inefficient, or faced natural calamities with which it could not deal, the way opened for insurgents, who sought to place a new emperor on the throne. The new dynasty might respond vigorously for a while, only to eventually succumb to the same insuperable challenges, after which its mandate, too, was withdrawn.[92] Thus the history of prerevolutionary China was one of periodic rebellion,[93] but none until the Taiping was genuinely millenarian. All previous uprisings took traditional categories for granted. Even natural disasters had their appointed place and could be borne with a certain equanimity. The combination of natural calamities with the sociopolitical disasters of the mid-nineteenth century changed that pattern. The infusion of millenarian ideas by Christian missionaries provided the missing doctrinal element. (The Chinese case is, by the way, one of those clear-cut instances in which the presence of missionaries proved critical to the rise of millenarianism.) Two charismatic figures were necessary to link ideas with social situations: first, Hung Hsiu-ch'üan, who introduced the Christian idea of a major break in the cyclical view of history; second, Mao Tse-tung, who drew in and Sinified Marxist doctrines.

Why did these three revolutionary movements—nazism, bolshevism, and Chinese communism—spread over such large areas? How was it possible for millenarian movements, in the past almost uniformly small-scale and rural, to take over the governance of nation-states?

One answer is that millenarian movements, like any other kind, exist within the limits of the existing technology of communications. They require the nurturance that only remote, relatively unurbanized areas can provide. This for a number of reasons: greater disaster vulnerability, more homogeneous population, greater difficulty of suppression, ease of attitudinal reinforcement. Among the cases with which we have been dealing, the preeminent example is, of course, Chinese communism, growing in the fastnesses of Yenan. To a somewhat lesser but still conspicuous degree the Nazi party was nonurban. It caught hold last in such cities as Hamburg, Frankfurt, and Berlin. In an analysis of the 1932

German election in cities of 25,000 or more, "the larger the city, the smaller the Nazi vote. . . . The ideal-typical Nazi voter in 1932 was a middle-class self-employed Protestant who lived either on a farm or in a small community, and who had previously voted for a centrist or regionalist political party strongly opposed to the power and influence of big business and big labor." [94]

The strong exception appears to be Russia. Indeed, the differences between Soviet and Chinese communism in part turn on the urban character of the former and the rural character of the latter. To what extent does the apparently city-oriented character of bolshevism invalidate our argument?

In fact, if we look closely at the distribution of bolshevism before the Revolution, we find that the patterns are in reality quite complex. It is true that in a broadly general sense bolshevism, like other forms of social-democracy, was exceedingly weak outside the towns. [95] However, the nature of the Bolshevik membership in combination with the more specific loci of activity provide a picture by no means at total variance with the characteristics of millenarianism presented earlier. On the basis of our discussion of urbanism earlier in this chapter, we should expect to find bolshevism in precisely those areas where urbanization is least typical; in settings, that is, least characterized by features of size, complexity, and diversity. Our earlier discussion mentioned, for example, the company town as a one form of disaster-prone urban anomaly.

In fact bolshevism was strongest in precisely such marginally urban locales. It was much stronger in the one-industry textile town of Ivanovo-Voznesensk, homogeneous and prone to economic fluctuations, than it was in the mixed industrial economy of Moscow. Workers in the former also appear to have been much more readily socialized to a sense of "class consciousness." [96] It seems likely as well that the larger the city, the more dispersed the residence patterns and the more powerful and efficient the opposition.

The early Bolsheviks, much more than was the case with other Russian parties, were likely to be of peasant stock and working-class status. They still maintained ties with the villages from which they had come, and any success they had in spreading dissident beliefs to the peasantry was as a result of these ties. The consequence was to create Bolshevik and other Social-Democratic enclaves outside large cities, in the villages or, more likely, in small industrial towns. In general, by economic position, social background, and even nationality, the Bolsheviks were notably more homogeneous than the Mensheviks.[97] This homogeneity derived from and was maintained by the homogeneous character of the communities of greatest Bolshevik strength.

Finally, two institutions in particular contributed to homogeneity and insularity. First, the government policy of exiling dissidents to Siberia could only serve to enhance the conditions necessary for a chiliastic movement. Exile spread the movement and intentionally concentrated its supporters in an isolated area. As might be expected, Siberia was one of the very few unurbanized areas which was strongly antigovernment.[98] The second institution was the factory itself. The factory was a potent if unintended device for the concentration of discontent. It brought together for long periods of time individuals who might otherwise have gone their separate ways. Together with the working-class neighborhood it produced a kind of ghettoization, again one of the urban exceptions where we should expect millenarianism to flourish. And in point of fact, the Bolsheviks did best "in areas of established large-scale factory production." [99] Thus while bolshevism does diverge from the rural and small-town milieu of other millenarian groups, its exploitation of the urban anomalies makes its success comprehensible.

As we have already seen, a major problem in the expansion of millenarian movements is one of communication, when the very conditions that allow a movement to develop also segregate it. It is, consequently, by no means surprising that the only millenarian movements to achieve control of large nation-states did so in the twentieth century. Nazism, of course, made conscious and highly effective use of all media of communications in a technologically sophisticated society. Russia and China, though their communications systems may now appear rudimentary, represented enormous advances over the essentially word-of-mouth systems that existed in

Münster and Florence. In part, the improvement was due to the sheer technology of the process. But it also reflects the development of effective organizational forms. The bureaucratically organized party combines small groups at the local level capable of offering support and reinforcement to the convert, with vertical and horizontal channels of communication giving a sense of participation in a larger whole.

But insofar as millenarianism is concerned, the sense of a larger whole, however communicated, stems from the manner in which disaster itself is perceived. The great millenarian movements of modern times may owe their existence as much to changes in the patterns of disaster and disaster perception as to any other causes. The conditions that we have seen operative in the cases of nazism and Soviet and Chinese communism may in the end be but enabling or facilitating conditions. We have seen that multiple disasters preceded each. It remains now to determine whether these disasters differed qualitatively from the cataclysms that beset earlier periods; if that proves to be true, it may provide the answer to the baffling problem of scale.

Chapter Seven

CHANGING PATTERNS OF DISASTER

In this concluding chapter, I wish to turn, however specula-
tively, to some large but critical questions concerning the
future of millenarian movements in modern life. One of these
questions has already been raised in the preceding chapter:
To what extent is totalitarianism attributable to changes in
patterns or modes of disaster? Allied to it are two other
problems, both of which grow out of the relationship between
social movements and technology: Can individuals not
directly affected by a disaster participate vicariously in it?
Can disasters be induced, more or less at will, to serve
conscious political or social purposes? Since these are relatively recent questions, they cannot be expected to yield to
ready answers. Indeed, a full exploration would require a
volume in itself. Nevertheless, not to face them at all would
be to evade the full implications of what has gone before.

If the questions are all answered positively, that is tanta-
mount to saying that the rural character of millenarianism
has undergone a basic change: that it has been made
compatible with forms of social organization in which, in the
past, it was unable to take root. In view of the upheavals
caused by revolutionary messianism when it existed on a
local scale in agrarian surroundings, that is a conclusion as
consequential as it is unsettling. If, on the other hand, the
queries are answered negatively, the implication is that
millenarianism is indeed a waning phenomenon, that its
twentieth-century representatives in Russia, Germany, and
China constitute historical flukes, unlikely to recur.

The answers, however, are unlikely to be definitive, either
on one side or the other. Where one seeks to, as it were, cast a
horoscope of this kind, the uncertainties are too great to yield
up much more than bits and pieces of an answer. Doubtless,
in this matter as in so many others, participation in events is
the victim of its virtues. We know at one and the same time
both too much and too little. One cannot avoid the gnawing

suspicion that what in retrospect appear to be the genuinely significant transformations proceed in a manner sufficiently subtle and insidious to bypass the perceptions of most of those they touch.

As we begin to compare the disaster patterns of preindustrial and industrial society, the differences that strike us first are the most trivial. The preindustrial age had its plagues, famines, and floods, while our own period has undergone colonization, war, and depression. In the past, catastrophe was more apt to be natural in origin. To be sure, actual impact often depended to a great extent on human agency; for example, the relationship between plague outbreaks and sanitation or floods and the maintenance of dikes. But overall, disaster occurred as a result of events in the natural world, with or without human complicity. As human beings learned how to predict, control, or defend against events in the physical world, it was reasonable to assume that the category of "disaster events" would gradually disappear.

In the event, however, that has proven untrue. In a solemn litany, Anthony Wallace constructs a typology of modern-day disasters,[1] and it is instructive to note the balance of natural to manmade. The strictly natural are: earthquake, epidemic, famine, flood, and storm. Prediction, control, or defense already exist for all but earthquake, and even in that case promising research on prediction is well under way. Such destruction as they cause can be ascribed to a temporary deficit of will or resources rather than to an inability in principle to deal with them.

All the rest of Wallace's disaster categories are made up, not of "acts of God" but of acts of man: atomic weapons, conventional bombing, combat, economic dislocations, expatriation and displacement, explosions, fires, invasion and conquest, massacre and pogrom, mine disasters, discrimination and restriction, revolution, riots and mob violence, siege, and strikes. One may quibble over the manner in which I have divided his list. Explosions, fires, and mine disasters might under certain circumstances be considered natural disasters. By the same token, had his catalog been compiled more recently, the manmade side would almost certainly have included ecological disasters. But in any case, the message should be clear: as the impact of natural disasters has waned, new categories of manmade disasters have arisen in their place. Indeed, the very social organization which has provided the means for defenses against the ravages of nature has made possible novel types of "unnatural" catastrophes.

There were, of course, always certain forms of manmade disasters in the past. Neither war nor mob violence nor persecution is a modern invention. We must, I think, operate on the assumption that man's psychological equipment, insofar as it bears upon his destructive and self-destructive propensities, has remained constant. The important point is that the manmade disasters in premodern societies were localized. All manmade and some natural disasters depend upon human beings to transmit them from person to person. Even in the case of plague, André Siegfried notes, disease spreads over space and time in a manner exactly corresponding to the manner and rate at which individuals move over the earth's surface.[2] The inability or unwillingness of persons to venture much beyond a small home area meant that they visited evils predominantly upon each other. Only exceptional expenditures of time and energy (one thinks, for example, of the Crusades) could alter this.

If one looks for master trends which characterize the modern age, surely one of the most obvious is an increase in scale. Increasing scale has been a hallmark of societies that are undergoing or have already undergone industrialization. The increase in scale does not simply involve economic life, where we are accustomed to point to the economies that so often accrue to increases in productive, distributive, or consumptive capacities. There has also been a scalar increase in disaster. Manmade disasters are no longer bound to a single town or locality. Some continue to be so, such as mine disasters, but as in so much else, catastrophe too mounts to the level attained by more benign events. Our inability to comprehend genocide[3] in part results from the fact that it represents such an unprecedented increase in scale. The extermination camps constitute, in a sense, the disaster counterpart to industrial production, a potentiality unforeseen because "normal men do not know that everything is possible." [4]

We can argue about whether and when quantitative change becomes qualitative change, and there will always be some who contend that shifts are merely of degree and not of kind. Yet one cannot escape the feeling that total war, economic depression, and genocide basically differ from the conflicts, instabilities, and persecutions of the past. The three differ greatly in the degree to which they are the products of human intention. But they are at one in their scope and their break with the past. Beginning with World War I, armed conflict, through rampant technological change, offered the possibility of rampant, uncontrolled expansion—a consequence of what Raymond Aron calls "technical surprise." [5] The qualitative transformation is precisely of the sort that signals a new type of disaster, in the magnitude of destruction, the inability to fully anticipate its onset and effects, and the inadequacy of defense. The vulnerability of civilian populations more and more resembles the manner in which, in the past, ordered social life stood in jeopardy before forces of nature:

> Total war has a very important political significance insofar as it contradicts the basic assumptions upon which the relationship between the military and the civilian branches of government rests: it is the function of the army to protect and to defend the civilian population. In contrast, the history of warfare in our century could almost be told as the story of the growing incapacity of the army to fulfill this basic function, until today the strategy of deterrence has openly changed the role of the military from that of a protector into that of a belated and essentially futile avenger.[6]

Economic depression, so heavily implicated in the rise of nazism, is of course a consequence of the very process of development that keeps older forms of deprivation at bay. Presumably, it is not an inevitable by-product. If one examines the relationships between economic forces and millenarian activity, one finds that mere economic fluctuation was not involved. As chapter two indicated, millenarian movements are not the simple consequences of relative deprivation. The deprivation involved must be environment-transforming disaster. For that reason, rises and falls in price levels, for example, cannot of themselves draw forth millenarian activity. George Rudé, in his examination of food riots in preindustrial France, clearly notes the limited, temporary, and surprisingly instrumental character of crowd behavior caused by price fluctuations.[7] On the other hand, the incorporation of local areas into new, remote, and incomprehensible national economies has a very different effect, which lies behind much of the millenarian ferment in southern Europe in the nineteenth and twentieth centuries.[8] In a similar vein, Kenelm Burridge argues that millenarian movements in the non-Western world, particularly the Cargo Cults, arose in reaction to the introduction of a money economy.[9] While it seems unlikely that such a broad spectrum of effects could spring from such a specific cause, it is again a structural economic change that is alleged to provide the trigger.

The concept of a world depression is a peculiarly modern notion. It is distinctive in its speed, in the lack of forewarning (excepting of course the perceptive few who are never listened to), and in the swiftness with which it draws in onlookers. Where movements of goods, labor, and capital have become extensive and are taken for granted, damage spreads along the same routes previously used to mutual profit and advantage. The scale of a depression only too easily rises to meet the scale of the most inclusive economic system.

Modern disaster is an artifact of interdependence. Where men are no longer able to encapsulate themselves in isolated communities, bad times, no less than good ones, soon become common property. Contemporary advocates of decentralization act out of a desire to increase damage control, whether they recognize it or not. The apocalyptic myths of the last several decades have been cast on a global scale: world depression, world war, nuclear holocaust, overpopulation, ecological disaster. The point here is not that these beliefs are either true or false, but that the "imagination of disaster" has become fixated on worldwide catastrophe. This is so because technology and the expansion of international transactions now makes it plausible.

The more optimistic conclusion one might draw is that only the exceedingly rare global disaster is representative of modern disaster patterns. For to an extent old vulnerabilities remain, often to surprising degrees. Tendencies toward diversity and integration, strong though they are, must be set against persistent anomalies, some of which we have already had occasion to discuss: the ghetto, the one-industry economy, the company town. What we may call institutions of concentration continue to grow, separating and isolating relatively homogeneous groups.[10] The factory, the university, and the ghetto all insulate their members and group like with like. They set up homogeneous population islands and resist diversity. Sources of stress and instability that might be readily absorbed in more heterogeneous communities may appear cataclysmic in less polyglot environments. The irony is that specialization produces in the end a social segmentation not unlike the relatively unspecialized rural milieu. Just as each rural locale may be physically separated from every other, so each specialized unit in an urbanized society is set off functionally from the others. When segmentation by function involves physical separateness or limited communications with other units, the effects common to agrarian societies are, as it were, imported into highly sophisticated urban settings.

The second major qualitative factor now operative in increasing the scope of disaster is the possibility for vicarious experience. We have all along been operating on the assumption that disaster communicates its effects along lines of physical proximity: one must be in the presence of plague germs and plague victims to be involved in a plague itself. Disasters in the past could be bounded in terms of their physical effects. Even economic depression spreads in a recognizable way, according to preexisting economic relationships. Mass media, however, particularly television, open the possibility that disaster can be communicated almost instantaneously to areas remote from the original source of stress. It is not a matter of transmitting information; one can know about a catastrophe elsewhere while pursuing one's life very much as usual. Instead, the question arises whether the psychological reactions to disaster, of the kind discussed in chapter two, can be induced in others through media of communication.

I wish to suggest that this may indeed be possible, that with the advent of television we are all potential disaster victims. The best evidence for this lies in individual reactions to the assassination of President John F. Kennedy. This event provides valuable insights into the process of the expansion of the disaster community for a number of reasons. First, one might suspect the normal area of impact to be relatively small. Even the death of a president does not inflict any immediate tangible deprivations upon most people. The impact, as in any individual death, falls upon a relatively small circle of loved ones, friends, and co-workers. Notwithstanding the symbolic significance of the presidency, one might suspect that the emotional effects of such an event might dissipate as they move outward from this circle of intimates. Second, the assassination of President Kennedy took place, as no similar acts had before, in the television era. Third, within hours social scientists had begun to systematically study reactions to the assassination, and as a result we know more about its consequences than we do about almost any other national event.

To many students of the assassination and its aftermath it became clear that it affected people very much as a conventional disaster would.[11] Despite surface dissimilarities, the assassination, like a flood, a sudden enemy attack, or a depression, became a collective stress experience for virtually the entire society.

The reason for this lies in the degree of participation afforded by marathon television coverage. Television created a sense of vicarious participation which made every viewer feel as if he were not merely a spectator at the sidelines but an active participant. This expansion of the public world to incorporate previously private lives has, of course, happened before. George Steiner argues that the great citizen armies of the French Revolution did the same thing.[12] The Kennedy assassination marked a quantum leap in the interpenetration of public and private, in the rapidity with which individuals found themselves within the ambit of great events: "There was apparently a compulsive need to glue oneself to television and thus vicariously take part in the events and the farewells." [13] There was a sharing of both information and emotions.[14] The strength of vicarious participation becomes clearer when, in the National Opinion Research Center study, individuals were asked to compare their present feelings with some past event: "The majority of all respondents could not recall any other time in their lives when they had the same sort of feelings. . . . Of those who could think of such an occasion (47 per cent of the public), the majority referred to the death of a parent, close friends, or other relative. Only a third of the group mentioned the death of any other public figure." [15]

One of the strongest indicators of vicarious participation is a comparison between the strength of reactions in Dallas and in the country at large. Curiously—although in light of our discussion perhaps predictably—there were practically no differences. Discrepancies in the percentage experiencing physical or emotional reactions are for the most part trivial. The only substantial difference was in the incidence of feelings of extreme nervousness and tension: 82 percent in Dallas against 68 percent in a national sample.[16] What is remarkable is not the magnitude of the difference so much as its smallness when one thinks of differences between the locations of the two groups.

But the most notable characteristic of the assassination was the degree to which vicarious participation produced observable, clinical reactions. In the NORC study, respondents were questioned concerning a wide range of possible reactions. More than 40 percent reported the following symptoms during the four days between the assassination and the funeral: loss of appetite, crying, difficulty sleeping, feelings of great nervousness and tension, unusual fatigue, and feelings of dazedness and numbness. Between 20 and 40 percent also experienced unusually frequent smoking, headaches, upset stomach, rapid heartbeat, and some memory loss.[17] Within a few days of the funeral, the symptoms disappeared very rapidly.

The most striking aspect of these reports is their correspondence with the findings of disaster research. For these psychological and psychosomatic symptoms, and their remission with the restoration of a stable environment, virtually reproduce the disaster syndrome. Yet they occurred in millions of people whose only contact with the events in question was prolonged exposure to the media, notably television, reinforced by interaction with persons similarly exposed. The data strongly suggest that the disaster syndrome is either not limited to those directly affected or, more likely, that we shall have to reexamine our understanding of what "directly affected" means. For television appears to have the potential of inducing a feeling of disaster impact in people remote from the source of disturbance and whose physical and social world remains otherwise intact.

Television temporarily created disaster victims. It obviously did so unintentionally. I wish to move now to the question of whether it is possible to induce disaster intentionally, for conscious political and social purposes. This possibility too characterizes the modern world and suggests yet another reason why millenarianism may be prolonged beyond what may have appeared to be its natural time. If mass media can, as it were, transmit the emotional effects of disaster to persons who otherwise would not experience them, cannot disasters themselves be willed into existence? But even if this could be done, why would anyone wish to? The answer is that to the extent that the group solidarity and emotional excitement of a millenarian movement are appealing to one, there is an incentive to create the kind of circumstances that make millenarian movements possible.

An interesting example comes from China. Approximately seventeen years after the Communists took power in a revolution with marked millenarian aspects, Chinese society underwent yet another upheaval: the so-called Cultural Revolution. Robert J. Lifton tells us that "it has meant nothing less than *an all-consuming death-and-rebirth experience, an induced catastrophe together with a prescription for reconstituting the world being destroyed.*" [18] Like most millenarian movements, the Cultural Revolution failed. Unlike others, however, it appears not to have arisen as a spontaneous response to the natural conditions of society. Its hallmark is not its fervor but its artificiality. Just as Mao's generation went through the formative disaster of the Long March, so successive generations must be marked by their own confrontations with disaster. And if the world has no disaster to offer, then one must be constructed.

The marauding Red Guards were unusual, but they were not unique. Totalitarian revolutions meet success by inducing disaster. That is the meaning of their use of terror. The French Revolution in this aspect as in so many others is paradigmatic. The Reign of Terror introduces us to purge and terror as a means of preserving instability and movement. The Nazis further institutionalized terror, moving past the SA "Blood Purge" to the constant terror of the camps. The Soviet Union, in the Stalin years, endured its periodic purges.

Terror begins in the unsettled, precarious atmosphere of revolutionary victory. It then appears, as Crane Brinton points out, a necessary step in the march to the millennium; it is as much a Reign of Virtue as a Reign of Terror.[19] At that point, it still has a kind of "naturalness," notwithstanding the appalling human costs and the extremes of nervous excitement. Postrevolutionary terror does seem to emerge out of the logic of the situation. Eventually, the terror runs its course: "large numbers of men can stand only so much interference with the routines and rituals of their daily existence."[20] The revolution is then on its way to the comparative normalcy of a Thermidorean reaction. The zealots die off, kill each other, seek exile, or otherwise fade into insignificance and the new regime makes its peace with the past.

However, this cycle is not, apparently, inevitable. The passage into Thermidor can be blocked or at least significantly delayed. Brinton, the great theorist of revolutionary cycles, himself recognized this. As late as 1952, he was troubled by the recurrence of Soviet purges and terror:

> The Russians may have found a way, a way not found by Puritans or Jacobins, of keeping the ordinary man forever keyed to the intensities, the conformities, the perpetual participation in state ritual, the exhausting sacramental devotion, the holy-rolling unrelieved, the constant transcending of common weaknesses and common sense, the *madness* we have sought to analyze as the "Reigns of Terror and Virtue."[21]

By 1956, he was reasonably satisfied that the Soviets had not in fact found the secret of permanent revolution, that with the death of Stalin, the Russian Revolution finally "ended."[22]

Events since 1956 have borne him out. But that still means
that the completion of the cycle was delayed some twenty-five
years. The purges were themselves cyclical, alternating periods of quiesence and upheaval.[23]

The Soviet purges and the Chinese Cultural Revolution
both sought to grasp the elusive secret of "permanent
revolution." So too did the Nazis. Hannah Arendt is correct
in her assertion that the concentration camps were central
rather than peripheral institutions.[24] They were a way of
trying to institutionalize permanent revolution. *For permanent
revolution is nothing more nor less than permanent disaster.* The
"Reign of Terror and of Virtue" appeals directly to the
millenarian, to the believer in the desirability and necessity of
total change. The imminent world of evil must be destroyed,
for only if it is can the new order be constructed. And if evil
remains, that only means we have been inefficient in destroying it. We must try again.

Disaster provides the illusion of fundamental change. If so
much of the visible world alters, then surely the period
afterward will be the new order. The slate will be clean. Since
spontaneous events cannot be counted upon to produce
disaster after disaster, men take it upon themselves to
generate catastrophe. They move populations, shift statuses,
and destroy alleged enemies with sufficient ferocity to give the
appearance—even to themselves—of a final passage from
corruption to perfection.

The reason why they can deceive themselves is that the
transient period of the disaster utopia does appear to
prefigure, in its perverse way, the total community of the
millennium. Men are suddenly liberated from the old ways,
given new commands, and plunged into an apocalyptic
struggle with evil. Ultimates are at stake. They must be; what
other possible justification could there be for the extremities
of political terror? In a final irony, the categories of disaster
and millennium collapse into each other. The former not only
prepares for the latter, disaster *is* the millennium. In their
"pursuit of the millennium" the new chiliasts generate
disaster not for the instrumental purpose of toppling the old
order but as something good in itself. In the long run, of
course, they will fail. Permanent disaster is as elusive as

permanent revolution. Even cycles of induced disaster and social peace require a tinkering with human propensities that, for the moment, appears mercifully beyond our capabilities. But to the extent that "all things are possible," this aspiration, too, may eventually find its bitter fruition.

The search for the millennium, then, is by no means simply a thing of the past. It has in the twentieth century broken out of its old rural confines, at precisely the point in social development when its old reservoirs of support were about to be overrun and absorbed in a flood of urbanism. The pull of a perfect future in one's own lifetime has been too great, and the ingenuity of man in generating disasters for himself is a capability that can hardly be underestimated. The millenarian quest has not, unfortunately, been simply a "religion of the oppressed." [25] As the means for inducing disaster at will have been developed and used, millenarianism has become as much the instrument of oppression as its by-product. Millenarianism has emerged from its old haunts—the ghetto, small town, and backland—into modern urban society. In the process, it has increasingly left behind the oppressed for whom it was the last resort in adversity and become the creature of those who seek power and dominion. The idea of the millennium, appropriated from those who most require it, now animates those who need it least. Once the unintended consequence of disaster, millenarian expectation now flourishes as its cause.

Notes

Introduction

1 Anthony F. C. Wallace, *Human Behavior in Extreme Situations*, p. 15.
2 Harry B. Williams, "Fewer Disasters, Better Studied," pp. 5–11.
3 Allen H. Barton, *Communities in Disaster*, p. 58.
4 Papers published in Sylvia L. Thrupp, ed., *Millennial Dreams in Action.*
5 Weston La Barre, "Materials for a History of Studies of Crisis Cults," pp. 3–44.
6 E.g. M. W. Smith, "Towards a Classification of Cult Movements," pp. 8–12. Anthony F. C. Wallace, Fred W. Voget, and Marian W. Smith, "Toward a Classification of Cult Movements," pp. 25–28.

Chapter One

1 Material for this section has been drawn primarily from the reports of the assistant government anthropologist F. E. Williams: *The Vailala Madness and the Destruction of Native Ceremonies in the Gulf Division*; and "The Vailala Madness in Retrospect," in E. E. Evans-Pritchard, Raymond Firth, Bronislaw Malinowski, and Isaac Schapera, eds., *Essays Presented to C. G. Seligman*, pp. 369–79. Williams's 1923 report also includes valuable appendixes by G. H. Murray, then the acting resident magistrate. A synoptic view of the entire Cargo Cult phenomenon may be obtained from two controversial but highly stimulating syntheses: Peter Worsley, *The Trumpet Shall Sound*; and I. C. Jarvie, *The Revolution in Anthropology*. Among the most detailed accounts of relatively recent Cargo Cults are: D. Glynn Cochrane, *Big Men and Cargo Cults*; Theodore Schwartz, *The Paliau Movement in the Admiralty Islands, 1946–1954*; and Margaret Mead, *New Lives for Old.*
2 Williams, *The Vailala Madness*, p. 10.
3 Information in this section has been drawn from: Frederic Wakeman, Jr., *Strangers at the Gate*, pp. 3, 126–30; Kwang-ching Liu, "Nineteenth Century China: The Disintegration of the Old Order and the Impact of the West," in Ping-ti Ho and Tang Tsou, eds., *China's Heritage and the Communist Political System*, 1: 93–178; P. M. Yap, "The Mental Illness of Hung Hsiu-Ch'uan, Leader of the Taiping Rebellion," pp. 287–304; Eugene P. Boardman, "Millenary Aspects of the Taiping Rebellion (1851–64)," in Thrupp, *Millennial Dreams in Action*, pp. 70–79.
4 Information in this section has been drawn from the principal source, James Mooney, *The Ghost-Dance Religion and the Sioux Outbreak of*

1890; and from Vittorio Lanternari, *The Religions of the Oppressed*, pp. 128–32; Weston La Barre, *The Ghost Dance*, pp. 229–33.

5   Mooney, *The Ghost-Dance Religion*, pp. 115, 118.

6   Information in this section has been drawn from: Norman Cohn, *The Pursuit of the Millennium*, pp. 205–22; Howard Kaminsky, "The Free Spirit of the Hussite Revolt," in Thrupp, *Millennial Dreams in Action*, pp. 166–86.

7   Norman Cohn, *The Pursuit of the Millennium*, pp. 31–43; Joseph F. Zygmunt, "Prophetic Failure and Chiliastic Identity," pp. 926–48; Yonina Talmon, "Millenarian Movements," pp. 159–200.

8   For a bibliographical essay, see La Barre, *The Ghost Dance*.

9   A. J. F. Köbben, "Prophetic Movements as an Expression of Social Protest," pp. 117–64.

10 Y. Talmon, "Millenarian Movements."

11 Michael Barkun, "Law and Social Revolution," pp. 113–41.

12 George Rosen, "Enthusiasm, 'a dark lanthorn of the spirit'," pp. 393–421; R. A. Knox, *Enthusiasm*.

13 Y. Talmon, "Millenarian Movements"; L. P. Mair, "Independent Religious Movements in Three Continents," pp. 113–36; Margaret Mead, "Comment on Independent Religious Movements," pp. 324–29; Worsley, *The Trumpet Shall Sound*, pp. 44, 247–49.

14 Worsley, *The Trumpet Shall Sound*, p. 75.

15 *The Paranoid Style in American Politics*.

16 Hannah Arendt, *On Revolution*, p. 35.

17 Max Gluckman, *Politics, Law and Ritual in Tribal Society*, p. 169.

18 Ibid., pp. 155–201; idem, *Order and Rebellion in Tribal Africa*, pp. 110–36.

19 George Rudé, *The Crowd in History*; Morris Janowitz, "Patterns of Collective Racial Violence," in Hugh Davis Graham and Ted Robert Gurr, eds., *Violence in America*, pp. 412–43. Cf. the concept of "primitive" collective violence adopted by Charles Tilly in "Collective Violence in European Perspective," in Graham and Gurr, *Violence in America*, pp. 4–45.

20 J. L. Talmon, *The Origins of Totalitarian Democracy*; idem, *Political Messianism*; Ernest Lee Tuveson, *Redeemer Nation*; David E. Apter, "Political Religion in the New Nations," in Clifford Geertz, ed., *Old Societies and New States*, pp. 57–104; Melvin J. Lasky, "The Meta-Physics of Doomsday," pp. 36–47.

21 David F. Aberle, *The Peyote Religion among the Navaho*, pp. 331–32.

22 Yonina Talmon, "Pursuit of the Millennium," pp. 125–48.

23 Mair, "Independent Religious Movements."

24 *The Anatomy of Revolution*, pp. 215–50.

25 Ibid., pp. 128–54.

26 Ibid., p. 153.

27 Ibid., p. 192.

28 Ibid., p. 207.

29 *The Revolution of the Saints*, pp. 309, 317–19.

30 Ibid., p. 309.

31 Knox, *Enthusiasm*, pp. 72–73; Jeffrey Burton Russell, *Witchcraft in the Middle Ages*, p. 151.
32 Bernard Lewis, *The Assassins*.
33 T. O. Ranger, "Connexions Between 'Primary Resistance' Movements and Mass Nationalism in East and Central Africa," pp. 437–53, 631–41.
34 Karl Mannheim, *Ideology and Utopia*, p. 211. Curiously, although Mannheim was one of the first scholars to recognize the significance of revolutionary messianism (having first published *Ideology* in 1929), contemporary millenarian scholars have generally ignored him.
35 Ernest Lee Tuveson, *Millennium and Utopia*.
36 Rosen, "Enthusiasm."
37 Tuveson, *Millennium and Utopia*, pp. v–vi.
38 David E. Smith, "Millenarian Scholarship in America," pp. 535–49.
39 Tuveson, *Redeemer Nation*, p. 213. It is only fair to point out that Tuveson sees the theme of withdrawal as dominant; messianism as "the generally less powerful idea."
40 Arthur Bestor, *Backwoods Utopias*, pp. 1–59.
41 Ibid., p. 38.
42 J. L. Talmon, *The Origins of Totalitarian Democracy*; idem, *Political Messianism*.
43 Ibid., p. 11.
44 J. L. Talmon, *Political Messianism*, p. 513.
45 "Introduction," in Elie Kedourie, ed., *Nationalism in Asia and Africa*, p. 103.
46 Ibid., p. 106.
47 Y. Talmon, "Millenarian Movements."
48 Worsley, *The Trumpet Shall Sound*, pp. 254–56.
49 Lanternari, *The Religions of the Oppressed*, pp. vi–vii.
50 Expressed in modified form in Worsley, *The Trumpet Shall Sound*, p. 245.
51 René Ribeiro, "Brazilian Messianic Movements," in Thrupp, *Millennial Dreams in Action*, pp. 55–69.
52 Bryan Wilson, "Millennialism in Comparative Perspective," pp. 93–114.
53 Kitsiri Malalgoda, "Millennialism in Relation to Buddhism," p. 439.
54 Ibid.
55 *The Pursuit of the Millennium* (1961), pp. xiii–xvi, 307–15. These passages do not appear in the most recent edition (1970). Cohn does deal with related themes in his *Warrant for Genocide*.
56 *The Pursuit of the Millennium* (1961), p. 309.
57 Ibid., p. 310.

Chapter Two

1 Aberle, *The Peyote Religion*, p. 323.
2 Ted Robert Gurr, *Why Men Rebel*, pp. 48–49, 203–04.
3 "America's Race Paradox," pp. 9–18.

4   Denton E. Morrison, "Some Notes toward Theory on Relative Deprivation, Social Movements, and Social Change," pp. 675–90.
5   Ibid.
6   *The Peyote Religion*, p. 329.
7   Y. Talmon, "Millenarian Movements"; Mair, "Independent Religious Movements"; Mead, "Independent Religious Movements"; Worsley, *The Trumpet Shall Sound*, pp. 44, 247–49.
8   "Revitalization Movements," pp. 264–81.
9   Samuel Z. Klausner, "The Intermingling of Pain and Pleasure: The Stress-Seeking Personality in Its Social Context," in Klausner, ed., *Why Man Takes Chances*, p. 139.
10 Anthony F. C. Wallace, "Stress and Rapid Personality Changes," pp. 761–74.
11 Wallace, *Revitalization Movements.*"
12 Anthony F. C. Wallace, "Mazeway Resynthesis," pp. 626–38.
13 "Stress and Rapid Personality Changes."
14 Jarvie, *The Revolution in Anthropology*, passim.
15 Expressed in modified form in Worsley, *The Trumpet Shall Sound*, p. 245.
16 David F. Aberle, "The Prophet Dance and Reactions to White Contact," pp. 74–83; Leslie Spier, Wayne Shuttles, and Melville J. Herskovits, "Comments on Aberle's Thesis of Deprivation," pp. 84–88.
17 Y. Talmon, "Pursuit of the Millennium."
18 E.g. Cohn, *The Pursuit of the Millennium* (1970), p. 17.
19 E. J. Hobsbawm, *Primitive Rebels*, p. 9.
20 Leon Festinger, Henry W. Riecken, and Stanley Schachter, *When Prophecy Fails*; John Lofland and Rodney Stark, "Becoming a World-Saver," pp. 862–75.
21 George Rosen, *Madness in Society*, pp. 9, 191, 223–25; H. B. M. Murphy, "Social Change and Mental Health," pp. 385–445.
22 P. M. Yap, "Mental Diseases Peculiar to Certain Cultures," pp. 313–27.
23 Anthony F. C. Wallace, "Cultural Determinants of Response to Hallucinatory Experience," pp. 58–69.
24 Alexander H. Leighton and Jane M. Hughes, "Cultures as a Causative of Mental Disorder," pp. 446–70.
25 Y. Talmon, "Pursuit of the Millennium."
26 Aberle, *The Peyote Religion*, pp. 331–32.
27 "Political Religion in the New Nations," in Geertz, *Old Societies and New States*, pp. 57–104.
28 Cohn, *The Pursuit of the Millennium* (1970), pp. 59–60; Cohn, in Thrupp, *Millennial Dreams in Action*; Hobsbawm, *Primitive Rebels*, p. 79; Köbben, "Prophetic Movements"; Y. Talmon, "Millenarian Movements."
29 Whitney R. Cross, *The Burned-Over District*, passim.
30 Bernard Berelson and Gary A. Steiner, *Human Behavior*, p. 588.
31 "Revitalization Movements."
32 E. D. Wittkower and J. Fried, "A Cross-Cultural Approach to Mental Health Problems," pp. 423–28.

33 Ibid.; Leighton and Hughes, "Cultures as a Causative of Mental Disorder"; P. M. Yap, "Words and Things in Comparative Psychiatry, with Special Reference to the Exotic Psychoses," pp. 163–69.

34 Murphy, "Social Change and Mental Health."

35 Wittkower and Fried, "A Cross-Cultural Approach."

36 Murphy, "Social Change and Mental Health."

37 "The Fate of Personal Adjustment in the Process of Modernization," pp. 81–114.

38 Local experts modified the test in each country to filter out questions which might elicit culture-bound responses. Every effort was made to control for phenomena which might appear pathological to a Western physician but are regarded as normal in the society in question.

39 Victor D. Sanua, "Immigration, Migration and Mental Illness: A Review of the Literature with Special Emphasis on Schizophrenia," in Eugene B. Brody, ed., *Behavior in New Environments*, pp. 291–352; Robert J. Kleiner and Seymour Parker, "Social-Psychological Aspects of Migration and Mental Disorder in a Negro Population," in ibid., pp. 353–74.

40 Elmer L. Struening, Judith G. Rabkin, and Harris B. Peck, "Migration and Ethnic Membership in Relation to Social Problems," in ibid., pp. 217–48.

41 Murphy, "Social Change and Mental Health"; Rosen, *Madness in Society,* p. 194.

42 John A. Honigmann, "Culture Patterns and Human Stress," p. 34.

43 Ibid., p. 31.

44 "Social Change and Mental Health," p. 417.

45 Gideon Sjoberg, "Disasters and Social Change," in George W. Baker and Dwight W. Chapman, eds., *Man and Society in Disaster*, p. 357.

46 Barton, *Communities in Disaster*, pp. 38, 41.

47 Wallace, *Human Behavior in Extreme Situations.*

48 Sjoberg, in Baker and Chapman, *Man and Society in Disaster.*

49 William Caudill, *Effects of Social and Cultural Systems in Reactions to Stress.*

50 E.g. Wallace, *Human Behavior in Extreme Situations*; idem, "Mazeway Disintegration," pp. 356–84; Dwight W. Chapman, "A Brief Introduction to Contemporary Disaster Research," in Baker and Chapman, *Man and Society in Disaster,* pp. 3–22; J. S. Tyhurst, "Individual Reactions to Community Disaster," pp. 764–69.

51 Irving L. Janis, "Problems of Theory in the Analysis of Stress Behavior," pp. 12–25.

52 Lewis M. Killian, "Some Accomplishments and Some Needs in Disaster Study," pp. 66–72.

53 Chapman, in Baker and Chapman, *Man and Society in Disaster.*

54 Robert N. Wilson, "Disaster and Mental Health," in ibid., pp. 124–50.

55 Immediate attention to the psychological consequences of disaster, while still uncommon, is less rare than it once was. See, for example, the work done in Corning, New York, after the 1972 flood: Ann S. Kliman, "Psychological First Aid in a Mass Disaster."

56   Bradford B. Hudson, "Anxiety Response to the Unfamiliar," pp. 53–60.
57   Martha Wolfenstein, *Disaster*, p. 79.
58   "The Physiology of Faith," pp. 505–18.
59   F. P. Kilpatrick, "Problems of Perception in Extreme Situations," p. 21.
60   *The Psychology of Social Movements*, pp. 74–77.
61   Hudson, "Anxiety Response to the Unfamiliar."
62   Ibid., p. 58.
63   Philip Ziegler, *The Black Death*.
64   Raul Hilberg, *The Destruction of the European Jews*, pp. 662–69.
65   *In Bluebeard's Castle*, p. 24.
66   Cantril, *The Psychology of Social Movements*, pp. 70–77.

Chapter Three

1   Cross, *The Burned-Over District*, passim.
2   Barton, *Communities in Disaster*, p. 20 and see generally pp. 11–21.
3   Robert D. Rossel, "The Great Awakening," pp. 907–25.
4   Eric Hoffer, *The True Believer*, p. 33.
5   F. Glenn Abney and Larry B. Hill, "Natural Disasters as a Political Variable," pp. 974–81.
6   Gurr, *Why Men Rebel*, pp. 79–83.
7   "Pursuit of the Millennium."
8   Cohn, *The Pursuit of the Millennium* (1970), pp. 53–60.
9   Rudé, *The Crowd in History*, p. 5.
10   Hobsbawm, *Primitive Rebels*; Tilly, in Graham and Gurr, *Violence in America*, pp. 4–45.
11   *The Religions of the Oppressed*, p. vi.
12   "On Materials for a History of Studies of Crisis Cults," pp. 387–90.
13   Tilly, in Graham and Gurr, *Violence in America*; Roger Lane, "Urbanization and Criminal Violence in the Nineteenth Century," in ibid., pp. 468–84.
14   In Graham and Gurr, *Violence in America*, p. 11.
15   *Primitive Rebels*, p. 65.
16   Cantril, *The Psychology of Social Movements*, pp. 135–37.
17   Bernard J. Siegel, "Defensive Structuring and Environmental Stress," pp. 11–32.
18   Frederic Cople Jaher, *Doubters and Dissenters*, p. 4; David Bennett, *Protectors and Fugitives*.
19   Rudé, *The Crowd in History*, pp. 103–04.
20   "The Utopian Side of the Indian Uprising," in David W. Plath, ed., *Aware of Utopia*, pp. 86–116.
21   Cochrane, *Big Men and Cargo Cults*, p. 161.
22   Boardman, in Thrupp, *Millennial Dreams in Action*, pp. 70–79.
23   In Plath, *Aware of Utopia*, p. 95.
24   Anthony Oberschall, "Group Violence," pp. 61–92.
25   In Graham and Gurr, *Violence in America*, p. 38.
26   *Political Man*, pp. 97–100.

27 Gideon Sjoberg, *The Preindustrial City*, p. 159.

28 Ibid., pp. 159–60.

29 George B. Bikle, Jr., "Utopia and the Planning Element in Modern Japan," in Plath, *Aware of Utopia*, pp. 33–54.

30 De Queiroz, "Studies of Crisis Cults."

31 Donald E. Curry, "Messianism and Protestantism in Brazil's Sertão," pp. 416–38.

32 Hobsbawm, *Primitive Rebels*, p. 79.

33 William L. Langer, "The Next Assignment," pp. 283–304; Ziegler, *The Black Death*, p. 234.

34 André Siegfried, *Routes of Contagion*, pp. 45–46.

35 Alexander Alland, Jr., "War and Disease: An Anthropological Perspective," in Morton Fried, Marvin Harris, and Robert Murphy, eds., *War*, pp. 65–75.

36 Cochrane, *Big Men and Cargo Cults*, passim.

37 Langer, "The Next Assignment," pp. 283–304.

38 Barton, *Communities in Disaster*, p. 332.

39 "Defensive Structuring and Environmental Stress," p. 29.

40 Ibid.

41 For a theory of religious development based on this idea, see La Barre, *The Ghost Dance*.

42 Siegel, "Defensive Structuring and Environmental Stress."

43 Hudson, "Anxiety Response to the Unfamiliar."

44 Russell B. Dynes and Daniel Yutzy, "The Religious Interpretation of Disaster," pp. 34–48.

45 Ibid.

46 *The Structure of Scientific Revolutions*, p. 77.

47 Michael Polanyi, *Science, Faith and Society*, pp. 90–94.

48 *Doubters and Dissenters*, p. 4.

49 Christopher Hill, *The World Turned Upside Down*, p. 86. See also William M. Lamont, *Godly Rule*, passim.

50 E. J. Hobsbawm, "The Crisis of the Seventeenth Century," in Trevor Aston, ed., *Crisis in Europe*, pp. 5–62; H. R. Trevor-Roper, "The General Crisis of the Seventeenth Century," in ibid., pp. 63–102.

51 Christopher Hill, *The World Turned Upside Down*, p. 74; Tuveson, *Millennium and Utopia*, passim, but especially pp. 1–70.

52 "Revitalization Movements."

53 Plath, *Aware of Utopia*.

54 Hoffer, *The True Believer*, p. 58.

55 Worsley, *The Trumpet Shall Sound*, pp. 251–52.

56 Ibid., p. 245; Kedourie, *Nationalism in Asia and Africa*.

57 Seiji Nuita, "Traditional Utopias in Japan and the West: A Study in Contrasts," in Plath, *Aware of Utopia*, pp. 12–32.

58 "Prophetic Movements"; Köbben speculates that Hinduism might have accommodated messianism in the form of future avatars of Vishnu.

59 In Plath, *Aware of Utopia*, pp. 86–116.

60 The rebels also included Muslims, but there is no evidence that they introduced motifs from Islamic messianism.

61 Chapman, in Baker and Chapman, *Man and Society in Disaster*, pp. 3–22.

62 Sjoberg, in ibid., pp. 356–84.

63 "Stress and Rapid Personality Changes."

64 Ibid.; and idem, "Mazeway Resynthesis."

65 Idem, "Stress and Rapid Personality Changes."

66 Ibid.

67 Rosen, *Madness in Society*, p. 63.

68 Max Weber, *Economy and Society*, ed. Guenther Roth and Claus Wittich, 3: 1111–12.

69 Ibid., p. 1143.

70 Daniel Bell, "Sociodicy," pp. 696–714; Richard R. Lingeman, "The Greeks Had a Word for It—But What Does It Mean?", pp. 28–32.

71 Rosen, *Madness in Society*, pp. 21–70.

72 E.g. Ranger, " 'Primary Resistance' Movements and Modern Mass Nationalism," pp. 437–53, 631–41.

73 Worsley, *The Trumpet Shall Sound*, p. xii.

Chapter Four

1 Cantril, *The Psychology of Social Movements*, pp. 139–43.

2 Mooney, *The Ghost-Dance Religion*, p. 73; Lanternari, *The Religions of the Oppressed*, p. 130.

3 Mooney, *The Ghost-Dance Religion*, pp. xxii–xxiii.

4 Ibid., pp. 157–61.

5 Worsley, *The Trumpet Shall Sound*, pp. 2–5.

6 *Enthusiasm*, pp. 72–74.

7 E.g. Köbben, "Prophetic Movements."

8 Richard E. Dawson and Kenneth Prewitt, *Political Socialization*, pp. 107–08, 118–19.

9 Gershom Scholem, *The Messianic Idea in Judaism*, pp. 78–141.

10 *Innovation*, p. 324.

11 See, for example, Dean Jaros, Herbert Hirsch, and Fredric J. Fleron, Jr., "The Malevolent Leader," pp. 564–75.

12 Lipset, *Political Man*, pp. 76, 104–05.

13 Ibid., p. 76.

14 H. R. Trevor-Roper, *The European Witch-craze of the Sixteenth and Seventeenth Centuries and Other Essays*, pp. 90–192; Russell, *Witchcraft in the Middle Ages*, pp. 200, 268–69.

15 Rosen, *Madness in Society*, p. 219.

16 A. D. Nock, *Conversion*, p. 7.

17 William Sargant, *Battle for the Mind*, p. xxi.

18 Ibid., pp. 86–90 and passim.

19 Ibid.

20 E.g. Ward Hunt Goodenough, *Cooperation in Change*, p. 302.

21 *Primitive Rebels*, pp. 83–84.

22 Sargant, *Battle for the Mind*, pp. 85, 142–43.
23 Raymond A. Bauer, "Brainwashing: Psychology or Demonology?", pp. 41–47.
24 *The True Believer*, p. 10.
25 Sargant, *Battle for the Mind*, pp. 4–5, 32–33, 225–26.
26 Robert Jay Lifton, *Thought Reform and the Psychology of Totalism*, p. 150.
27 Ibid., pp. 150, 129.
28 Erik H. Erikson, "Wholeness and Totality—A Psychiatric Contribution," in Carl J. Friedrich, ed., *Totalitarianism*, pp. 156–70.
29 Ibid.
30 Lifton, *Thought Reform*, p. 436.
31 Ibid., pp. 150–51.
32 Cantril, *The Psychology of Social Movements*, pp. 65–69.
33 L. S. Penrose, *On the Objective Study of Crowd Behaviour*, p. 33.
34 Sargant, *Battle for the Mind*, pp. 74, 131.
35 Hudson, "Anxiety Response."
36 Wallace, "Stress and Rapid Personality Changes."
37 Quoted in Sargant, *Battle for the Mind*, pp. 141–42.
38 George Rosen, "Emotion and Sensibility in Ages of Anxiety," pp. 770–84.
39 *The Waning of the Middle Ages*; Langer, "The Next Assignment."
40 Rosen, "Emotion and Sensibility."
41 Jaher, *Doubters and Dissenters*, pp. 4, 7.
42 *In Bluebeard's Castle.*
43 Lifton, *Thought Reform*, pp. 82–84.
44 Wallace, "Mazeway Resynthesis."
45 Barton, *Communities in Disaster*, pp. 11–21.
46 "Independent Religious Movements."
47 Sargant, *Battle for the Mind*, passim.
48 Ibid., pp. 52–54, 120.
49 Honigmann, "Culture Patterns and Human Stress."
50 Anthony F. C. Wallace, *The Death and Rebirth of the Seneca*, pp. 239–302.
51 Leighton and Hughes, "Cultures as a Causative of Mental Disorder."
52 Rosen, "Emotion and Sensibility."
53 Quincy Wright, *A Study of War*, p. 60.
54 Hudson, "Anxiety Response"; Kilpatrick, "Problems of Perception."
55 Kilpatrick, "Problems of Perception," p. 21.
56 Wilson, in Baker and Chapman, *Man and Society in Disaster*, pp. 124–50.
57 Wolfenstein, *Disaster*, p. 79.
58 Edgar H. Schein, "Reaction Patterns to Severe, Chronic Stress in American Army Prisoners of War of the Chinese," pp. 21–30.
59 Sargant, *Battle for the Mind*, pp. 144–45.
60 *Man and Society in Calamity*, pp. 27–47.
61 Wolfenstein, *Disaster*, p. 79; Chapman, in Baker and Chapman, *Man and Society in Disaster*; Barton, *Communities in Disaster*, p. 70.

62 Sjoberg, ibid.

63 Baker and Chapman, *Man and Society in Disaster.*

64 Albert Biderman and Herbert Zimmer, eds., *The Manipulation of Human Behavior,* pp. 1–18; Lifton, *Thought Reform,* pp. 236–37.

65 Lifton, *Thought Reform,* p. 400; Sargant, *Battle for the Mind,* p. 161.

66 Sargant, *Battle for the Mind,* pp. 219–24.

67 Rosabeth Moss Kanter, "Commitment and Social Organization," pp. 499–517. For an expanded analysis, see Kanter, *Commitment and Community.*

68 Festinger, Riecken, and Schachter, *When Prophecy Fails,* p. 28; see also Zygmunt, "Prophetic Failure and Chiliastic Identity."

69 Wallace, *Death and Rebirth,* pp. 235–318.

70 Cohn, *The Pursuit of the Millennium* (1970), pp. 226–31.

71 Ibid., pp. 235, 237. For a less psychologically oriented approach to Muntzer, see Steven E. Ozment, *Mysticism and Dissent,* pp. 64–67.

72 Justus M. van der Kroef, "Messianic Movements in the Celebes, Sumatra, and Borneo," in Thrupp, *Millennial Dreams in Action,* pp. 80–121.

73 Donald L. Barnett and Karaji Njama, *Mau Mau from Within,* pp. 125–26.

74 Takie Sugiyama Lebra, "Religious Conversion as a Breakthrough for Transculturation," pp. 181–96.

75 Kanter, "Commitment and Social Organization."

76 I am indebted to Glynn Cochrane for this insight.

77 Brinton, *The Anatomy of Revolution,* p. 163.

78 Lifton, *Thought Reform,* p. 423.

79 *Order and Rebellion,* p. 145.

80 *The Trumpet Shall Sound,* pp. 249–50.

81 *The Origins of Totalitarianism,* p. 372.

82 For a demonstration of the link between size and legal institutions, see Richard D. Schwartz, "Social Factors in the Development of Legal Control," pp. 471–91.

83 Cohn, *The Pursuit of the Millennium* (1961), p. 100.

84 Ibid., p. 101; Hobsbawm, *Primitive Rebels.*

85 *Economy and Society,* p. 1121.

86 Reinhard Bendix, *Max Weber, an Intellectual Portrait,* p. 301.

87 Worsley, *The Trumpet Shall Sound,* p. xix.

88 Zygmunt, "Prophetic Failure and Chiliastic Identity; Aberle, *The Peyote Religion,* pp. 331–32.

89 Festinger, Reicken, and Schachter, *When Prophecy Fails,* p. 27.

90 Zygmunt, "Prophetic Failure and Chiliastic Identity"; Scholem, *The Messianic Idea in Judaism.*

91 Lamont, *Godly Rule,* passim.

92 "The Next Assignment."

93 For a review of the sparse literature, see Neal E. Cutler, "Generational Analysis in Political Science."

94 "An End to European Integration?", pp. 91–105.

95 "The Problem of Generations in Finnish Communism," pp. 190–202.

96 "The Psychohistorical Origins of the Nazi Youth Cohort," pp. 1457–502.
97 Ibid., p. 1463.
98 "The Cohort as a Concept in the Study of Social Change," p. 851.
99 Cutler, "Generational Analysis in Political Science."
100 Philip Abrams, "Rites de Passage," p. 179.
101 Ibid.
102 Loewenberg, "Nazi Youth Cohort." See also Hans Gerth, "The Nazi Party," pp. 517–41. On the general relationship between youth and revolution, see Herbert Moller, "Youth as a Force in the Modern World," pp. 237–60.
103 Cantril, *The Psychology of Social Movements*, pp. 169–209.
104 Barnett, *Innovation*, pp. 385–87.
105 Robert Levine, "Political Socialization and Culture Change," in Geertz, *Old Societies and New States*, pp. 280–303.

Chapter Five

1 "Epidemic Malaise," pp. 1–2.
2 P. 32.
3 Rosen, "Enthusiasm," p. 399. See also, C. Hill, *The World Turned Upside Down*, pp. 237, 287; Susie I. Tucker, *Enthusiasm*, pp. 52, 93.
4. Rosen, "Enthusiasm," p. 421.
5 Leon Bramson, *The Political Context of Sociology*, p. 53.
6 Ibid.
7 Elliott Currie and Jerome H. Skolnick, "A Critical Note on Conceptions of Collective Behavior," pp. 34–45.
8 Jarvie, *The Revolution in Anthropology*, p. 110.
9 Frances R. Hill, "Nationalist Millenarians and Millenarian Nationalists," pp. 269–88.
10 Ranger, " 'Primary Resistance' Movements and Mass Nationalism."
11 Ibid.; F. Landa Jocano, *Ideology and Radical Movements in the Philippines*.
12 *Nationalism in Asia and Africa*, p. 106.
13 *Madness in Society*, pp. 195–225.
14 Ibid., p. 224.
15 *The Dancing Mania of the Middle Ages*, p. 34.
16 *Objective Study of Crowd Behaviour*, pp. 2, 15, 16.
17 LeBon, *The Crowd*, p. 47.
18 Colin P. McEvedy and A. W. Beard, "Royal Free Epidemic of 1955"; Alan C. Kerckhoff and Kurt W. Back, *The June Bug*, pp. 7–11.
19 F. K. Taylor and R. C. A. Hunter, "Observations of a Hysterical Epidemic in a Hospital Ward," pp. 821–39; "Epidemic Malaise."
20 McEvedy and Beard, "Royal Free Epidemic"; idem, "Concept of Benign Myalgic Encephalomyelitis," pp. 11–17.
21 "Epidemic Malaise," p. 2.
22 Pp. 24–25.

23 Ibid., p. v.
24 "Epidemic Malaise."
25 Ibid.; J. Knight, "Epidemic Hysteria," pp. 858–65; Rosen, *Madness in Society*, pp. 217–24.
26 "Epidemic Malaise."
27 Taylor and Hunter, "Observations of a Hysterical Epidemic."
28 Ibid., p. 829.
29 G. J. Ebrahim, "Mass Hysteria in School Children," pp. 437–38.
30 Taylor and Hunter, "Observations of a Hysterical Epidemic," p. 834.
31 Murphy, "Social Change and Mental Health."
32 *The June Bug.*
33 "Epidemic Malaise."
34 *The June Bug*, pp. 158–88.
35 Cf. ibid.; and Penrose, *Objective Study of Crowd Behaviour*, p. 15.
36 Rosen, *Madness in Society*, pp. 4–5; Ernest M. Gruenberg, "Socially Shared Psychopathology," in Alexander H. Leighton, John A. Clausen, and Robert N. Wilson, eds., *Explorations in Social Psychiatry*, pp. 201–29.
37 "Epidemic Malaise"; Trevor-Roper, *The European Witch-craze.*
38 Berelson and Steiner, *Human Behavior*, p. 623; Charles E. Fritz and Eli S. Marks, "The NORC Studies of Human Behavior in Disaster," pp. 26–41.
39 Charles E. Fritz and Harry B. Williams, "The Human Being in Disaster," pp. 42–51.
40 Fritz and Marks, "Human Behavior in Disaster."
41 Calvin S. Drayer, "Psychological Factors and Problems, Emergency and Long-Term," pp. 151–59.
42 Cantril, *The Psychology of Social Movements.*
43 Langer, "The Next Assignment."
44 Penrose, *Objective Study of Crowd Behaviour*, p. 33.
45 G. M. Gilbert, "Social Causes Contributing to Panic," in Iago Galdston, ed., *Panic and Morals*, pp. 152–61.
46 Penrose, *Objective Study of Crowd Behaviour*, p. 34.
47 Evidence summarized in Brent M. Rutherford, "Psychopathology, Decision-Making, and Political Involvement," pp. 387–407.
48 "The Mental Illness of Hung Hsiu-Ch'uan."
49 *Major Trends in Jewish Mysticism*, p. 290.
50 For a defense of the validity of psychiatric or psychoanalytic approaches to history, see Langer, "The Next Assignment."
51 In Leighton, Clausen, and Wilson, *Explorations in Social Psychiatry*, p. 222.
52 I. M. Lewis, *Ecstatic Religion*, p. 191. See also J. B. Loudon, "Psychogenic Disorder and Social Conflict among the Zulu," in Marvin K. Opler, ed., *Culture and Mental Health*, pp. 351–69.
53 Rosen, *Madness in Society*, pp. 54–55.
54 *Psychopathology and Politics.* See also Morton Levitt and Ben Rubenstein, "Normality as a factor in Contemporary Political Life," pp. 171–86.

55 Rutherford, "Psychopathology, Decision-Making, and Political Involvement."

56 Cantril, *The Psychology of Social Movements;* Rudé, *The Crowd in History.*

57 "Psychopathology and Political Recruitment," pp. 913–31.

58 Rosen, *Madness in Society,* p. 109.

59 Penrose, *Objective Study of Crowd Behaviour,* p. 28.

60 *Warrant for Genocide.*

61 *The Paranoid Style,* p. 4.

62 Ibid., p. 38.

63 *The Pursuit of the Millennium* (1970), p. 87.

64 *The Paranoid Style,* p. 39.

65 *The European Witch-craze.* Although the subject of some initial criticism, this essay is now receiving much more sympathetic consideration from historians. See, for example, Russell, *Witchcraft in the Middle Ages,* p. 42.

66 Christopher Hill, *Antichrist in Seventeenth-Century England,* p. 170.

67 Trevor-Roper, *The European Witch-craze,* pp. 165–66.

68 Rosen, "Emotion and Sensibility."

69 Trevor-Roper, *The European Witch-craze.* Trevor-Roper's argument becomes even more significant in light of evidence that many putative medieval witches may have held millenarian beliefs; Russell, *Witchcraft in the Middle Ages,* pp. 136–42.

70 *The Pursuit of the Millennium* (1970), p. 109.

71 Trevor-Roper, *The European Witch-craze,* p. 192.

72 Kerckhoff and Back, *The June Bug,* p. 160.

73 Murray Edelman, *The Symbolic Uses of Politics,* pp. 6–7.

74 *The Paranoid Style,* p. 36.

75 Penrose, *Objective Study of Crowd Behaviour,* p. 61

76 An apparent exception is Hans Toch, *The Social Psychology of Social Movements,* pp. 55–57.

77 Rutherford, "Psychopathology, Decision-Making, and Political Involvement"; Penrose, *Objective Study of Crowd Behaviour,* p. 61.

78 Toch, *Social Psychology,* pp. 56–57.

79 Hofstadter, *The Paranoid Style,* p. 30.

80 Rosen, *Madness in Society,* pp. 223–24.

81 Worsley, *The Trumpet Shall Sound,* p. 44.

82 Cohn, *The Pursuit of the Millennium* (1970), pp. 133–34, 179–80.

83 Hecker, *The Dancing Mania;* Rosen, *Madness in Society,* pp. 197–203.

84 *Big Men and Cargo Cults,* p. 164.

85 Jarvie, *The Revolution in Anthropology,* pp. 127–28.

86 Wallace, "Cultural Determinants."

87 *Madness in Society,* pp. 49–50.

88 *Battle for the Mind,* pp. 14–15.

89 I. M. Lewis, *Ecstatic Religion,* p. 39.

90 Ibid.

91 "The Social Causation of Affective Mysticism," pp. 305–38.

92 Cross, *The Burned-Over District.*

93 Ibid., p. 13.
94 Lebra, "Religious Conversion."
95 *The June Bug*, pp. 103–05.
96 Ibid., p. 115.
97 Ibid., p. 35; Penrose, *Objective Study of Crowd Behaviour*, p. 15.
98 Siegfried, *Routes of Contagion*, pp. 85–98.
99 *The Trumpet Shall Sound*, pp. 249–50.
100 Lebra, "Religious Conversion."
101 Ibid, p. 187.
102 *Ecstatic Religion*, pp. 131–32.
103 Lipset, *Political Man*, p. 100.
104 I. M. Lewis, *Ecstatic Religion*, p. 195.
105 Edelman, *The Symbolic Uses of Politics*, p. 16.
106 *Order and Rebellion.*
107 I. M. Lewis, *Ecstatic Religion*, p. 127.
108 H. L. Nieburg, "Agonistics—Rituals of Conflict," pp. 56–73.
109 Wolfenstein, *Disaster*, p. 189.
110 Russell R. Dynes and E. L. Quarantelli, "The Absence of Community Conflict in the Early Phases of Natural Disasters"; Russell R. Dynes, "Organizational Involvement and Changes in Community Structure in Disaster," pp. 430–39.
111 Dynes, "Organizational Involvement."
112 Dynes and Quarantelli, "Absence of Community Conflict."
113 Wolfenstein, *Disaster*, pp. 197–98.

Chapter Six

1 Geoffrey Barraclough, *An Introduction to Contemporary History*, p. 88.
2 Peter Farb, "Ghost Dance and Cargo Cult," pp. 58–64.
3 Sjoberg, *The Preindustrial City*, p. 83.
4 George H. Williams, *The Radical Reformation*, p. 364.
5 Philippe Dellinger, *The German Hansa*, p. 121.
6 Cohn, *The Pursuit of the Millennium* (1970), pp. 256–57; G. H. Williams, *The Radical Reformation*, pp. 363–64.
7 Cohn, *The Pursuit of the Millennium* (1970), pp. 257, 282.
8 G. H. Williams, *The Radical Reformation*, p. 356.
9 Knox, *Enthusiasm*, p. 137.
10 Cohn, *The Pursuit of the Millennium* (1970), pp. 259–60; Knox, *Enthusiasm*, p. 127.
11 G. H. Williams, *The Radical Reformation*, pp. 364, 368.
12 *Enthusiasm*, p. 127.
13 Ibid.
14 Sjoberg, *The Preindustrial City*, p. 84.
15 Cf. Cecil Roth, *The Last Florentine Republic*, pp. 76, 184, 320. Roth estimates 100,000–120,000 for the period 1527–30.
16 Weinstein, in Thrupp, *Millennial Dreams in Action*, pp. 187–203.
17 Donald Weinstein, *Savonarola and Florence*, passim.
18 Ibid., p. 35.

19 Ibid., pp. 64–65.
20 Ibid., p. 34.
21 John N. Stephens, "Heresy in Medieval and Renaissance Florence," pp. 25–60.
22 Weinstein, in Thrupp, *Millennial Dreams in Action*, pp. 187–203.
23 Stephens, "Heresy in Florence."
24 Ibid.
25 Ibid., p. 41.
26 Weinstein, in Thrupp, *Millennial Dreams in Action*, p. 199.
27 Stephens, "Heresy in Florence."
28 B. S. Capp, *The Fifth Monarchy Men*, p. 76.
29 Ibid., p. 14.
30 Ibid., p. 80; C. Hill, *The World Turned Upside Down*, pp. 68–69.
31 Capp, *The Fifth Monarchy Men*, p. 82.
32 Ibid., pp. 88–89.
33 Sjoberg, *The Preindustrial City*, p. 12.
34 S. Kitzinger, "The Rastafarian Brethren of Jamaica," pp. 33–39.
35 De Queiroz, "Studies of Crisis Cults."
36 Essien-Udom, *Black Nationalism,* p. 390.
37 Ibid., pp. 72–73.
38 Cf. Cedric J. Robinson, "Malcolm Little as a Charismatic Leader." Robinson is not inclined to attach much importance to West Indian origins.
39 Lanternari, *The Religions of the Oppressed,*" p. 133.
40 George Shepperson, "The Comparative Study of Millenarian Movements," in Thrupp, *Millennial Dreams in Action*, pp. 44–54.
41 Quoted in Essien-Udom, *Black Nationalism,* p. 49.
42 Lanternari, *The Religions of the Oppressed,* pp. 134–37.
43 Shepperson, in Thrupp, *Millennial Dreams in Action*, pp. 44–54.
44 Siegel, "Defensive Structuring and Environmental Stress."
45 Lamont, *Godly Rule,* p. 25.
46 Tuveson, *Millennium and Utopia.*
47 *The Trumpet Shall Sound,* p. xi.
48 *Antichrist in Seventeenth-Century England,* p. 1.
49 Ibid., p. 3.
50 *The Trumpet Shall Sound,* p. 225.
51 Ibid., p. 255; Tilly, in Graham and Gurr, *Violence in America,* pp. 4–45.
52 Cf. David W. Plath, "Foreword," in Plath, *Aware of Utopia,* pp. ix–xvi.
53 *The Anatomy of Revolution,* pp. 192–207, but especially, pp. 204, 207.
54 Kedourie, *Nationalism in Asia and Africa*; J. L. Talmon *The Origins of Totalitarian Democracy.*
55 Kedourie, *Nationalism in Asia and Africa,* pp. 103, 106.
56 Arendt, *On Revolution,* pp. 43–46.
57 Quoted in Salo Wittmayer Baron, *Modern Nationalism and Religion,* p. 209.
58 Tuveson, *Redeemer Nation,* p. 213.
59 James C. Davies, "The J-Curve of Rising and Declining Satisfactions

as a Cause of Some Great Revolutions and a Contained Rebellion," in Graham and Gurr, *Violence in America*, pp. 690–730.

60 Brinton, *The Anatomy of Revolution*, p. 33.
61 Loewenberg, "Nazi Youth Cohort."
62 Gerth, "The Nazi Party," pp. 530–31. After 1918 there was sporadic civil violence undertaken by private armies.
63 Ibid., p. 530.
64 Moller, "Youth as a Force."
65 James P. Harrison, *The Communists and Chinese Peasant Rebellions*, p. 106.
66 Ch'ien Tuan-sheng, *The Government and Politics of China*, p. 76.
67 J. L. Talmon, *Political Messianism*, p. 15.
68 *In Bluebeard's Castle*, pp. 11–12.
69 J. L. Talmon, *Political Messianism*, p. 25.
70 Ibid., p. 514.
71 Baron, *Modern Nationalism and Religion*, pp. 210–11.
72 Vatro Murvar, "Messianism in Russia," pp. 277–338.
73 Ibid.
74 Ibid.
75 Ibid.
76 Ibid.
77 Peter Viereck, *Meta-Politics*, p. 226; George L. Mosse, *The Crisis of German Ideology*, p. 281.
78 Mosse, *The Crisis of German Ideology*, p. 281; Fritz Stern, *The Politics of Cultural Despair*, pp. 310–11.
79 Cohn, *The Pursuit of the Millennium* (1970), pp. 138–39, 285.
80 Mosse, *The Crisis of German Ideology*, pp. 19–20, 35.
81 Harrison, *The Communists*, pp. 162–63, 174.
82 *Warrant for Genocide.*
83 Arendt, *The Origins of Totalitarianism*, pp. 11–120 passim.
84 Hajo Holborn, "Origins and Political Character of Nazi Ideology."
85 Ibid.
86 For a discussion of the social and political context of the Taiping Rebellion, see chapter one. An intriguing but imperfectly understood aspect of the rebellion concerns the relationship between the Taipings and the older secret societies. Since the secret societies incorporated Buddhist millenarian doctrines, it is possible that Taiping millenarianism received some of its chiliastic thrust from them. If this proves to be the case, it frees the Taipings from doctrinal dependence upon the Christian missions. See Jean Chesneaux, "Secret Societies in China's Historical Evolution," in Chesneaux, *Popular Movements and Secret Societies in China 1840–1950*, pp. 1–21; Guillaume Dunstheimer, "Some Religious Aspects of Secret Societies," in ibid., pp. 23–28; Jean Chesneaux, *Secret Societies in China in the Nineteenth and Twentieth Centuries*, pp. 89–94.
87 Kwang-ching Liu, in Ho and Tsou, *China's Heritage*, pp. 93–178.
88 Albert Feuerwerker, "Comments," in Ho and Tsou, *China's Heritage*, pp. 179–93.

89 Mary Clabaugh Wright, *The Last Stand of Chinese Conservatism.*
90 Harrison, *The Communists*, pp. 80–81.
91 Ibid., pp. 82–83. M. C. Wright, *Chinese Conservatism*, pp. 300–03.
92 S. Y. Tong, *The Nien Army and Their Guerilla Warfare*, pp. 231–32.
93 For a summary of major uprisings, see Harrison, *The Communists*, pp. 279–304.
94 Lipset, *Political Man*, pp. 144, 148.
95 David Lane, *The Roots of Russian Communism*, p. 207.
96 Ibid., pp. 210–12.
97 Ibid., pp. 50, 131–32, 210.
98 Ibid., p. 206.
99 Ibid., p. 212.

Chapter Seven

1 *Human Behavior in Extreme Situations.*
2 *Routes of Contagion.*
3 Cf. Steiner, *In Bluebeard's Castle*, pp. 29–56; H. Stuart Hughes, "The Experience of Recent History," in Seymour M. Farber and Roger H. L. Wilson, eds., *Control of the Mind*, pp. 133–43.
4 David Rousset, quoted in Arendt, *The Origins of Totalitarianism*, p. 303.
5 *The Century of Total War*, pp. 19–22.
6 Arendt, *On Revolution*, p. 5.
7 *The Crowd in History*, passim, especially pp. 19–31.
8 Hobsbawm, *Primitive Rebels*, pp. 57–107. Tilly, in Graham and Gurr, *Violence in America*, pp. 4–45.
9 *New Heaven New Earth*, pp. 145–46.
10 For the concept of the concentrating institution, I am indebted to David Easton, "Children and Political Instability," paper prepared for presentation at Syracuse University, n.d., who applies it to those institutions which concentrate by age.
11 From Bradley S. Greenberg and Edwin B. Parker, eds., *The Kennedy Assassination and the American Public.* See especially the following: Wilbur Schramm, "Introduction: Communication in Crisis," pp. 1–28; Paul B. Sheatsley and Jacob J. Feldman, "A National Survey of Public Reactions and Behavior," pp. 149–77; S. Thomas Friedman and John Pierce-Jones, "Attitudinal Strategies in American Undergraduates' Interpretations of the Assassination," pp. 240–54; and Sidney Verba, "The Kennedy Assassination and the Nature of Political Commitment," pp. 348–60.
12 *In Bluebeard's Castle*, p. 13.
13 Schramm, in Greenberg and Parker, *The Kennedy Assassination*, p. 8.
14 Verba, in ibid., pp. 348–60.
15 Sheatsley and Feldman, in ibid., p. 154.
16 Bradley S. Greenberg and Edwin B. Parker, "Summary: Social Research on the Assassination," in ibid., pp. 361–84.
17 Ibid.

18 *Revolutionary Immortality*, p. 32.
19 *The Anatomy of Revolution*, pp. 212–13.
20 Ibid., p. 213.
21 Ibid., p. 249.
22 Ibid., p. vi.
23 Jerzy Gliksman, "Social Prophylaxis as a Form of Soviet Terror," in Friedrich, *Totalitarianism*, pp. 60–74.
24 *The Origins of Totalitarianism*, pp. 437–59.
25 Lanternari, *The Religions of the Oppressed.*

Bibliography

A note on sources: Space considerations preclude anything approaching an exhaustive survey of the primary source literature, although some of the most important items are included (Mooney's report on the Ghost Dance, F. E. Williams's description of the Vailala Madness). For more extensive listings of relevant materials, see Cohn (1970), Lanternari, La Barre (1971), and Worsley, all cited below.

Aberle, David F. "The Prophet Dance and Reactions to White Contact." *Southwestern Journal of Anthropology* 15 (1959): 74–83.
———. *The Peyote Religion among the Navaho.* Viking Fund Publications in Anthropology, no. 42. New York: Wenner-Gren Foundation for Anthropological Research, 1966.
Abney, F. Glenn, and Hill, Larry B. "Natural Disasters as a Political Variable: The Effect of a Hurricane on an Urban Election." *The American Political Science Review* 60 (1966): 974–81.
Abrams, Philip. "Rites de Passage: The Conflict of Generations in Industrial Society." *The Journal of Contemporary History* 5 (1970): 175–90.
Arendt, Hannah. *The Origins of Totalitarianism.* New York: World, 1958.
———. *On Revolution.* New York: Viking, 1965.
Aron, Raymond. *The Century of Total War.* Boston: Beacon, 1955.
Aston, Trevor, ed. *Crisis in Europe, 1560–1660.* Garden City, N.Y.: Doubleday Anchor, 1967.
Baker, George W., and Chapman, Dwight W., eds. *Man and Society in Disaster.* New York: Basic Books, 1962.
Barkun, Michael. "Law and Social Revolution: Millenarianism and the Legal System." *Law and Society Review* 6 (1971): 113–41.
Barnett, Donald L., and Njama, Karari. *Mau Mau from Within: Autobiography and Analysis of Kenya's Peasant Revolt.* New York: Monthly Review Press, 1966.
Barnett, H. G. *Innovation: The Basis of Cultural Change.* New York: McGraw-Hill, 1953.
Baron, Salo Wittmayer. *Modern Nationalism and Religion.* New York: Meridian, 1960.

Barraclough, Geoffrey. *An Introduction to Contemporary History.*
Baltimore: Penguin, 1967.

Barton, Allen H. *Communities in Disaster: A Sociological Analysis of
Collective Stress Situations.* Garden City, N.Y.: Doubleday, 1969.

Bauer, Raymond A. "Brainwashing: Psychology or Demonology?"
The Journal of Social Issues 13, no. 3 (1957): 41–47.

Bell, Daniel. "Sociodicy: A Guide to Modern Usage." *American
Scholar* 35 (1968): 696–714.

Bendix, Reinhard. *Max Weber, an Intellectual Portrait.* 1960. Reprint. Garden City, N.Y.: Doubleday Anchor, 1962.

Bennett, David. *Protectors and Fugitives: Anti-Alien Extremism in
American History.* New York: Holt, Rinehart and Winston,
forthcoming.

Berelson, Bernard, and Steiner, Gary A. *Human Behavior: An
Inventory of Scientific Findings.* New York: Harcourt, Brace and
World, 1964.

Bestor, Arthur. *Backwoods Utopias: The Sectarian Origins and the
Owenite Phase of Communitarian Socialism in America, 1663–1829.*
2d ed. Philadelphia: University of Pennsylvania Press, 1970.

Biderman, Albert, and Zimmer, Herbert, eds. *The Manipulation of
Human Behavior.* New York: Wiley, 1961.

Bramson, Leon. *The Political Context of Sociology.* Princeton, N.J.:
Princeton University Press, 1961.

Brinton, Crane. *The Anatomy of Revolution.* New York: Vintage,
Press, 1950.

Brody, Eugene B., ed. *Behavior in New Environments: Adaptation of
Migrant Populations.* Beverly Hills, Calif.: Sage Publications, 1970.

Burridge, Kenelm. *New Heaven New Earth: A Study of Millenarian
Activities.* Oxford: Basil Blackwell, 1969.

Cantril, Hadley. *The Psychology of Social Movements.* 1941. Reprint.
New York: Science Editions, 1967.

Capp, B. S. *The Fifth Monarchy Men: A Study in Seventeenth-Century
English Millenarianism.* London: Faber and Faber, 1972.

Caudill, William. *Effects of Social and Cultural Systems in Reactions
to Stress.* New York: Social Science Research Council, 1958.

Chesneaux, Jean. *Secret Societies in China in the Nineteenth and
Twentieth Centuries.* Ann Arbor, Mich.: The University of Michi-
gan Press, 1971.

―――, ed. *Popular Movements and Secret Societies in China,
1840–1950.* Stanford, Calif.: Stanford University Press, 1972.

Chien Tuan-sheng. *The Government and Politics of China.* Cambridge: Harvard University Press, 1950.

Cochrane, D. Glynn. *Big Men and Cargo Cults.* London: Oxford
University Press, 1970.

Cohn, Norman. *The Pursuit of the Millennium: Revolutionary Messianism in Medieval and Reformation Europe and Its Bearing on Modern Totalitarian Movements.* 2d ed. New York: Harper Torchbooks, 1961.

————. *Warrant for Genocide: The Myth of the Jewish World Conspiracy and the Protocols of the Elders of Zion.* New York: Oxford University Press, 1967.

————. *The Pursuit of the Millennium: Revolutionary Millenarians and Mystical Anarchists of the Middle Ages.* 3d ed. New York: Oxford University Press, 1970.

Cross, Whitney R. *The Burned-Over District: The Social and Intellectual History of Enthusiastic Religion in Upper New York State, 1800–1850.* Ithaca, N.Y.: Cornell University Press, 1950.

Currie, Elliott, and Skolnick, Jerome H. "A Critical Note on Conceptions of Collective Behavior." *The Annals* 391 (September 1970): 34–45.

Curry, Donald E. "Messianism and Protestantism in Brazil's Sertão." *Journal of Inter-American Studies and World Affairs* 12 (1970): 416–38.

Cutler, Neal E. "Generational Analysis in Political Science." Paper read at the Annual Meeting of the American Political Science Association, September 7–11, 1971. Mimeographed.

Dawson, Richard E., and Prewitt, Kenneth. *Political Socialization.* Boston: Little, Brown, 1969.

Dellinger, Philippe. *The German Hansa.* Stanford, Calif.: Stanford University Press, 1970.

De Queiroz, Maria Isaura Pereira. "On materials for a History of Studies of Crisis Cults." *Current Anthropology* 12 (1971): 387–90.

Drayer, Calvin S. "Psychological Factors and Problems, Emergency and Long-Term." *The Annals* 309 (January 1957): 151–59.

Dynes, Russell R. "Organizational Involvement and Changes in Community Structure in Disaster." *American Behavioral Scientist* 13 (1970): 430–39.

Dynes, Russell R., and Quarantelli, E. L. "The Absence of Community Conflict in the Early Phases of Natural Disasters." Mimeographed. Columbus, Ohio: Disaster Research Center, the Ohio State University, n.d.

Dynes, Russell R., and Yutzy, Daniel. "The Religious Interpretation of Disaster." *Topic 10: A Journal of the Liberal Arts,* Fall 1965, pp. 34–48.

Ebrahim, G. J. "Mass Hysteria in School Children: Notes on Three Outbreaks in East Africa." *Clinical Pediatrics* 7 (1968): 437–38.

Edelman, Murray. *The Symbolic Uses of Politics.* Urbana, Ill.: University of Illinois Press, 1964.

"Epidemic Malaise." *British Medical Journal* 1 (January 3, 1970):
1–2.

Essien-Udom, E. U. *Black Nationalism: A Search for Identity in
America.* Reprint. New York: Dell, 1964.

Evans-Pritchard, E. E.; Firth, Raymond; Malinowski, Bronislaw;
and Schapera, Isaac, eds. *Essays Presented to C. G. Seligman.*
1934. Reprint. Westport, Conn.: Negro Universities Press, 1970.

Farb, Peter. "Ghost Dance and Cargo Cult." *Horizon* 11 (Spring
1969): 58–64.

Farber, Seymour M., and Wilson, Roger H. L., eds. *Control of the
Mind.* New York: McGraw-Hill, 1961.

Festinger, Leon; Riecken, Henry W.; and Schachter, Stanley. *When
Prophecy Fails: A Social and Psychological Study of a Modern
Group That Predicted the Destruction of the World.* New York:
Harper Torchbooks, 1966.

Fried, Morton; Harris, Marvin; and Murphy, Robert, eds. *War: The
Anthropology of Armed Conflict and Aggression.* Garden City,
N.Y.: The Natural History Press, 1968.

Friedrich, Carl J., ed. *Totalitarianism.* 1954. Reprint. New York:
Universal Library, 1964.

Fritz, Charles E., and Marks, Eli S. "The NORC Studies of Human
Behavior in Disaster." *The Journal of Social Issues* 10, no. 3
(1954): 26–41.

Fritz, Charles E., and Williams, Harry B. "The Human Being in
Disaster: A Research Perspective." *The Annals* 309 (January
1957): 42–51.

Galdston, Iago, ed. *Panic and Morals.* New York: International
Universities Press, 1958.

Geertz, Clifford, ed. *Old Societies and New States.* New York: The
Free Press of Glencoe, 1963.

Gerth, Hans. "The Nazi Party: Its Leadership and Composition."
The American Journal of Sociology 45 (1940): 517–41.

Glazer, Nathan. "America's Race Paradox." *Encounter* 31 (October
1968): 9–18.

Gluckman, Max. *Order and Rebellion in Tribal Africa.* London:
Cohen and West, 1963.

————. *Politics, Law and Ritual in Tribal Society.* 1965. Reprint.
New York: Mentor, 1968.

Goodenough, Ward Hunt. *Cooperation in Change.* New York:
Science Editions, 1966.

Graham, Hugh Davis, and Gurr, Ted Robert, eds. *Violence in
America: Historical and Comparative Perspectives.* New York:
Bantam, 1969.

Greenberg, Bradley S., and Parker, Edwin B., eds. *The Kennedy Assassination and the American Public: Social Communication in Crisis.* Stanford, Calif.: Stanford University Press, 1965.

Gurr, Ted Robert. *Why Men Rebel.* Princeton, N.J.: Princeton University Press, 1970.

Harrison, James P. *The Communists and Chinese Peasant Rebellions: A Study in the Rewriting of Chinese History.* London: Gollancz, 1970.

Hecker, J. F. C. *The Dancing Mania of the Middle Ages.* Translated by B. G. Babington. 1865. Reprint. New York: J. Fitzgerald, 1885.

Hilberg, Raul. *The Destruction of the European Jews.* Chicago: Quadrangle, 1967.

Hill, Christopher. *Antichrist in Seventeenth-Century England.* London: Oxford University Press, 1971.

————. *The World Turned Upside Down: Radical Ideas during the English Revolution.* New York: Viking, 1972.

Hill, Frances R. "Nationalist Millenarians and Millenarian Nationalists." *American Behavioral Scientist* 16 (1972): 269–88.

Ho Ping-ti and Tang Tsou, eds. *China's Heritage and the Communist Political System.* Chicago: University of Chicago Press, 1968.

Hobsbawm, E. J. *Primitive Rebels: Studies in Archaic Forms of Social Movements in the Nineteenth and Twentieth Centuries.* New York: Norton, 1959.

Hoffer, Eric. *The True Believer.* New York: Mentor, 1958.

Hofstadter, Richard. *The Paranoid Style in American Politics.* New York: Knopf, 1965.

Holborn, Hajo. "Origins and Political Character of Nazi Ideology." Paper read at the Annual Meeting of the American Political Science Association, 1963.

Honigmann, John A. "Culture Patterns and Human Stress: A Study in Social Psychiatry." *Psychiatry* 13 (1950): 25–34.

Hudson, Bradford B. "Anxiety Response to the Unfamiliar." *The Journal of Social Issues* 10, no. 3 (1954): 53–60.

Huizinga, Johan. *The Waning of the Middle Ages.* 1949. Reprint. Garden City, N.Y.: Doubleday Anchor, 1954.

Inglehart, Ronald. "An End to European Integration?" *The American Political Science Review* 61 (1967): 91–105.

Inkeles, Alex, and Smith, David H. "The Fate of Personal Adjustment in the Process of Modernization." *International Journal of Comparative Sociology* 11 (1970): 81–114.

Jaher, Frederic Cople. *Doubters and Dissenters: Cataclysmic Thought in America, 1885–1918.* New York: The Free Press of Glencoe, 1964.

Janis, Irving L. "Problems of Theory in the Analysis of Stress Behavior." *The Journal of Social Issues* 10, no. 3 (1954): 12–25.

Jaros, Dean; Hirsch, Herbert; and Fleron, Frederic J., Jr. "The Malevolent Leader: Political Socialization in an American Subculture." *The American Political Science Review* 62 (1968): 564–75.

Jarvie, I. C. *The Revolution in Anthropology.* Chicago: Regnery, 1969.

Jocano, F. Landa. *Ideology and Radical Movements in the Philippines: A Preliminary View.* Singapore: Institute of Southeast Asia Studies, 1971.

Kanter, Rosabeth Moss. "Commitment and Social Organization: A Study of Commitment Mechanisms in Utopian Communities." *American Sociological Review* 33 (1968): 499–517.

————. *Commitment and Community: Communes and Utopias in Sociological Perspective.* Cambridge: Harvard University Press, 1972.

Kedourie, Elie, ed. *Nationalism in Asia and Africa.* New York: Meridian, 1970.

Kerckhoff, Alan C., and Back, Kurt W. *The June Bug: A Study of Hysterical Contagion.* New York: Appleton-Century Crofts, 1968.

Killian, Lewis M. "Some Accomplishments and Some Needs in Disaster Study." *The Journal of Social Issues* 10, no. 3 (1954): 66–72.

Kilpatrick, F. P. "Problems of Perception in Extreme Situations." *Human Organization* 16 (Summer 1957): 20–22.

Kitzinger, S. "The Rastafarian Brethren of Jamaica." *Comparative Studies in Society and History* 9 (1966): 33–39.

Klausner, Samuel Z., ed. *Why Man Takes Chances: Studies in Stress-Seeking.* Garden City, N.Y.: Doubleday Anchor, 1968.

Kliman, Ann S. "Psychological First Aid in a Mass Disaster: The Corning Flood Project." Mimeographed. White Plains, N.Y.: The Center for Preventive Psychiatry, September 25, 1972.

Knight, J. "Epidemic Hysteria." *American Journal of Public Health* 55 (1965): 858–65.

Knox, R. A. *Enthusiasm: A Chapter in the History of Religion: with Special Reference to the Seventeenth and Eighteenth Centuries.* New York: Oxford University Press, 1950.

Köbben, A. J. F. "Prophetic Movements as an Expression of Social Protest." *International Archives of Ethnography* 49, part 1 (1960): 117–64.

Kuhn, Thomas S. *The Structure of Scientific Revolutions.* Chicago: University of Chicago Press, 1962.

La Barre, Weston. *The Ghost Dance: The Origins of Religion.* Garden City, N.Y.: Doubleday, 1970.

————. "Materials for a History of Studies of Crisis Cults: A Bibliographic Essay." *Current Anthropology* 12 (1971): 3–44.

Lamont, William M. *Godly Rule: Politics and Religion, 1603–60.* London: Macmillan, 1969.

Lane, David. *The Roots of Russian Communism: A Social and Historical Study of Russian Social-Democracy 1898–1907.* Assen, The Netherlands: Van Gorcum, 1969.

Langer, William L. "The Next Assignment." *The American Historical Review* 63 (1958): 283–304

Lanternari, Vittorio. *The Religions of the Oppressed: A Study of Modern Messianic Cults.* 1963. Reprint. New York: Mentor, 1965.

Lasky, Melvin J. "The Meta-Physics of Doomsday: John Rogers and Oliver Cromwell." *Encounter* 32 (January 1969): 36–47.

Lasswell, Harold D. *Psychopathology and Politics.* Reprint. New York: Viking, 1966.

LeBon, Gustave. *The Crowd: A Study of the Popular Mind.* 1895. Reprint. New York: Viking, 1960.

Lebra, Takie Sugiyama. "Religious Conversion as a Breakthrough for Transculturation: A Japanese Sect in Hawaii." *Journal for the Scientific Study of Religion* 9 (1970): 181–96.

Leighton, Alexander H.; Clausen, John A.; and Wilson, Robert N., eds. *Explorations in Social Psychiatry.* New York: Basic Books, 1957.

Leighton, Alexander H., and Hughes, Jane M. "Cultures as a Causative of Mental Disorder." *Milbank Memorial Fund Quarterly* 39 (1961): 446–70.

Levitt, Morton, and Rubenstein, Ben. "Normality as a Factor in Contemporary Political Life." *Political Science Quarterly* 85 (1970): 171–86.

Lewis, Bernard. *The Assassins: A Radical Sect in Islam.* New York: Basic Books, 1968.

Lewis, I. M. *Ecstatic Religion: An Anthropological Study of Spirit Possession and Shamanism.* Middlesex, England: Penguin, 1971.

Lifton, Robert Jay. *Thought Reform and the Psychology of Totalism: A Study of "Brainwashing" in China.* New York: Norton, 1963.

————. *Revolutionary Immortality: Mao Tse-tung and the Chinese Cultural Revolution.* New York: Vintage, 1968.

Lingeman, Richard R. "The Greeks Had a Word for It—But What Does It Mean?" *New York Times Magazine,* August 4, 1968, pp. 28–32.

Lipset, Seymour Martin. *Political Man: The Social Bases of Politics.* Garden City, N.Y.: Doubleday Anchor, 1963.

Loewenberg, Peter. "The Psychohistorical Origins of the Nazi Youth Cohort." *American Historical Review* 76 (1971): 1457–502.

Lofland, John, and Stark, Rodney. "Becoming a World-Saver: A Theory of Conversion to a Deviant Perspective." *American Sociological Review* 30 (1965): 862–75.

McEvedy, Colin P., and Beard, A. W. "Concept of Benign Myalgic Encephalomyelitis." *British Medical Journal* 1 (January 3, 1970): 11–17.

————. "Royal Free Epidemic of 1955: A Reconsideration." *British Medical Journal* 1 (January 3, 1970): 7–11.

Mackay, Charles. *Extraordinary Popular Delusions and the Madness of Crowds.* 1841. Reprint. New York: Noonday, 1966.

Mair, L. P. "Independent Religious Movements in Three Continents." *Comparative Studies in Society and History* 1 (1958–59): 113–36.

Malalgoda, Kitsiri. "Millennialism in Relation to Buddhism." *Comparative Studies in Society and History* 12 (1970): 424–41.

Mannheim, Karl. *Ideology and Utopia.* 1936. Reprint. New York: Harcourt, Brace and World, 1965.

Marcus, George. "Psychopathology and Political Recruitment." *Journal of Politics* 31 (1969): 913–31.

Mead, Margaret. "Comment on Independent Religious Movements." *Comparative Studies in Society and History* 1 (1958–59): 324–29.

————. *New Lives for Old: Cultural Transformation, Manus, 1923–1953.* New York: William Morrow, 1956.

Moller, Herbert. "Youth as a Force in the Modern World." *Comparative Studies in Society and History* 10 (1968): 237–60.

————. "The Social Causation of Affective Mysticism." *Journal of Social History* 4 (1971): 305–38.

Mooney, James. *The Ghost-Dance Religion and the Sioux Outbreak of 1890.* Abridged by Anthony F. C. Wallace. 1896. Reprint. Chicago: University of Chicago Press, 1965.

Morrison, Denton E. "Some Notes toward Theory on Relative Deprivation, Social Movements, and Social Change." *American Behavioral Scientist* 14 (1971): 675–90.

Mosse, George L. *The Crisis of German Ideology: Intellectual Origins of the Third Reich.* New York: Grosset and Dunlap, 1964.

Murphy, H. B. M. "Social Change and Mental Health." *Milbank Memorial Fund Quarterly* 39 (1961): 385–445.

Murvar, Vatro. "Messianism in Russia: Religious and Revolutionary." *Journal for the Scientific Study of Religion* 10 (1971): 277–338.

Nieburg, H. L. "Agonistics—Rituals of Conflict." *The Annals* 391 (September 1970): 56–73.

Nock, A. D. *Conversion.* Reprint. London: Oxford University Press, 1961.

Oberschall, Anthony. "Group Violence: Some Hypotheses and Empirical Uniformities." *Law and Society Review* 5 (1970) 61–92.

Opler, Marvin K., ed. *Culture and Mental Health: Cross-Cultural Studies.* New York: Macmillan, 1959.

Ozment, Steven E. *Mysticism and Dissent: Religious Ideology and Social Protest in the Sixteenth Century.* New Haven: Yale University Press, 1973.

Penrose, L. S. *On the Objective Study of Crowd Behaviour.* London: H. K. Lewis, 1952.

Plath, David, ed. *Aware of Utopia.* Urbana, Ill.: University of Illinois Press, 1971.

Polanyi, Michael. *Science, Faith and Society.* Chicago: University of Chicago Press, 1964.

Ranger, T. O. "Connexions between 'Primary Resistance' Movements and Modern Mass Nationalism in East and Central Africa." *Journal of African History* 9 (1968): 437–53, 631–41.

Rintala, Marvin. "The Problem of Generations in Finnish Communism." *The American Slavic and East European Review* 17 (1971): 190–202.

Robinson, Cedric J. "Malcolm Little as a Charismatic Leader." Paper read at the Annual Meeting of the American Political Science Association, September 8–12, 1970.

Rosen, George. "Emotion and Sensibility in Ages of Anxiety: A Comparative Historical Review." *American Journal of Psychiatry* 124 (1967): 770–84.

―――. "Enthusiasm, 'a dark lanthorn of the spirit.' " *Bulletin of the History of Medicine* 42 (September–October 1968): 393–421.

―――. *Madness in Society: Chapters in the Historical Sociology of Mental Illness.* New York: Harper Torchbooks, 1969.

Rossel, Robert D. "The Great Awakening: An Historical Analysis." *American Journal of Sociology* 75 (1970): 907–25.

Roth, Cecil. *The Last Florentine Republic.* New York: Russell and Russell, 1968.

Rudé, George. *The Crowd in History, 1730–1848.* New York: Wiley, 1964.

Russell, Jeffrey Burton. *Witchcraft in the Middle Ages.* Ithaca, N.Y.: Cornell University Press, 1972.

Rutherford, Brent M. "Psychopathology, Decision-Making, and Political Involvement." *The Journal of Conflict Resolution* 10 (1966): 387–407.

Ryder, Norman B. "The Cohort as a Concept in the Study of Social Change." *American Sociological Review* 30 (1965): 843–61.

Sargant, William. *Battle for the Mind.* Baltimore: Penguin, 1961.
————. "The Physiology of Faith. The Forty-Third Maudsley
Lecture." *British Journal of Psychiatry* 115 (1969): 505–18.
Schein, Edgar H. "Reaction Patterns to Severe, Chronic Stress in
American Army Prisoners of War of the Chinese." *The Journal of
Social Issues* 13, no. 3 (1957): 21–30.
Scholem, Gershom. *Major Trends in Jewish Mysticism.* New York:
Schocken, 1961.
————. *The Messianic Idea in Judaism.* New York: Schocken, 1971.
Schwartz, Richard D. "Social Factors in the Development of Legal
Control: A Case Study of Two Israeli Settlements." *Yale Law
Journal* 63 (1954): 471–91.
Schwartz, Theodore. *The Paliau Movement in the Admiralty Islands,
1946–1954.* Anthropological Papers, vol. 49, no. 2. New York:
American Museum of Natural History, 1962.
Siegel, Bernard J. "Defensive Structuring and Environmental
Stress." *American Journal of Sociology* 76 (1970): 11–32.
Siegfried, André. *Routes of Contagion.* New York: Harcourt, Brace
and World, 1965.
Sjoberg, Gideon. *The Preindustrial City: Past and Present.* New
York: The Free Press, 1960.
Smith, David E. "Millenarian Scholarship in America." *American
Quarterly* 17 (1965): 535–49.
Smith, M. W. "Towards a Classification of Cult Movements." *Man*
59 (1959): 8–12.
Sorokin, Pitrim A. *Man and Society in Calamity.* New York: E. P.
Dutton, 1943.
Spier, Leslie; Shuttles, Wayne; and Herskovits, Melville J. "Com-
ments on Aberle's Thesis of Deprivation." *Southwestern Journal of
Anthropology* 15 (1959): 84–88.
Steiner, George. *In Bluebeard's Castle: Some Notes Towards the
Re-definition of Culture.* New Haven: Yale University Press, 1971.
Stephens, John N. "Heresy in Medieval and Renaissance Florence."
Past and Present 54 (February 1972): 25–60.
Stern, Fritz. *The Politics of Cultural Despair: A Study in the Rise of
the Germanic Ideology.* Garden City, N.Y.: Doubleday, 1965.
Talmon, J. L. *The Origins of Totalitarian Democracy.* New York:
Praeger, 1960.
————. *Political Messianism: The Romantic Phase.* New York:
Praeger, 1960.
Talmon, Yonina. "Pursuit of the Millennium: The Relation between
Religious and Social Change." *Archives Européènes de Sociologie* 3
(1962): 125–48.

————. "Millenarian Movements." *Archives Européènes de Sociologie* 7 (1966): 159–200.

Taylor, F. K., and Hunter, R. C. A. "Observations of a Hysterical Epidemic in a Hospital Ward: Thoughts on the Dynamics of Mental Epidemics." *Psychiatric Quarterly* 32 (1958): 821–39.

Thrupp, Sylvia L., ed. *Millennial Dreams in Action: Essays in Comparative Study.* Comparative Studies in Society and History, suppl. 2. The Hague: Mouton, 1962.

Toch, Hans. *The Social Psychology of Social Movements.* Indianapolis: Bobbs-Merrill, 1965.

Tong, S. Y. *The Nien Army and Their Guerilla Warfare, 1851–1868.* Paris: Mouton, 1961.

Trevor-Roper, H. R. *The European Witch-craze of the Sixteenth and Seventeenth Centuries and Other Essays.* New York: Harper Torchbooks, 1969.

Tucker, Susie I. *Enthusiasm: A Study in Semantic Change.* Cambridge: Cambridge University Press, 1972.

Tuveson, Ernest Lee. *Millennium and Utopia: A Study in the Background of the Idea of Progress.* New York: Harper Torchbooks, 1964.

————. *Redeemer Nation.* Chicago: University of Chicago Press, 1968.

Tyhurst, J. S. "Individual Reactions to Community Disaster: The Natural History of Psychiatric Phenomena." *American Journal of Psychiatry* 107 (1951): 764–69.

Viereck, Peter. *Meta-Politics: The Roots of the Nazi Mind.* New York: Capricorn, 1961.

Wakeman, Frederic, Jr. *Strangers at the Gate: Social Disorder in South China, 1839–1861.* Berkeley: University of California Press, 1966.

Wallace, Anthony F. C. *Human Behavior in Extreme Situations.* Committee on Disaster Studies, Disaster Study No. 1; Division of Anthropology and Psychology, Publication 390. Washington, D.C.: National Academy of Sciences–National Research Council, 1956.

————. "Mazeway Resynthesis: A Bio-cultural Theory of Religious Inspiration." *Transactions of the New York Academy of Sciences,* 2d ser. 18 (1956): 626–38.

————. "Revitalization Movements." *American Anthropologist* 58 (1956): 264–81.

————. "Stress and Rapid Personality Changes." *International Record of Medicine* 169 (1956): 761–74.

————. "Mazeway Disintegration: The Individual's Perception of

Socio-Cultural Disorganization." *Human Organization* 16 (Summer 1957): 23–27.
———. "Cultural Determinants of Response to Hallucinatory Experience." *AMA Archives of General Psychiatry* 1 (1959): 58–69.
———. *The Death and Rebirth of the Seneca.* New York: Knopf, 1970.
Wallace, Anthony F. C.; Voget, Fred W.; and Smith, Marian W. "Toward a Classification of Cult Movements: Some Further Contributions." *Man* 59 (1959): 25–28.
Walzer, Michael. *The Revolution of the Saints: A Study in the Origins of Radical Politics.* Cambridge: Harvard University Press, 1965.
Weber, Max. *Economy and Society: An Outline of Interpretive Sociology.* Edited by Guenther Roth and Claus Wittich. 3 vols. New York: Bedminster Press, 1968.
Weinstein, Donald. *Savonarola and Florence: Prophecy and Patriotism in the Renaissance.* Princeton, N.J.: Princeton University Press, 1970.
Williams, F. E. *The Vailala Madness and the Destruction of Native Ceremonies in the Gulf Division.* Anthropology Report, no. 4. Port Moresby, New Guinea: Government Printer, 1923.
Williams, George H. *The Radical Reformation.* Philadelphia: Westminster Press, 1962.
Williams, Harry B. "Fewer Disasters, Better Studied." *The Journal of Social Issues* 10, no. 3 (1954): 5–11.
Wilson, Bryan. "Millennialism in Comparative Perspective." *Comparative Studies in Society and History* 6 (1963): 93–114.
Wittkower, E. D., and Fried, J. "A Cross-Cultural Approach to Mental Health Problems." *American Journal of Psychiatry* 116 (1959): 423–28.
Wolfenstein, Martha. *Disaster: A Psychological Essay.* Glencoe, Ill.: The Free Press, 1957.
Worsley, Peter. *The Trumpet Shall Sound: A Study of "Cargo" Cults in Melanesia.* 2d ed. New York: Schocken, 1968.
Wright, Mary Clabaugh. *The Last Stand of Chinese Conservatism: The T'ung-Chih Restoration, 1862–1874.* Stanford, Calif.: Stanford University Press, 1957.
Wright, Quincy. *A Study of War.* Abridged ed. Chicago: University of Chicago Press, 1965.
Yap, P. M. "Mental Diseases Peculiar to Certain Cultures: A Survey of Comparative Psychiatry." *Journal of Mental Science* 97 (1951): 313–27.
———. "The Mental Illness of Hung Hsiu-Ch'uan, Leader of the Taiping Rebellion." *Far Eastern Quarterly* 13 (1953–54): 287–304.

————. "Words and Things in Comparative Psychiatry, with Special Reference to the Exotic Psychoses." *Acta Psychiatrica Scandanavica* 38 (1962): 163–69.

Ziegler, Philip. *The Black Death.* London: Collins, 1969.

Zygmunt, Joseph F. "Prophetic Failure and Chiliastic Identity: The Case of Jehovah's Witnesses." *American Journal of Sociology* 75 (1970): 926–48.

Index

Anabaptists. *See* Münster, Anabaptists in

Anarchism, 101–02

Black Death, 58, 74, 113
Bohm, Hans, 115
Brainwashing, 102, 104, 112, 114. *See also* Conversion
Burned-Over District, 45, 62–63, 157–58

Cargo Cults, 12–14, 71, 75, 92, 117–18, 155
Chinese Revolution, 187–99 passim; Cultural Revolution as extension of, 208. *See also* Taiping Rebellion
Cohn, Norman, 3, 31–32, 186
Collective psychopathology, 134–45 passim
Communism, Russian, 126, 187–99 passim, 209–10
Conspiracy thinking, 145–54 passim; role in millenarian movements, 151–54
Conversion: defined, 98–99; causes of, 102–05, 108; ecstatic behavior and, 108–09; prophets and, 109; disaster and, 110–14

Defensive structuring, 77–78, 177–78
Disaster: study of, 2; defined, 51; effects of, 52–55, 122, 157, 159, 207–08; anticipation of, 57–61, 153; vulnerability to, 68–70, 72–73, 176–78; single versus multiple, 74–84; explanations of, 79–84; utopia, 163–65; totalitarianism and, 187–99 passim; types of, 201–05; war as, 203; depression as,

203–04; mass communications and, 205–08. *See also* Conversion; Millenarian movements; Revolution; Socialization
Disaster syndrome. *See* Disaster, effects of

Erikson, Erik, 104

Fifth Monarchy Men, 173–74
Florence, 170–71; Savonarolan movement in, 171–72
France: millenarianism in, 28–29; *Grand Peur* in, 70

Garvey, Marcus, 175
Germany. *See* Nazism
Ghost Dance, 15–16, 42, 92
Gould, Harold, 85–86
Great Awakening, 63

Handsome Lake, 109, 115
Haymarket Riot, 60, 81
Hecker, J. F. C., 135
Hoffer, Eric, 103
Hofstadter, Richard, 20, 145–46
Hysteria, 136–39

Inglehart, Ronald, 123
Ireland, 63–64

Jaher, Frederic, 81
Jehovah's Witnesses, 121
Joachim of Fiore, 119, 192

Kennedy, John F.: assassination of, 206–07
Kerckhoff, Alan, and Back, Kurt, 138–39, 158–59
Kuhn, Thomas, 80–81

LeBon, Gustave, 129, 135
Lifton, Robert Jay, 104

245